POWER CONSULTING

POWER CONSULTING

Using the Media to Expand Your Business

RUDOLPH C. KEMPPAINEN

JOHN WILEY & SONS

NEW YORK   CHICHESTER   BRISBANE   TORONTO   SINGAPORE

Copyright © 1988 by John Wiley & Sons, Inc.

All rights reserved. Published simultaneously in Canada.

Reproduction or translation of any part of this work beyond that permitted by Section 107 or 108 of the 1976 United States Copyright Act without the permission of the copyright owner is unlawful. Requests for permission or further information should be addressed to the Permissions Department, John Wiley & Sons, Inc.

This publication is designed to provide accurate and authoritative information in regard to the subject matter covered. It is sold with the understanding that the publisher is not engaged in rendering legal, accounting, or other professional service. If legal advice or other expert assistance is required, the services of a competent professional person should be sought. *From a Declaration of Principles jointly adopted by a Committee of the American Bar Association and a Committee of Publishers.*

Library of Congress Cataloging in Publication Data:

Kemppainen, Rudolph C., 1952-
   Power consulting: using the media to expand your business/Rudolph C. Kemppainen

     p.   cm.
   Bibliography: p.
   ISBN 0-471-63148-5
    1. Consultants—Marketing. I. Title.
HD69.C6K46 1988   88-2664
658.4′6′0688—dc19   CIP

Printed in the United States of America
10 9 8 7 6 5 4 3 2 1

PREFACE

Successfully marketing any business can be difficult. This challenge is often harder when the business's product is an "intangible."

This is the challenge of marketing a consulting business. Most of what a consultant offers cannot be touched or seen by the customer—at least, not immediately. Because of this perceptual problem, the business consultant must be able to create confidence in the "intangible."

To create that confidence, the business consultant must sell an image to the potential client. The *prestige image* is exactly what is required. This book is designed to help you to build this prestige image and to sell it effectively. This tandem, building and selling of the image, must work together. Neither element, standing alone, will get the job done.

In many ways, your marketing challenge is similar to that of a politician seeking public office. You know what you are capable of doing for your constituents (clients), but you won't be able to prove it until you are elected (hired).

Because your image building and selling task is so similar to a politician's, you will have to formulate your marketing strategy in much the same way. Although word-of-mouth advertising, when it's favorable, is always an asset, you can't count on this factor alone to get the job done for you. It is merely a single factor in the total package.

HOW THIS BOOK WILL HELP YOU

The assumption made in writing this book is that you know little in the way of marketing—you are literally at the starting point in your efforts. To begin, you'll learn how to: assess your personal image and use it to your best advantage; build your prestige image by increasing your strengths and reducing your weaknesses; and outline a marketing strategy and select the right medium or combination of media to project your prestige image to prospective clients.

Here are some of the many topics this book will cover:

- An image marketability checklist for your current image
- How prospective clients view marketing strategy
- Building image to meet prospective needs

- Effective outlining techniques for marketing strategy
- How to conduct a market survey
- Stage implementation of marketing strategy
- Overviews of all major available promotion media
- How to promote through press releases
- Special secrets of newspaper advertising
- Common mistakes to avoid in newspaper advertising
- Marketing strategy through trade and professional journals
- How to write image-building articles in trade journals
- How to use radio advertising effectively
- Writing the effective radio commercial
- How to develop public service programs for television
- How to expand your market through cable and satellite television
- Powerful promotion through the internal newsletter
- How to deliver effective speeches
- Seminar organization secrets
- How to write seminar instruction materials
- How to connect seminars and individual consulting efforts for ultimate success

In fourteen information-packed chapters this book will show you how to promote your consulting business as far as your ambition and your stamina will allow. The secrets of the top consultants will be revealed and combined with the author's personal experiences and information gained from numerous case examples of consultants (many of whom are outrageously successful), to show you how to duplicate their success.

This book will open the curtains and take you behind the scenes to show you how the best promoters in the business make great things happen. Some of the things which you'll read in this book will surprise you, but nothing presented here is untested.

This book is designed to help you in promoting yourself to your ultimate potential. Reading this book may be your ticket to the success which you've only dreamed about in the past.

A SPECIAL NOTE ON ETHICS

Consultants in some fields may feel restricted, because of ethical considerations, from using some of the recommendations that have been included in this book. Consider all recommendations with an open mind. If you still have reservations, after giving appropriate consideration to the evidence presented, contact your applicable professional organization for their advice. This will assure you that your marketing efforts will not be viewed as inappropriate by your peers.

RUDOLPH C. KEMPPAINEN

Chassell, Michigan
June 1988

CONTENTS

1
ASSESSING YOUR PERSONAL IMAGE   1

2
THE PROVEN IMAGE-BUILDING TECHNIQUES   11

3
OUTLINE APPROACH FOR MARKET STRATEGY   27

4
MEDIA SELECTION AND EMPHASIS:
KEYS TO FINANCIALLY EFFECTIVE PROMOTION   41

5
EFFECTIVE NEWSPAPER MARKETING TECHNIQUES   55

6
TARGET MARKETING THROUGH TRADE JOURNALS   69

7
POWER PROMOTION THROUGH RADIO ADVERTISING   81

8
TELEVISION ADVERTISING AND PROMOTION:
THE CRITICAL EDGE IN IMAGERY   95

9
CABLE TELEVISION AND SATELLITE SYSTEMS: EXPANDING TO THE NATIONAL FOCUS 113

10
ORGANIZING THE PROMOTIONAL NEWSLETTER 129

11
SPEECHES: KEY TO EFFECTIVE PUBLIC RELATIONS 153

12
SEMINAR POWER: PRESTIGE BUILDER FOR A CONSULTING BUSINESS 169

13
WRITING SEMINAR AND INSTRUCTION MANUALS 189

14
PROMOTING INDIVIDUAL CONSULTING: KEY TO LONG-TERM SUCCESS 205

INDEX 213

POWER CONSULTING

CHAPTER 1

ASSESSING YOUR PERSONAL IMAGE

Because professional consulting is predominantly a service as opposed to a tangible product, the image of the service provider is one of the most critical aspects in effectively reaching a target market. Your personal image, rather than an image of a tangible product, is the primary criterion on which a prospective consumer of your services will base his or her buying decision. Your purchaser will often be required to have faith in the quality of your work with no prior experience of it. This factor will be particularly in evidence if you do not have a lengthy track record in providing consulting services.

How do you put together the right "image package" to get the job done? Where do you begin the process?

The most important part of this process is to conduct an accurate self-appraisal of your *current* qualities. What is your current image? If it is not as favorable as you might like, how do you go about changing it?

In the first three chapters of this book, we will focus on these critical questions within which lie the secrets of your success. When these elements have been thoroughly defined, and modified when necessary, the remaining chapters will go into the use of various promotional vehicles to project this image to prospective clientele.

To begin the process, this chapter focuses on the self-assessment phase of the process. I will show you the important points involved in analyzing your personal and professional image. Further, I will help you check out your current marketability. As the final part of this process, I will show you how to step up your priorities for any needed image improvement.

ANALYZING YOUR CURRENT IMAGE

Top professional consultants are, by necessity, very public figures. This is one of the keys to their success. But this public stature has a price. They face the same measuring stick as politicians, and almost every facet of their lives, both professional and personal, becomes a factor in how they are viewed. Unfortunate as this may seem, it is a fact of life that must be dealt with effectively.

In making an accurate judgment about your image, you should recognize that you are "playing to an audience." What I mean by this is that your words, appearance, and actions are being scrutinized by clients and prospective clients alike.

First impressions are usually the most indelible. Making a good first impression is critical to a long-term, smooth, working relationship. It's human nature not to readily relinquish the first impressions that we obtain about others. Don't require this process from prospective clients.

Most people will make these first judgments within a few minutes. They are most likely to notice the basic four cornerstones of personal image. These are

1. Hairstyle
2. Fashion sense
3. Body language
4. Voice projection quality

Each of these four items, taken individually, may not be critical. But they can either add or detract from the total package. If one is negative, another facet may have to be twice as good to make up for it.

To help you judge yourself, let's take a look at how each of these items can have either a negative or positive impact on your projected image.

Hairstyle

Although we can't do much about whether or not we have hair, we can work effectively with what we do have. Some of us may have a full head of hair. Others, like myself, have found that time has gradually increased the amount of face that has to be washed in the morning.

Assuming you have something to style, what should you do about hairstyle? The decision should be based on the most conservative elements of your target market. Unless you're specializing in consulting to the rock music industry, you're going to be better off with a tasteful hairstyle that is not longer than customary norms.

Avoid hairstyles that seem to go against the natural way in which your hair tends to grow. This will help your hair to stay in place more naturally, avoiding the "messed-up look" that could happen during the course of a busy day.

Unless you're dealing with extremely upper-echelon professionals, it would also be wise to avoid a "glamour" look in hairstyling. Anyone who is integrally involved in the hands-on portions of a business is likely to feel out of place if your appearance suggests that you're headed for a party at the fanciest spot in the city.

For our female readers, it is a good idea to keep hairstyles smooth-flowing and not excessively long. Especially in the conservative business realm, the use of excessively tight curls isn't recommended unless your face is naturally long and needs a rounding effect for a more balanced appearance.

The key here is to avoid making your hair the center of attention, either positively or negatively. You want your client to think about what you're saying, not about how your hair looks.

Fashion Sense

Much of the advice given for hairstyles also applies in your selection of a business wardrobe. For most prospective markets, you don't need formal attire to make a favorable impression. Even in that bastion of conservative living, the banking community, this is not absolutely essential.

There is a marked tendency to overspend in this area when it isn't truly necessary. With a little bit of smart planning, an entire business wardrobe can be structured at minimal cost and project an image that makes you look like a million.

One of the quickest ways to get the "business suit" look is to assemble a wardrobe around a couple of tastefully tailored sport coats. With these, select matching slacks when a more formal appearance is desired and use contrasting colors when a more informal appearance is desirable. Darker colors are usually best in selecting coats. This will help you to appear conservative enough in almost any environment.

It's generally a good idea to go for solid colors in coats. You can always coordinate prints for slacks to vary the look. But prints in coat fabrics will tend to restrict your freedom of selection in slacks and cut down on the variety of looks that you can obtain from your wardrobe.

For women, the equivalent suit, consisting of a skirt (usually straight) and matching jacket over a plain or print blouse, seems to be the standard for business wear. The guidelines for men's clothing apply, with the exception that women have more leeway in questions of color, style, and accessories. Regular dresses can also be appropriate in many business situations, of course, but avoid low-cut tops or skirts above the knee.

Avoid excessive flashiness in attire. Flashiness might have worked for Liberace on stage, but it will appear strange in the office of a bank president. Common sense here is usually the best guide for how to proceed.

This approach may be varied somewhat if you decide to conduct seminars. In this setting, you must think about showmanship. In seminars, you need to consider methods of holding audience attention. A small amount of "flash" in this area might help. But don't overwhelm people with it. You don't want this to drown out the message that you wish to deliver.

As a final note, don't overdo it on flashy jewelry. One consultant and public speaker I know wears rings with mounted stones on almost every finger and diamond-studded gold cufflinks. This display of open wealth can sometimes cause prospective clients to resent the fees that they are asked to pay; they assume that the person receiving the money is much richer than the one paying it out.

Having the right fashion image is really a delicate balancing act. You want to appear successful without triggering resentment and excessive envy from your audience. Maintaining a tasteful middle ground in your approach is your best assurance of meeting this objective.

Body Language

After your prospective client has seen you and judged your appearance, the next key to establishing faith in you is projecting self-confidence. Body language, or how you carry yourself, is an essential part of this projection process.

People who sit completely still with their hands folded while they speak tend to appear lacking in essential confidence. Lack of animation creates an appearance of uncertainty that is readily picked up by the audience, whether it's one person or a hundred.

I could easily cite numerous examples of the positive influence that animated speech can have, but two examples from the national political arena clearly illustrate how this works.

In the 1960 compaign for the U.S. presidency, Vice-President Richard Nixon went up against John Kennedy. In a face-to-face debate, Nixon was stiff and unanimated in his presentation. By contrast, Kennedy used effective body language to accentuate the points that he made. Kennedy won the presidency.

Some experts felt that Nixon had a superior command of governmental facts. But he didn't make much of an impression. In 1968, Nixon wisely chose not to confront Hubert Humphrey in a similar debate. This was probably the key to his winning the presidency in his second effort.

Again in 1980, this same principle came forward in the presidential contest between Jimmy Carter and Ronald Reagan. Jimmy Carter stood at the podium, grasping it as though it were the last straw of a drowning man. By contrast, Ronald Reagan projected a relaxed, animated, and confident image. Although many felt that President Carter was more knowledgeable, Reagan won the debate—and the presidency in a landslide—by projecting himself better.

Take time to study the body language of successful public speakers. An excellent example is the evangelist Billy Graham. He holds audience attention by effectively combining speaking skills and delivery style. Whether or not we agree with what he has to say, few can disagree that he is *very* capable in delivering his message.

The secret of such effective speakers as Graham and Reagan is simple. They have developed their own comfortable forms of animated behavior, deeply rooted in the confidence they have in their command of the subjects on which they speak. Knowing your subject well is *not* enough. In animating your delivery, you convince your listener of the confidence you feel inside.

As a consultant, you are often called on to convince others to modify procedures, habits, or other behaviors. You will usually have greater success if your audience feels that *you* believe what you say. Animation in delivery is a key to attaining this important objective.

Voice Projection Quality

The final key is how you sound to your listener. Voice projection quality, like body language, helps to impress your listener regarding your information.

One of the deadliest "sins" that anyone in a position to persuade others can commit is to speak in a monotone. Anyone who fails to vary their tone of voice, at least minimally, is likely to bore their audience to sleep—even on an otherwise interesting subject.

If you've never done so before, consider delivering a speech into a tape recorder for practice. Then play it back and listen to how you sound. The result could be very revealing.

Pay special attention to your delivery of the most important points you want to make. Does the tone of your voice indicate that *you* think they're important? Does your voice indicate any emotion at all?

Often we fail to see (or hear) ourselves as others do. This exercise will help you to perfect your delivery style, eliminating any hesitancies that you might have, and to deliver with a better speaking quality that persuades your audience.

> **SPECIAL HINT**
>
> If you have access to a videotape camera and recorder, consider videotaping yourself to observe your body language as well as hear your speech patterns. The resulting tape will help you to pinpoint specific areas of weakness—and it could be the key to effective presentations in the future.

HOW MARKETABLE ARE YOU?

Based on the information just reviewed, you should have a pretty good idea of how you measure up. If this was the first time that you saw yourself as others see you, you may have been either pleasantly surprised or rudely awakened. In my case, that first look did *not* yield any pleasant surprises. But it pointed to needed improvements in numerous areas.

Let's take a quick review of points, using a checklist, to see how your total picture shapes up. Check each item that applies to your particular case.

Marketability Checklist

( ) 1. Possess firm grasp of subject matter.
( ) 2. Have confidence in your own abilities.
( ) 3. Project confidence without being cocky.
( ) 4. Wear tasteful attire.
( ) 5. General appearance is pleasant.
( ) 6. Voice patterns are capable of generating listener interest.
( ) 7. Get along well with a variety of people.
( ) 8. Capable of honest analysis of self and others.

Checking Your Results

Ideally, if you can check all eight items on the marketability checklist, you are an ideal candidate for marketing. But few of us, if we're truly honest with ourselves, can check off all eight. At least that's true when we're first starting out.

After you've gained experience, you probably can hit 100 percent. Initially, however, getting six of the eight items can be considered a fairly good score.

The first three qualities in the checklist are absolutely essential if any person is to be marketed with *any* measure of success. The fourth through sixth qualities on the list are items that can be learned, if they are not already present. Possessing the final two qualities will separate you from the pack in terms of marketing longevity. These two assets will determine your ability to generate repeat business from clients and to adjust to changing conditions.

Because people in our society are so visually oriented, you should be particularly aware of points 3 through 5 on the list. These qualities are central to successful initial marketing. You want potential customers to be attracted to your services.

After you have attracted them as customers, possession of the first three qualities, along with the seventh, will usually be sufficient to keep them loyal to you for years to come. Being able to check off those four points indicates that you can produce results when it counts.

ESTABLISHING DEVELOPMENTAL PRIORITIES

Although there may be some of us lucky enough not to need any improvements, most of us are likely to need at least one rough edge smoothed out. A thorough self-appraisal sometimes creates a discouragingly long list of necessary changes.

If you're faced with a long list of faults based on your review of the preceding subsection, don't try to make all the improvements at once. Changes of habit are often very difficult to make. Eliminating one shortfall at a time can be difficult enough, particularly if it has become deeply ingrained as habit. Taking on a whole group of problems at once could prove impossible psychologically.

Just as we can only live our lives one day at a time, we can only solve our problems one step at a time. Take a serious look at your list of needed improvements. Tackle the one that you consider the toughest first. Be determined to overcome this first problem. Your success here will give you an immeasurable boost psychologically in facing the remainder of your list. If you can topple the toughest problem, the rest will seem like the proverbial piece of cake by comparison to it.

Treat your list with the same attitude displayed by a marathon runner toward a race. Pace yourself. Set realistic time goals for accomplishment.

Your author is an excellent case in point. I had an unconscious habit, whenever I was waiting for a meeting to start, to rhythmically tap my heel on the floor. This habit could be enough to drive people around me crazy.

Rather than chastise myself for it, making myself more tense and making the problem more likely, I taught myself to relax. Although it took me almost two months to break the habit, I was successful. The rest of my "rough edges" were relatively easy, by comparison, to conquer.

By tackling your toughest problem first, while your resolve and enthusiasm for the assignment is at its strongest, you are more likely to succeed.

As you progress to the end of your personal list, don't hesitate to congratulate yourself. Find some small way to reward yourself for success. This will help you to maintain adequate motivation to complete the task before you. Don't let up your drive, simply because the final tasks are easier than the starting ones. Maintain your momentum. This is the secret to developing positive habits that will effectively replace the negative ones you wished to change.

As a final note, don't be surprised—or discouraged—if you experience an occasional episode of backsliding. You may find that some of your old habits may want to reassert themselves into your life. This really isn't all that unusual. But if you are determined to control your life, instead of letting your life control you, you should be able to finally eliminate these problems completely.

> **SPECIAL HINT ON MAINTAINING PERSONAL PERSPECTIVE**
>
> Whenever we embark on a personal improvement program, it can be tempting to be *too* hard on ourselves. We become so focused on the negatives in our lives that we run the risk of viewing our total beings negatively. This can effectively defeat your objective to developing and projecting a positive self-image.
>
> To keep your outlook positive, make a list of both your strengths and your weaknesses. Write them down in a two-column list, a variation on the listing technique mentioned earlier.
>
> Doing this gives you a graphic summary to read and review and will help you to maintain a perspective on your life while you are striving for self-improvement. As you make needed changes in your life, put these changes on the positive side of your list. Periodically revise this list as tangible proof of your progress.
>
> Seeing the positive side of the list gradually grow while the negative side shrinks will further motivate you to continue your self-improvement program. Don't hesitate to use any aids you can think of to motivate you further. Any long-term program can benefit from this technique.
>
> Positive reinforcement always works wonders. Don't focus your attention on what you are giving up. Instead, think of what you are gaining. Focus on the increased income and what it can buy for you and your family, and on the increased community prestige that you will gain through your efforts. Looking back rarely benefits us measurably, except when we strive to correct past mistakes. Keeping our eyes on the future usually works better.

CLOSING THOUGHTS

Through the course of this book, we will be reviewing and discussing various methods of projecting personal and professional image to prospective clients for your consulting services. But we really can't do that until we have a clear definition of what your image is.

This is why this first chapter is so important to your success. A common pitfall of self-improvement programs is the failure to identify practical applications for the improvements we make. In order to achieve any goal, whether it is self-improvement or a distant vacation destination, you have to know where you currently stand before you can map out your journey.

When you have identified the separate elements of your image and are satisfied with them, you can begin the process of promoting it. The next two chapters will deal with transforming an intangible image into a marketable "product" for your prospective service consumer.

If you have studied this chapter thoroughly and followed its suggestions, you should have a solid idea of exactly what you can offer to your clientele in both image and tangible service. The next step is to identify the market need and mold your image to fit that need. The practical applications, mentioned a moment ago, are discussed in the next chapter.

CHAPTER 2

THE PROVEN IMAGE-BUILDING TECHNIQUES

It's been said that one of the quickest lessons in humility is gained when one looks into a mirror the first thing in the morning. What stares back at us isn't always that complimentary.

Even when we perceive the reflected image as flattering, it may not be the way that other people view us. When we have a positive self-image, the real trick becomes to get people around us to view us the way we see ourselves.

In this chapter, we'll take a closer look at the differences between these two views and how you can narrow the gap. We'll discuss how prospective clients analyze marketing strategies presented for their consumption, and how to gear your efforts to meet client needs. One of the most common problems that you will face in your marketing efforts is the natural skepticism that any sophisticated businessperson is likely to have. Your assignment, in gearing your marketing efforts, is to turn the natural skeptic into a firm believer.

ANALYZING THE PERCEPTUAL DIFFERENCE

Quite often, in the course of our busy lives, we don't pay enough attention to the way in which people around us react to our presence. There is a strong tendency to focus on a particular objective—and to ignore peripheral matters completely.

This makes the split-second analysis of a situation almost impossible to complete accurately. You may be achieving your objectives in one way or another, but you may be choosing courses of action that don't yield responses as quickly—or as easily—as possible. That can make a dramatic difference in the hourly monetary yield for your efforts.

Let's take a quick look, in checklist form, at how you view your business capabilities. Check off each item that you feel accurately describes you.

Self-Perception Checklist

( ) 1. Able to quickly and accurately judge the value of ideas.
( ) 2. Have the ability to get ideas across to others.
( ) 3. Circle of close friends seems to grow steadily.
( ) 4. Able to implement others' ideas accurately.
( ) 5. Associates value your opinions.
( ) 6. Relationship with associates is harmonious.

If you were able to check off each of the items in the preceding checklist, your self-image is quite high. If your self-estimation is correct, you have a considerable ability to influence people to do what you want them to do.

Now the important question is whether or not others see you in the same way. Let's do a comparative reaction test to see whether the results are the same.

Colleague Influence Checklist

( ) 1. Associates frequently review their ideas with you in their formulative stages.
( ) 2. Associates quickly demonstrate their understanding of ideas that you present.
( ) 3. Friends often confide personal details of their lives to you.
( ) 4. You often receive compliments from associates on your work quality.
( ) 5. Colleagues seek your advice frequently.
( ) 6. Any disagreements with associates are quickly resolved on a friendly basis.

At this point, it would be valuable to compare your two lists. It is one thing to view yourself favorably—and quite another to have that image translate itself into tangible action. Let's put the two checklists side by side and compare the responses.

In the self-perception checklist, you may have checked off the first item and not done the same in the colleague influence checklist. The difference here is quite obvious. You may feel very capable of evaluating ideas effectively, but this ability has not been translated and communicated to the people around you. They do not recognize your ability as you do. If they did, they would be bringing their ideas to you, even in their formulative stages, to get your suggestions.

The second item is of equal importance. People may listen to you, politely nod their heads, and go off to do as they please. They don't remember what you said, and they couldn't care less about it. As a result, you've wasted your wind on them—and you have no results to show for your efforts.

If, by contrast, your listeners show their comprehension through more than polite nods of their heads, you've made some very tangible progress in gearing their responses appropriately. You can very readily judge this by seeing whether people act in ways that you recommend to them. Do they follow instructions that you provide? Or, by contrast, does it take several abortive efforts before something is accomplished to specifications?

If you have problems in this particular area, you may be too sparing in your use of descriptive phrasing. If you want someone to perform a swan dive, you don't simply tell them to "jump in the lake." You have to be specific.

In the rush to get through a larger group of details, you may be guilty of giving the light brush to specificity. Then you're frustrated by inadequate results— and by having to go back to provide more direction. Being specific at the beginning reduces the time between directive and accomplishment in almost every case. That translates itself into higher dollar yields for your time.

The third item on each list really centers on the true quality of the friendships that you develop. There is often a tendency, particularly in the business environment, to emphasize quantity over quality in the friendships we develop. You may end up with a lot of acquaintances and very few true friends.

The real test is whether people are equally willing to interact with you on a social basis as they are on business matters. If they aren't, they probably view your value primarily on the basis of what benefits their association with you will bring to them. They don't really care about you as a person and, because of that, they shouldn't be considered in your true circle of friends.

It's important to recognize the difference between the two groups—and to know which person goes into which group. When you need something accomplished quickly, a true friend is most likely to accommodate you. Others will act out of a sense of obligation and, as a result, may leave much to be desired in both promptness and quality.

Comparing your responses to the fourth item on both lists really cues you in on whether your efforts are recognized in the same way that you see them. You may figure that you're doing a good job, but your associates may not necessarily share such a glowing appraisal.

If someone comes up to you and volunteers a positive response to your work, you know that you've made a positive impression. There is a valid caution to be made here, though. Don't put a whole lot of stock into compliments that you fish out of people. If they don't volunteer favorable comments, they may be giving you the response they figure you want to hear— not what they truly feel about your efforts.

The fifth item concerns a sticky problem for many of us, particularly those of us in executive positions. People may respond to your advice favorably—and even respond with relative cheerfulness to your directives. But that may be because you're seen as their meal ticket, and nothing else.

Publicly, they may be very agreeable to your volunteered advice. But, privately, they may wish you'd lose face or, even worse, your job.

When associates seek your advice on their own initiative, you know that they value it. Your advice isn't merely being forced down their throats because of your position in the power structure.

Item 6 on both checklists concerns the same problem as the fifth. You may perceive that your relationship with associates is harmonious, simply because they are agreeing with you. Even a cat will purr contentedly when it's petted according to the natural lay of its hair. But that can change quickly if you pet it against the grain.

True harmony in your business relationships is best judged when differences of opinion occur. If you can settle them in ways that provide a measure of satisfaction for everyone—the noble art of compromise—you do indeed have the ability to have a harmonious relationship. This will assure that your associates' smiles will be genuine—and not immediately erased when you leave the room.

TRANSLATING PERCEPTIONS INTO RESULTS

Studying the preceding section may have knocked the stuffing out of your self-image. If so, take heart. Most of us flunk out on a point or two in that group.

The important thing is that we begin with a dose of reality and honesty as a starting point in our efforts. If we hope to influence large groups of people, we must have the ability, first, to influence people individually.

Establishing a Personal Approach with a Client

The most common failure of mass marketing approaches is a tendency toward impersonality. This is based on a failure to recognize that, while the message is going out to a large number of people, each response is on an *individual* basis.

This book is an excellent example of this principle in action. We may never meet personally. I may never get to know your name. But there is no question about one thing. I am talking directly to you—through the words on these pages. There will probably be a large number of people with interests similar to yours who will also read this book. But there is no question that when you're reading these words, I'm not talking to a group of other people. My attention is focused on your interests and the needs of your professional life.

This is the essential secret in converting the skeptical recipient of your promotional message into a loyal customer. Our society has become, to a major degree, very impersonal. Defying that trend is one of the surest ways to get anyone's attention. You must make that person realize that you are interested in their success. Don't address that person as a corporation. Speak to him or her as an individual.

Get down-home and personal with a prospective client in your marketing approach, regardless of whether you use a mass market letter or other method. To illustrate, here's a sample of a letter opening that sets a personalized tone.

Sample Letter Opening

Dear Colleague:

I'm sure that you, as I do, receive a lot of advertising mail. Over 90 percent of it quickly ends up in that "round file" next to your desk, headed for the incinerator or garbage truck.

Before you send my letter to that fate, I hope that you'll share a few minutes of your time with me. I would consider it a personal honor if you did. They could be some of the most profitable minutes you've invested in a long time.

I'm the president of a consulting firm that specializes in helping professionals manage their offices more effectively. Through the use of my company's resource bases, I've helped many people just like you to gain the major personal satisfaction that comes from professional success.

Here are some of the ways in which I could help you . . .

The letter would go on to tell about some of your consulting benefits to the prospective consumer.

You probably noted the conversational, very informal tone of the letter's opening. It's done that way for a very specific reason. Consumers are used to the hard sell—and have developed a psychological resistance to it. Your recipient has also been frustrated by a lot of mail that really doesn't do much to help his or her business efforts.

This letter recognizes, and emphathizes with, that frustration. Then it delivers an important message. It says, "Sure, I understand they've frustrated you. I can understand why. *But I'm different!*"

Once that bold statement has been made, the rest of the letter has to deliver on that promise. If you've done your homework, you will be able to do exactly that.

Consumer skepticism is a difficult hurdle for any marketing effort. That's the way people are. We're naturally inclined to believe that the advertiser's primary interest is not us—but getting their hands on our money.

Although that skepticism is a major problem in advertising a product, it is even more of a problem for a service-related business. If you're offering something to consumers that they can't hold in their hands, they will naturally wonder exactly when they've received what they've paid for.

This is one reason why many professional service providers are particularly wary about mass-market advertising approaches. They feel that it would sacrifice the personal touch that is extremely important in overcoming consumer skepticism. As we've seen here, it's truly possible to have the best of *both* worlds.

TWO TIPS FOR DIRECT MAIL

Tip No. 1
When forming address files, always use a person's name before a corporate name. An example:

Joseph Blank, President
Blank Machine Company, Inc.

The difference may seem very subtle. But there's a reason for it. You are addressing your mail to a person—not to a company. That will complement the personal approach of the envelope's contents.

Tip No. 2
Whenever possible, avoid the use of postage meters. Take the time to put standard postage stamps on the envelopes.

The mark of a postage meter on an envelope tends to identify it as something that has been ground out mechanically. The envelope lacks the personal feeling that comes when it's obvious that someone has taken the time to affix a stamp to it. When time is a priority in opening mail, the letter that looks like junk mail will not get attention—even if you invested first class postage to send it.

A SPECIAL NOTE TO REMEMBER

One currently used but consumer-resistant ploy is to mark envelopes with the words "Personal and Confidential" in an effort to get mail in to the person addressed—and past that watchful secretary in the front office. Unfortunately, this has been used quite extensively by advertisers for so-called adult products.

For this reason, I wouldn't recommend its use for consultants. An uptight secretary may throw your envelope into the wastebasket as a matter of principle, thinking that it's a condom advertisement. That would be unfortunate, particularly if that isn't what you're selling. The ploy rarely achieves its desired objective anymore and isn't really worth seriously considering for standard business usage.

A NOTE ON A PC TRICK

If you have a personal computer (PC) at your disposal, you have an excellent opportunity to make your marketing letters truly personalized with a minimum of time and effort. Most PCs have word processors with "mail-merge," a function that can customize letters with the recipient's name and address. Each recipient gets the same basic letter text, individually addressed. When you combine this approach with printing on your business letterhead, the recipient isn't likely to ever be able to tell that the letter wasn't produced for an individual customer. That illusion is bound to impress any recipient.

KEYS TO THE PRESTIGE IMAGE

Although most of us in the consulting business are searching for that elusive quality called prestige, few of us really understand its primary components. We recognize those individuals and companies that have it, but the underlying formula for acquiring it seems elusive to pin down.

Earlier in this chapter, we reviewed two separate checklists in which the qualities that effectively influence others were described. These qualities are some of the main elements that go into the development of the prestige image.

Gaining the Respect and Trust of a Client

To simplify these qualities to some degree, let's reduce them to a letter-designated principle—the *RTP Principle*. Expressed in equation form, it is:

Respect + Trust = Prestige

There is *no way* that any businessperson can enjoy the benefits of true prestige if either of these two elements are missing. They must be together, and firmly interlocked, in the same person's characteristics to achieve prestige.

The central problem, however, is that we may have a faulty perception of what constitutes respect and trust. Particularly in the case of respect, we may misinterpret the reactions that we receive.

As an example, an executive may wield a tremendous amount of personal and professional power because of his or her position in a corporate structure. That power, however, is not true respect. An employee may respond with *apparent* respect because he has five kids and a wife to feed and monthly mortgage and car payments to make, and the thought of losing employment scares the living daylights out of him. This is respect created by fear.

More effective respect is created through a sense of trust. That's the type of respect that will be of most benefit in your consulting efforts.

A dairy farmer friend once told me that cows and people aren't really too much different from each other. "If the cow trusts you," he told me, "you don't have to pull as hard to get the milk out. If people trust you, they're likely to tell you more than you'd ever want to know about them."

The "milk" on which your efforts thrive is the information that your clients provide about their business activities. You don't want your client to withhold important facts from you that could affect your recommendations. But your client has to be able to trust you.

How do you achieve that sense of trust? One of the best ways is to maintain a strict policy of discretion and confidentiality. If your client perceives *any* inclination in you to spread business gossip, he or she won't feel free to discuss important competitive factors about the business situation.

The objective is to relax your client, not to get too relaxed on the job yourself. If you do, you might end up getting too "chatty" in the relationship. When you start telling things like, "Did you hear how so-and-so got themselves into trouble?" you may get an attentive audience for the business gossip, but you close off the source of information available from your listener. Why should a client tell you something that you might repeat in the offices of another client? That wouldn't be to his or her advantage, particularly if your other client is a direct competitor.

Look at your relationship with your client in the same way as clergy should view information received in a confessional. What your client tells you in the privacy of a business office should *never* leave there. I make it a personal policy never to divulge names of business associates who deal with me—except by their expressed permission. I never actively solicit that permission. I'll only accept it if it is clearly volunteered by the client, as in a referral of a colleague to me.

This is the reason why any techniques that I've recommended to any of my clients—or any success secrets that I might share in this book—will be shared in an anonymous form. Unless the source has given me specific permission, no names will be used within these covers. I'd seriously recommend that you adopt an equally stringent policy in this key area.

As a final note, don't succumb to the temptation to become too cocky or overbearing with a client, in a vain effort to make an impression. There is a fine line between confidence and arrogance. Sometimes in the process of learning the difference, we can step into some pitfalls that can alienate us from clients.

An overbearing attitude won't be a display of confidence. Most people will assume that you're trying to compensate for some type of personal insecurity. A calm, nonfidgety approach will go much further in your effort to display confidence.

When you talk with a client or prospective client personally, don't avoid eye contact. If you're looking everywhere but at the woman client you're talking to, she'll start wondering who you're talking to—her or the decorations on the wall. Eye contact tells your listener that you believe in what you're saying—and want them to believe it, too.

BENEFITS AND PROBLEMS OF THE PRESTIGE IMAGE

One of the nicest things about the prestige image is that, once established, it tends to grow with the passage of time. As long as you continue to deliver positive results and don't do something that reflects badly on your reputation, your good reputation will precede you into almost any situation.

Of course, there's another side to that coin. When your good name has been established in the business community, expectations for your performance will also rise. Sometimes a consultant may be viewed as a "miracle worker" who can rescue even the business that's a lost cause. None of us can walk on water—or rescue a client who has gone past the point of no return.

When this type of situation is present, an important part of maintaining prestige is to accurately appraise the problem—and honestly tell a prospective client that the situation is not salvageable. If you take on a no-win situation, simply for the associated fee involved, you will develop a reputation as someone who will do anything for a price. That can quickly throw your prestige image out of the nearest window.

Prestige, and the publicity that often comes with it, also will put an increased responsibility on your shoulders. Whatever you do, don't take that responsibility lightly. Be certain that prospective clients have realistic expectations for obtainable results. You might cause some prospective clients to look elsewhere for service. After being taken for a financial ride by someone less scrupulous, clients will end up singing your praises for your honesty. Over the long term, you will reap the benefits through increased business volume.

Consider the benefits that can accrue. One example is a medical practice consultant who spent several of her first years accepting every call that came her way. She developed the image of being "hungry" for the business. Despite that image, she rarely topped the $100,000 annual income range.

That changed dramatically when she turned down a few clients who requested her services. Word soon spread that her services were quite "exclusive"—and that prospective clients were truly fortunate if they were able to retain her services. With that information out in the target market, her business volume jumped to the $250,000 annual mark with very little modification in her advertising budget.

Most of us place more value on things that are more difficult to acquire. The same idea applies, in many cases, to consultant services. Being perceived as "selective" only serves to add to your consulting prestige.

UNDERSTANDING YOUR MARKET'S NEEDS

Although the results of detailed market surveys are nice to have as a starting point, there are other ways to get useful preliminary market data. Doing some homework on a given metropolitan or geographical area usually yields valuable clues on what types of consulting services are most likely to be in demand.

Metropolitan areas are usually the most prolific hunting ground for prospective clients. But, with a measure of study, any area can provide a considerable pool of available business. The primary difference is that, outside the metropolitan area, where the density of prospective clients is lower, travel time between contacts will be longer.

The first step, of course, is to determine your preliminary market area. This can be a section of a city, as might be the case in New York, or an area as wide as four or five counties in more rural areas. Check available business directories to see which professional or business groups are most prolifically represented in your area. This basic research will give you a good idea whether or not it will pay to specialize in a narrower consulting field. A larger pool of potential clients can make specialization a feasible option, making your marketing approach easier to sharply define.

The second step is to determine what concerns are most prevalent in your target market. This can be done in one of two ways. The most popular is by survey, either by telephone canvass polling or by mailing questionnaires.

Another effective method is to check out the trade or professional journals that cover your chosen field. These journals will usually reflect the most dominant concerns, on a national level, that these people have. Although national concerns of a professional or business group may not affect each individual prospect equally, there is usually enough commonality of interests to assure that addressing these concerns will get the prospective client's attention.

The most likely pitfall in this process is to excessively narrow your market focus. Whenever you narrow the focus you reduce the pool of prospective clients. If you have only a few hundred potential clients, you don't have a sufficient base from which to draw an adequate clientele to make a consulting business thrive. No one, regardless of their marketing savvy, can expect to get *every* potential client as a customer.

TAILORING YOUR IMAGE TO THE TARGET MARKET

When you have made the basic decisions regarding definition of your target market, the next step is to do the "snip and tuck" tailoring of your image to appeal to that market. The most important consideration here is to thoroughly understand the group's approximate location on the political spectrum and any ethics, restrictions or considerations that might be involved.

In general, promotion aimed at any group shouldn't be much flashier than that which the group itself uses. If you use more flash than your prospective clients, they may feel that you don't understand the needs and restraints of their business or profession. As a result, they may not even bother to inquire about your services.

I am not saying that no humor or attention-getting vehicle is allowed in consultant advertising. Not so! It's up to you to develop your instinct about where and when to apply such devices.

As an example, I know of an attorney, specializing in contract negotiations, who serves as the representative for management at bargaining tables on a regional basis. On the back of his business card is a cartoon of two fellows in conversation. One of them has had his buttocks quite obviously carved out. The less fortunate fellow is being asked, "How'd you do on your last business deal?"

On the front of the card is the attorney's name and the words, "Contract Negotiations My Specialty." Just beneath are two lines that read, "We won't let THAT happen to you / See back of card."

With just a pinch of humor, this attorney is delivering a very serious message to a prospective client. Any prospect considering his services fears precisely what has happened on the back of the card. The attorney is telling the prospect that, if they retain his services, that won't happen.

This illustration is available from several different printing companies that handle business cards. Whenever I see the illustration, I get a small chuckle out of it. I always remember how that attorney used it.

Of course, this approach wouldn't be appropriate for everyone. The standard rule is that you won't have a problem if you err slightly on the side of conservatism. But, as my example showed, every rule seems made to be broken. The real impact comes when you observe the rules generally, breaking them only for special effect. The variance is what makes the presentation memorable.

As an example, if the earlier mentioned attorney had used humor in *everything* he presented to a prospective client, he would end up looking like a fool. No client would take him seriously. But that's not the case. All of his other materials are as straight-laced and conservative as possible. His letterhead has so much sobriety and dignity that even a funeral director would embrace it with open arms.

Humor, like salt, should be used sparingly. If they aren't, they will both leave a bad taste behind. A little of both goes a long way.

Good taste is the key to success here. Unfortunately, it, like beauty, is in the eye of the beholder. If in doubt, stay conservative. Knowing your "beholder" is important to being sure that presentations don't offend those whom you wish to attract. That's what makes studying your target market so important. It will help you to avoid adding too much "salt"—and driving away many prospective clients (and their dollars) from your consulting business.

PACKAGING YOUR IMAGE

So far, we've reviewed the key determinants in how prospective clients will see you—and decide whether they will retain your services as a consultant. That *first* positive decision by a prospective client is often the most difficult to acquire. When a client knows your skill level from past experience, and finds it satisfactory, getting repeat business from that client isn't likely to be that difficult.

It's that first decision that is addressed by prestige image development and its surrounding packaging. With no experience, a new client has to take a "leap of faith." Without some reasonably good rationale for action, this decision could seem like jumping from a high-flying plane without a parachute. Few of us are willing to commit commercial "suicide."

That's where image packaging plays an important role. Your assignment is to bring all your positive attributes together into a coherent presentation that will make that first leap less scary for the prospective client.

The process is very similar to assembling a job résumé. As an independently employed person, you're constantly "looking for a job." You have to approach prospective clients as if they were prospective employers. They must be convinced of qualifications in several general areas, including the following:

1. Educational background
2. Experience with subject matter involved
3. Prior positive results
4. Reliability

Although each of these factors is relatively important individually, you won't convince anyone of your suitability without qualifying in every factor. As an example, it doesn't matter that clients can count on you to show up—if you don't know what you're talking about when you get there.

You may have an exceptionally good educational background, but if you haven't shown an ability to adapt your knowledge to a given field, you won't be of as much value to the client. This is where, sometimes, experience can carry a whole lot more weight than education.

When you package your image for mass market consumption, it is usually best not to get too specific about any of these factors. Like a fisherman, you are dangling bait out there to attract fish (clients). Neither fish nor clients can be hooked until they bite the bait.

In fishing, the size of fish being attracted is usually directly proportional to the size of bait being offered. The same principle, in general terms, applies to attracting clients.

The important thing is to know the size and population (demographics) of the lake (client pool) that you're fishing in. If there are a lot of large "fish" in either one, it pays to increase the size of your bait.

By contrast, if you're only fishing where small fish reside, a bait that is too large will bring no results at all. Smaller clients will view the situation from a strictly financial viewpoint. They will feel that they won't be able to afford your fees—and decide that even an inquiry would be a waste of time.

CLOSING THOUGHTS

Most consultants start their careers on a restricted and localized basis in which a strong, direct, interpersonal selling approach can effectively meet the initial needs of their business. In many ways, this is the best approach for the beginner in the consulting field. We all have to get established some way, and this is as good as any.

Eventually, most of us become frustrated with a limited client base and begin dreaming of expanding our businesses to enjoy the income we feel we deserve. That is the point when mass marketing strategies become *mandatory* to achieving our objectives.

Facing this reality, we find ourselves on the horns of a dilemma. To maintain reasonable costs in mass marketing, we are forced to communicate our promotional message as quickly as possible—while maintaining a satisfactory measure of coherency.

This requires us to crystallize and condense our thinking, deciding what things are the most important to our message. This means that we have to know our strengths, select those most likely to convince prospective clients, and project them through the media that these clients are most likely to contact.

In these first two chapters, our attention has been concentrated on helping you to decide what strengths are the most important to project. You have to have a firm knowledge of your starting point before you can commence with your journey to success. We've also taken a look at some ways in which vital areas could be strengthened, if necessary.

In the chapters that follow, we focus our attention on honing a marketing strategy based on your specific business goals—whether they are regional or national in scope. As we review these various promotional vehicles, you will discover how to make the intelligent choices that will fit your individual needs and objectives.

I want you to go as far as your strength, talent, and ambition will carry you. The information that follows will help you toward that important objective.

CHAPTER 3

OUTLINE APPROACH FOR MARKET STRATEGY

With the clear definition of your personal image—both its strengths and weaknesses—that you've gained in the first two chapters, it's time to begin planning your comprehensive marketing strategy to effectively project that image to prospective clients. The key to success lies in the comprehensiveness of your total approach.

One of the most common pitfalls in marketing professional services is the lack of a long-term plan that won't be outgrown by the business. This is one of the essential weaknesses of one-on-one marketing strategies: You can't reach out to enough potential clients to assure more than nominal short-term growth, and you severely limit your options for long-term growth.

In this chapter, we will assume that you have no current marketing program in place that does more than touch one potential client at a time. As we progress in this chapter, you will see that the approach advocated here is radically different from that used in the one-to-one operational mode.

This chapter covers such important areas as establishing the need for consultant services, conducting the fast preliminary market survey, assessing survey results, and deciding where to begin your marketing thrust. The chapter also presents a special "stage" marketing outline process and shows you how to establish priorities and implement an outline plan. The contents of this chapter are geared to convert your consulting practice into a mass marketing product. Every step in this chapter is aimed at this important high-profit objective.

ESTABLISHING THE NEED FOR CONSULTING SERVICES

Far too many consulting practices today are opened on the premise that having a better mousetrap will bring the world to their doors. Unfortunately, this nonaggressive premise, like the trap, gets you only one "mouse" at a time. Practice growth remains quite lethargic.

The better route is to establish consultant service need in a given area *before* you open up the office. Your key determinant will be the range of knowledge on which your services are based. Examine the immediate locality of the proposed practice location to see whether enough potential clients exist for your services in the immediate vicinity.

This is an important factor, especially in the preliminary stages of practice development, to assure that your initial promotional costs are controlled. Your first promotional efforts will, by necessity, be of modest scope. You won't want to mortgage everything just for the initial promotional budget.

After you have established that a potential client base exists in a small radius, check surrounding communities. In this early stage, let various Chambers of Commerce know about your plans. These organizations can be an excellent source for preliminary client base data that will be useful in your planning process.

This process will require some research time for data collection, but you'll have the knowledge to make a decision on where to concentrate your preliminary advertising efforts. Collecting data within a 50-mile radius of your proposed practice location is a manageable operation at this initial point.

Determination of client-base size is strictly grounded on your preliminary capability to handle business. In the mass market approach, which is hinged on passive audience receptivity and subsequent motivation to action, an initial response rate of 3 to 4 percent on an available client base is considered fairly good.

With this in mind, decide how many clients you will need to get things rolling properly. As an example, you may want to start out with a client list numbering approximately 30. To achieve this, you need approximately 750 to 1,000 potential clients in the proposed market area to get an initial clientele of 30 quickly into your practice. The central question becomes whether this number of potential clients exists in your initial market area.

You may well receive considerably more responses to your advertising efforts than that, but the key lies in converting them from preliminary interest into firm clients. The percentages noted above refer to contractually sealed clients.

As part of your research, check into the number of potential competitors for these same consulting dollars. Most will probably not be direct competitors for you, but they may be tangentially involved in similar areas. This factor has to be considered as you promote in this market.

CONDUCTING THE FAST MARKET SURVEY

After you have determined that potential clients exist for your services, the next step is a quick market survey to assess consumer interest. A common pitfall of these preliminary surveys is to emphasize so much detail that a data deluge sometimes inhibits the decision-making process.

The fast preliminary market survey involves two essential steps: (1) development of a mailing list and (2) sending out a consulting firm profile and coupon of interest. This mailing will be quite adequate to get a reasonably accurate feel for your ability to reach these potential clients.

When you develop this first mailing, offer preliminary information to the respondents about what services you are offering. Include a reply coupon that has a space to indicate whether they feel that they can make use of such services at some point in the future. Emphasize, in this mailing, that response does not create an obligation to contract for services. This will assure a higher percentage rate of survey response.

This survey technique will also help you to refine your internal mailing lists to focus future marketing efforts on companies that responded favorably. Whenever marketing mailings are conducted, these will receive priority treatment.

Another technique is a telephone canvass of the market area. If you have the resources to conduct this approach, you can compile data much more quickly than you could otherwise. Inform the respondents of your preliminary plans to locate services in the area. Ask respondents to rate the importance to them of a new consulting service for the area.

The only caution in this technique is that, because respondents are passive (no purchase decision required), some responses should be taken with a grain of salt. Major polling organizations that regularly conduct telephone surveys have a built-in error factor for their surveys to take this passivity into account. This error factor is generally plus or minus 5 percentage points.

Avoid burdening respondents with an extensive list of questions. This will help to reduce the emotional fatigue factor, which can adversely taint survey results. If people feel that you're asking too many questions, they will likely tell you what you want to hear—just to get rid of you.

Regardless of which technique you choose to use for surveys, avoid artificially restricting the number of potential respondents. The effectiveness of any survey expands in direct proportion to the number of people being surveyed.

Respondents who are interested should be asked what their specific priorities for service are. This will give you a more concise profile of the mass market that you are attempting to reach with your message. As an important adjunct, you should also ask the approximate business volume size of the respondent. That will tell you how extensive services can be—and what potential clients can afford.

Few other details are really necessary in this preliminary survey. You aren't compiling corporate life histories here. Your primary goal is to determine whether these potential clients have interest in, and can afford, the services that you will offer.

ASSESSING SURVEY RESULTS

After you have received survey responses, your next step is to compile these responses to form indicative keys to your next steps. Generally, the responses to larger blanket surveys of a market area will tell you only about basic receptivity to a new promotional effort, and not convertibility into established clients.

Within this context, you should receive a minimum 30-percent positive response to your survey regarding need for services. A response less than that indicates a serious misjudgment of the market area—and a clear warning to go back to the drawing board. In most instances, you can reasonably expect positive response to be in the neighborhood of 65 to 75 percent.

As a practical guideline, we might use the 50-percent-positive response level as a determinant. A response above this level is a reasonably clear green light to proceed. A positive response level between 30 and 50 percent should be taken as a caution light, indicating that either the proposed service is not marketable or the way in which it was introduced is faulty.

Also, be careful to assess the level of positive responses in terms of the rate of responses. This is particularly applicable to the mail-in survey system. If you're not getting a fairly high rate of survey returns, you can safely assume that you aren't generating interest.

Unlike general advertising, surveys generally create a fairly high rate of response when no purchase obligation is attached to the effort. People are naturally inclined to give you their opinions (even uninvited, sometimes) on various subjects. If you can personalize the tone of your survey, you will capitalize on the flattery factor to further enhance the response rate.

If you've done your job well, you are likely to receive about a 30-percent response rate for a mail-in survey. This is especially true when the market radius is relatively small. This response percentage rate tends to decline as the radius of the area increases. When a survey is local, the response rate is generally much higher than could be expected from a more regional approach.

Taking these guidelines into account, review your compiled survey statistics. If they fall into the positive action range, you're all set to get your total marketing programming rolling on the road to success.

SURVEY RESULTS AS A PROMOTIONAL STARTING POINT

Division of survey results into community-based clusters is probably the best preliminary step to assure the success of your first promotional efforts.

Levels of interest indicated in each cluster will show you where your advertising dollars will be most soundly invested.

Many consultants, like other businesspersons, tend to start their promotional efforts in the media closest to their base of operations. This most often includes their hometown newspapers. This approach is usually dictated by sentiment, not concrete marketing data.

Assuming that you've analyzed your survey results with an eye to communities, you will be in a better position to decide whether that favorite hometown publication is *really* the best choice for your first advertising. If your best survey results come from another community, especially one nearby, you might be better served by advertising there first. Since it's nearby, you're likely to receive some promotional benefits in your home area as well.

In showing interest in you, the people in this area have paid you a compliment. Advertising in that community's newspaper is, in a sense, returning the compliment by showing your primary interest in them as well. This "flattery factor" shouldn't be discounted for its positive business-building effects.

KNOWING WHERE TO BEGIN

As you begin your promotional effort, call public attention to the survey that you conducted. Recipients of the survey will have their memory refreshed regarding your community presence. Respondents will have a natural curiosity about how their responses affected, or failed to affect, the business that you launched. That factor alone may be sufficient to draw them in as clients.

If the radius of your initial marketing survey was large enough to reflect the reach of the local electronic media, you might make preliminary plans concerning its use at this point. Please note that this should involve plans *only*. I do not advocate any significant outlay in electronic media advertising until your marketing effort has brought in some preliminary results.

An established consulting business has a clearly defined advantage in this marketing planning process over any that are just starting out. If you're in the former category, you have an established business dollar volume in place on which to base your advertising budget calculations. The business launching its maiden voyage in the marketing waters has no such advantage.

This advantage is not enjoyed by the established professional practice that changes its base location to a new market area. If this is your situation, you have prior experience in the other market, but you don't have the same clear idea of potential client expectations in the new market area. Essentially, you are "starting from scratch" again.

In previous writings to professional practice audiences, I have advocated an advertising and promotional budget ranging between 3 and 5 percent of gross business revenues. Although these professional audiences had generally higher business overhead considerations than consultants do, the recommendation remains valid as a conservative, but reasonable, approach to setting preliminary advertising budget objectives.

Using the traditional parameters of consulting practice operations, you may not even be in a position initially to handle a major influx of new business. Consulting strictly on a one-to-one basis restricts the number of people that your consulting firm can adequately service.

As we undergo the conversion from the old marketing psychology to the new, we must also make appropriate adjustments in our operational modes. The mass market technique generally reduces the average fees received from each client. This reduction is, however, more than offset by the vast increase in the number volume of clients served.

Rather than dealing individually with clients, you will be dispensing information to multiple client groups. For example, you might record an instructional videotape for your consulting clients. You would only be doing the essential work once, but your widened client base would give this tape multiple coverage.

In terms of actual fees, say your basic consulting fee is $250 per hour. You price your one-hour videotape at $60 per copy. Selling 50 copies of that videotape will bring in $3000 for your one hour of consulting time, rather than the $250 that you earned previously.

To summarize, your first step is setting your promotional mechanism in place—and preparing yourself operationally for a mass market response. Although you will retain the individualized consulting aspect of business for those clients needing special attention, your reliance on this aspect of the business will gradually be reduced.

This fundamental change in marketing and operational strategy tends to make your services more affordable to clients, attracting a greater number to your practice. That places you at a considerable competitive advantage in the consulting business. Many clients will be adequately served through this means—and totally satisfied. Although they will not have a high level of personal contact with their consultant, these clients will consider this an acceptable trade-off for the reduction in service costs.

To cite an actual example, one consultant assembled a two-hour videotape seminar package, offering it for sale at $150 per unit. Advertising the package on a regional basis, the consultant sold over *5,000 copies* of the package in less than two months! You don't need your pocket calculator to recognize the considerable impact this program has had on that consultant's practice.

As an added benefit, this consultant has sold many individualized consulting service contracts to purchasers of the seminar videotapes. Having seen this product, these clients have been presold on the value of the consultant's services.

Development of an extensive market base is an excellent "security blanket" for any consultant. Even if you choose to keep the level of individualized contact high in your consulting practice, this rapid expansion of your client list will assure a level of income security that few businesses ever enjoy.

When you have gained this advantage, your primary remaining challenge will be to maintain this client base adequately. For this reason, you'll find it necessary to maintain your ability to reach a mass market. Later in this book, we will discuss two of the best techniques for achieving this objective, the newsletter and the in-person seminar. Both of these avenues will serve well in this process while retaining the fundamentals of mass market service, which is most profitable for your consulting business.

THE STAGE MARKETING OUTLINE

Earlier in this chapter, we discussed the acceptable level for an advertising budget, placing it at approximately 3 to 5 percent of gross revenue. Maintaining control over advertising costs necessitates the use of a disciplined approach. This need is the basis for a *stage marketing outline*.

As a general rule, a total marketing package involves the use of a multimedia presentation. Reliance on only one form of promotion for the life of a consulting practice is almost tantamount to professional suicide. If you fail to attract new clients on a continuing basis, your practice eventually faces certain death.

The stage marketing outline is based on the expected growth of your consulting practice revenues. Development of your outline begins with the collection of data for costs of various media within your market area.

During the early stages of your marketing effort, you are likely to concentrate on mass direct mailings to prospective clients and the use of newspaper advertising (or that of a professional journal). Basically, your initial stage in the marketing outline will strongly emphasize cost control within each individual medium used.

As your practice dollar volume expands, making more money available for your advertising budget, you can gradually turn your attention to other media resources. Your next stage upward will be the use of radio advertising and/or programming to reach clients. These costs are inherently higher than those of print media, but they will be worthwhile if the individual station has a solid audience base within your professional interest group.

The final stage is graduation to television. The costs here are the highest of all media, but the impact of the medium can create explosive practice growth. I would, however, caution you against using television until annual practice volume gets over at least the $200,000 level. There is no way that you can launch a reasonably effective and respectable television campaign on a shoestring budget. Even a nominal effort here will likely cost you around $500 per month. Unless you're willing to put all your promotional eggs in the television basket (usually not a very wise choice), you need the higher practice volume to justify the expense.

The most important characteristic of this final stage is that it has an almost infinite number of substages within it. As practice dollar volume increases, you can expand promotional efforts to continue the process of practice growth. The only cautionary note here is to make sure that you have your practice logistics nailed down to accommodate this growth. You won't be enhancing your prestige image if you fail to provide the services that you advertise.

To help you better visualize the stage marketing outline concept, you might best divide the outline according to the scope of market area focus. This would be in three essential parts:

1. Local
2. Regional
3. National

When your focus is local, rely mostly on the print media for advertising. Although you might make limited use of low-end electronic media advertising, this won't play a significant role in your total plan.

At the regional focus stage, put increasing reliance on the electronic media, probably to the point that it uses half or slightly more of your total advertising budget. At this point, your practice dollar volume should already be well above average. If you intend to maintain a considerable measure of in-person contact with individual clients, this will probably be the last stage of expansion for your promotional efforts. As a practical matter, you can't expect to provide much one-on-one service to a national clientele. There just aren't enough hours in each working day.

Consultants who reach the national stage in practice growth generally have multimillion-dollar annual practice volume and have an aura about them that tends to discourage personal client contact. National marketing tends to create an image that seems larger than life itself.

The key to successful national marketing is the development of a solid reputation in the first two stages. A negative image generated in early stages, when magnified to the national focus, could literally crush the future marketability of a consultant's services at any level.

This is the major danger of graduating to the national scene. If you make a serious mistake, your public visibility will magnify the extent of your error. This will make it extremely difficult to go back and redevelop a practice at a lower level. It is almost impossible to restore the shine to a tarnished reputation.

Before you decide to go national with your promotional efforts, you have to be sure that your situation lends itself well to predominant use of television. There is no other way to effectively reach the mass audience at this level.

Take stock of your consulting career carefully. Be certain that there are no serious hidden skeletons in either your personal or professional closet. As you gain national prominence, the news media inevitably tends to focus on success.

Nothing seems to give journalists more pleasure than to dismantle a prominent person's reputation. This is especially true if a prominent consultant does any work for a public entity, particularly the federal government. Far more often than any of us care to remember, we've seen great careers laid to ruin by the smell of scandal.

I'm not trying to scare you away from the national marketing scope, but you should be aware of the threats you might face as you attain the loftier career levels. These are occupational hazards—and the price of fame when gained on a national level.

ESTABLISHING YOUR PRIORITIES

As you develop your marketing outline and total plan, the most important aspect of the process is to clearly define your professional and personal priorities. Everything in life is a process of trade-offs, including all significant career choices.

On the professional level, there's little doubt that prominence has significant benefits. You gain immediate financial benefits. More important, you set the stage for greater future growth of the consulting practice.

The personal side of the situation is, however, a significant consideration as you begin your expansion efforts. The demands on your time will inevitably increase. If you are married, it's important to have the support and understanding of your spouse and family for your decisions.

If you don't have that support, the increasing demands on your time could adversely affect relationships at home. Such added stress inevitably affects professional performance. Strife at home could sow the seeds of personal scandal. Advancing to the national scene could cause those seeds to germinate.

Within this context, you should set realistic objectives that will give you the balance to satisfy both professional and personal concerns. These decisions will determine what termination level you choose for your marketing outline.

Understanding these priorities thoroughly will also give you another benefit. You will be able to focus on your professional goals with a sense of purpose. Sometimes we can act without any understanding of our prevalent motivations. This lack of understanding can cause a serious loss of control over our actions.

As you advance through various levels of your career, the pressures will inevitably increase. Without firm goal focusing, errors in judgment can frequently happen. This happens because no yardstick exists on which to measure decisions. You can end up making progress, but in the wrong direction. That's a waste of time and resources that benefits no one and slows true progress to legitimate career objectives.

OUTLINE PLAN IMPLEMENTATION

After your marketing outline has been formulated, disciplined implementation remains the primary key to success. Any plan, regardless of its quality, will be of little value if you lack the discipline for follow-up.

There is a common tendency, particularly among the more creative types, to use outline plans as merely a preliminary sketch. All too often, the final result bears little resemblance to the initial outline. Although flexibility is necessary to deal with changing circumstances, it can be carried to the extreme in some cases.

Your outline's purpose is to clearly channel your productive energies to a designated objective. If you make changes without clear and compelling reasons, you face the clear danger of losing your marketing focus.

A marketing outline, designed on the basis of clear research data, is the result of careful analysis of the market's prevailing patterns. Unless there is a clear indication that a market's patterns have changed, you have no specific reason for changing your marketing strategy.

As you begin to implement your marketing plan, you may encounter circumstances when minor procedural changes are indicated. If that's true, you can make these minor course corrections without disrupting your total marketing plan.

One of the most prevalent errors in marketing outline implementation is to designate progression in terms of time instead of the business revenue being generated by the marketing effort. For example, a new consultant might plan on using newspapers for three months, then moving on to radio for a designated time period, and then going forward to television. This "elapsed time" method is not the correct way to proceed.

Moving forward in outline implementation should always be based on clear business revenue indicators. Building a financial base for your consulting business is the only responsible way to assure that you have sufficient revenue to maintain your promotional effort. If you proceed beyond these legitimate financial indicators, you face the distinct possibility of being forced to curtail promotional efforts at some point as a drastic course correction. This action can prove to be extremely demoralizing—and can have a destructive impact on your discipline.

Basing your strategy on the correct indicators is the best way to keep your perspective intact. As you progress along the outline path, you will have a tangible measure of your success that will serve to reinforce your internal discipline. This support mechanism will be a key factor in assuring that you will be a continuing star, not a meteor that burns up as it falls out of the marketing sky.

CLOSING THOUGHTS

In this chapter, our primary effort has been centered on focusing your energies in a productive way to assure that you will be headed in the right direction. This focus will also help you to make the greatest possible use of the materials that follow in this book.

Each subsequent chapter will focus attention on the mechanics of implementing some portion of the marketing outline that you should have formulated by now as the result of reading this chapter. If you haven't assembled this marketing outline yet, you'll find it very beneficial to do so before reading much further in this book.

Preliminary Market Sketch Outline

Phase One: Newspaper classifieds

Phase Two: Newspaper display advertising (start small—build with revenue)

Phase Three: Short radio commercial

Phase Four: Combination of Phases 2 and 3

Phase Five: Short (10–15 minutes) radio program (if results of Phase 3 are favorable)

Phase Six: Longer radio program (based on good results from Phase 5)

Phase Seven: Short television commercial (based on revenue results of earlier steps)

Phase Eight: Television program (proven results from Phase 7 a prerequisite)

Having an outline, even in the roughest form, will help you to better visualize the methods being discussed. Information, when not put into tangible practice, has very little practical value.

With a rough outline in place, each subsequent chapter will help you to fill in the outline to serve as a detailed marketing plan. Depending on the prevailing philosophy that you bring to the marketing process, you will choose those techniques that will best reflect your personality and your specific professional objectives.

Within the marketing context, creativity can be the greatest asset that you possess. But, like an uncontrolled machine gun, it can have as much negative potential as positive if there is no control or no aiming at a specific target.

This chapter, and those that follow, will help to give your creativity this needed targeting. Controlled innovation is an important key to creating an effective consultant marketing program. Having defined our target, it's time to select our arsenal. That process begins with the next chapter.

CHAPTER
4

MEDIA SELECTION AND EMPHASIS: KEYS TO FINANCIALLY EFFECTIVE PROMOTION

In the last three chapters we concentrated on what image to project and began to outline a marketing strategy. Any journey needs a vehicle to carry its voyagers to the desired destination. That's the objective of this chapter: to give you an overview of the media and show you how to select the right ones for you. We will review their relative merits and touch upon some key indicators to give you an idea of what media will give results geared to your business objectives. In future chapters we get into more detail about each media.

Most of these media will prove useful at different stages in your marketing and professional growth. The key to success is knowing which media to select at a particular stage. Some media are best while your focus is local, but this changes as you expand your focus to a regional, state, or national level.

The key factor is the audience per dollar delivery that results from your efforts. This factor will help you decide which media to choose for reaching each group of clients.

MEDIA BASICS

Most of us have put a small classified advertisement in the newspaper or called for a listing in the local phone directory. Phone directories are a good idea, especially if you're in a large metropolitan area. A listing in these directories gives your business a fairly strong local focus, which is particularly valuable if you're in a city like New York or Los Angeles.

The negative side of newspaper and phone directory advertising, especially in metropolitan areas, is that having more than your name, address, and phone number listed costs a fair amount of money, while keeping your message in a locally confined area. Phone directory advertising holds an additional problem. You have to commit yourself to a year's worth of advertising fees *in advance*—without the opportunity to alter your presentation if it isn't bringing in the results you want.

Newspapers give you considerable flexibility to change according to market conditions. However, the length of exposure to the market is limited. After a few days, your message may become the target for some bird in a cage. Repetition is the key to building name recognition, but that costs money.

The need for repetition is especially true in both phone directories and larger newspapers in metropolitan markets. There are a lot of people out there who are also competing for attention. Simple classified advertisements are great if you're selling a used car or refrigerator. Bargain hunters are accustomed to digging for the hidden gems.

Your prospective customers shouldn't be expected to conduct this type of treasure hunt. Most of them are busy people. They need to spot you easily. That takes a slightly larger advertisement. Unfortunately, that also escalates costs.

Because of high advertising costs, larger companies generally spend a smaller percentage of their gross income on advertising than their smaller counterparts. They put their advertising dollars into media with a large audience base. Their names and services are being exposed to a larger number of potential clients. They may not be doing a better job of formulating their advertising message. It's simply the law of averages. More prospective clients seeing their message equals more customers.

The repetition factor is particularly applicable when an advertiser moves to the more "perishable" advertising vehicles, radio and television. You're there for 30 seconds or a minute, deliver your message, and you're gone! To succeed in these media, you must achieve one of two objectives: (1) reach a lot of people, or (2) deliver a very memorable message. You'll have the best success if you can combine both objectives in your efforts.

The critical issue in radio and television promotion is the output power and effective broadcasting range. You want a fairly large broadcasting range during the prime listening or viewing hours. The question of delivering your message during prime hours is also critical to advertising effectiveness.

Some radio stations, as an example, can have a range of over 1000 miles—at 2 or 3 o'clock in the morning. The critical question is whether the people you want to reach will be listening at that hour. If they aren't, your advertising dollars aren't going to be providing benefits for your consulting business.

Regardless of which media you select, ask the representative to provide data on the number of people they reach. That can give you a good idea of how likely you'll be to reach your client base. Most media also have a profile of their average reader, listener, or viewer. They also know, generally, whether professional people pay attention to their articles or programming.

It may seem obvious, but you'll never get the customer whom you don't reach with your message. The world's best message won't do you any good—if nobody's listening.

Once you know where people are paying attention, it's time to gear your message to the media. Now is when an understanding of the delivery strengths and weaknesses of each media is very important. The rest of the chapter focuses on those factors that are important in planning your media marketing strategy.

KEYS TO NEWSPAPER PROMOTION

Newspaper promotion can operate to your benefit on two basic levels. Newspapers are most effective in the communication of ideas and, secondarily, in visual impact. The key here is to recognize your personality type and use your advertising to augment it.

As an example, one management consultant really enjoys going out on the town, spending a considerable number of his evenings at fashionable night spots. Wisely, he has chosen to make himself instantly recognizable within his community. He hasn't done that through audacious advertising methods. Quite to the contrary, his advertising space is relatively small, but he has included a photo of himself in *every* advertisement that he runs. No matter where he is, people immediately recognize him and know who has walked through the front door.

He related one incident to me. He and his wife were having dinner at a restaurant. A man came to their table, introduced himself, and said, "Aren't you so-and-so, the management consultant?" The consultant said yes. The man scribbled his name and office phone number on a napkin and put it on the table, asking the consultant to call the next day. The subsequent phone call and meeting resulted in the consultant's securing an account valued at over $20,000 annually. That was several years ago—and the money still keeps coming in.

The consultant's advertising wasn't flashy. His photo was in the advertisement along with his name, the tag line "Management Consultant," and a line that read, "When being the best really matters, call (phone number)." His entire advertisement was one column wide and about five inches long. But facial recognition worked for this consultant.

If you aren't out on the town a lot, select some other device that will make an impression. If you like people to come to your office, show the front of your office in your advertising. This is particularly beneficial if the building facade has an especially distinguishing feature that the reader will remember.

It's important to realize that neither words or pictures, standing alone, will work as effectively as a blend of the two. They must work cooperatively with each other to get the most results for the least money.

As an example, you might want to project an image of being a very hard working person. Have a picture taken with your suit coat off and your sleeves rolled up. Combine it with a message like, "I'll dig out the right answers for you."

Use words that either portray action or help the reader to visualize a favorable result from contacting you. This second element is illustrated in the aforementioned consultant's advertising line, "When being the best really matters, call. . . ."

This advice is useful in any print media advertising, but it's absolutely crucial to newspapers. They are perishable, and you have to get a forceful, but understated, message across. That's really the way to do it.

TRADE JOURNAL ADVERTISING

The same advertising principles discussed for newspapers apply to trade journal advertising, with one exception. The focus of trade journal advertising has to be more sharply defined than for general newspapers. This is because the focus of the readership is more clearly defined.

Trade and professional journals have a very specific audience to whom all their materials are addressed. This is, at the same time, both a benefit and an adverse consequence of advertising in this media. If you specialize your consulting efforts to a specific subgroup of a business, as in an individual profession, use of professional journals is ideally suited to addressing prospective clients on a regional or national level.

Trade and professional journal promotion is not so ideal if your consulting approach is more generalized. If you use this media, you may have to advertise in several different journals to get the necessary coverage. That can increase your advertising costs per client acquired considerably.

The best way to get the most from your expenditures is to combine advertising in professional journals with authorship of articles for them. This gives you a considerably expanded forum, gives the readers a better sample of your opinions, and develops your image far better in the readers' minds than could be done with advertising alone.

Advertisers inevitably have a *slight* advantage with the editors in placing articles in journals. Editors recognize who pays their bills, and are naturally biased toward an advertiser. The important thing to remember is that your article is not strictly self-serving. If it is blatantly so, editors must, on basic principle, reject it. Publishing articles that aren't service-oriented, simply to please an advertiser, would alienate subscribers and cause nothing but trouble for the journal that crosses this ethical line.

This subject is covered in greater detail in Chapter 6, but it should be noted here that most of these journal editors primarily focus on information that helps readers perform some of their work either easier or with better quality. Give readers a *little bit* of the same information that they would receive if they retained your professional services. This makes the best possible impression on editors.

PROMOTING YOURSELF ON RADIO

As mentioned earlier, radio promotion is essentially perishable. You don't have long to discuss things. You give your message directly, and you're well on your way.

The essential difference in using radio is that your message must be accomplished through words alone. Writing commercials for radio requires the use of descriptive phrasing to deliver a message to the listener. We'll discuss this further in Chapter 7.

At this point, the focus is on how, or if, radio fits into your basic marketing strategy. Will it serve your business objectives?

The answer to this question is a qualified yes. Because of its limitations, you shouldn't rely on it as your *only* promotional vehicle. Instead, it should be viewed as an adjunct to your promotional program.

The primary value of radio advertising is to focus attention on your opinions and your skills as a communicator. That's why you should definitely consider going before the microphone yourself to record your advertising. This gives potential clients a voice recognition to go with the name recognition that you're seeking to build, and it puts you in an excellent position whenever you make an oral presentation to a prospective client.

It probably isn't wise to overinvest in short radio commercials. A better vehicle is the occasional "public service program" that gives you a 5- to 10-minute forum where you can offer more detail and make a better impression on your listener. This can be quite expensive if you do it often. Use it sparingly for maximum effect. The radio station promotes such special programming with short announcements to spur listener interest. That would probably come as part of the total package deal that you make with the station.

Even if you use radio advertising, don't put all your eggs into this single basket. It's only a part of the total mosaic comprising effective promotion.

The print media and television are likely to serve as your primary vehicles for promotion, because of the readily apparent visual advantages they offer. The role of radio in the total marketing package is to give a less expensive opportunity to gain voice recognition and to reach potential clients who might not be in contact with your other promotional efforts. Include radio, but invest in it sparingly, to assure a blanket approach for your efforts.

TELEVISION ADVERTISING IN THE TOTAL PACKAGE

General television stations are, by their nature, regional media for your advertising message. The main problem with television, as with general interest newspapers, is that your message reaches a considerable number of people who will never have use for your services.

The primary use of television advertising is in markets that have a fairly high concentration of potential clients. When this is true, television offers you the best vehicle for combining all the factors of image projection. Potential clients will hear your voice, see your face, judge your level of confidence, and evaluate your information and how well you can serve them.

Depending on television alone as an advertising media isn't recommended. You would have to spend a considerable amount of money to get the job done. Your best course of action, particularly if you have a strict advertising budget, is to use cable television, which has a more sharply defined market area. We'll look at television marketing in more detail in Chapter 8.

To judge the financial viability of using general television, closely examine how sharply defined your consulting objectives are. As your consulting specialization increases, the promotion value of a general television station decreases—unless you have a high concentration of your specific market in the station's viewing radius.

As with anything else, you get what you pay for here. Television advertising rates are determined primarily by viewer ratings (the estimated number of people who watch the station at any given time of the day). Popular television stations can easily put a substantial strain on your advertising budget.

Because of costs, a longer program at a general television station may not be financially feasible. An alternative might be to approach a station affiliated with a college. Many of them have reasonably good production facilities and a substantially lower cost for advertising. The main drawback is that ratings are likely to be substantially lower with these stations.

This disadvantage is offset by the definite tendency of professional audiences, particularly those of a more intellectual inclination, to actively support and watch the programming of these stations. This places your programming into a higher concentration of your target market, particularly if your consulting efforts are geared to cut across the borders of various professional or business groups. That could make a PBS (Public Broadcasting System) affiliate an excellent choice.

It's important to note that here, as with articles written for professional journals, the orientation must be strictly service-oriented and instructional. The PBS image dictates that programming does not appear to be a prolonged commercial. Keeping this in mind will be very helpful in placing a program on a PBS affiliate's schedule.

USING THE CABLE AND SATELLITE ALTERNATIVES

Like the PBS affiliate stations, cable and satellite stations also tend to have a more sharply defined viewer population. The major difference is that the broadcasting range of cable and satellite television is likely to be considerably larger than that of a PBS station. This is especially true for satellite stations. Their range could make your message truly national in scope.

Despite this fact, the overall ratings (i.e., the percentage of households tuned in within the viewing range) are likely to be much lower here. The advantage is that, in strictly numerical terms, you're reaching a larger concentration of consumers in your interest area.

The larger cable networks, Turner Broadcasting System being an excellent example, have advertising rates rivaling those of the major networks. The key is to choose the source that delivers the largest concentration of potential clients for your advertising message.

The important thing is that, when you step up into these big leagues of advertising, you have the budget to handle it. It costs thousands of dollars for a broadcasting minute. It's definitely *not* a cheap effort. Viewer demographics have to be *very* favorable before the expenditure can be justified.

As an alternative to a large cable network, look into the lesser known, but reasonably well circulated, cable and satellite outlets. They give you the wider viewing area advantage—without the extremely high price tag. This can be your stepping-stone until you're financially ready to tangle with the big league outfits.

Smaller cable and satellite stations often offer rates that are in approximately the same range as the local general interest television stations. There are two differences in choosing this alternative: First, you are projecting your message and image over a considerably larger market area, making your name and skills known to more potential clients. Second, the concentration of special interest viewers is likely to be higher in these stations. This could easily translate itself into far more inquiries than might be generated from a general interest station—although you are investing the same number of dollars. We will explore cable and satellite television advertising further in Chapter 9.

TAPPING THE NEWSLETTER OPTION

Although many consulting firms use brochures as part of their total advertising programs, the scope of a newsletter is generally very limited and offers little information of value to the recipient. The general rationale favoring this approach is that putting too much information into printed matter reduces the prospect's need to become a client.

Using the newsletter option is actually to bring an adjunct source of income, not expense, for a consulting firm. By making the material primarily informational, you have a product to sell. You are actually being *paid by the customer* to advertise to them. That's a rather ironic twist to the process, but it's proven in many cases to work very well.

The newsletter isn't advertising in the true sense. Your consulting firm name is featured, but the primary thrust is informational.

The other benefit is that you can maintain an ongoing communication process with your current clients. In purchasing the newsletter service, they get additional information. As a side benefit, the newsletter often raises additional questions—which create additional need for consulting services by the client.

A newsletter is an excellent adjunct to a broadcast of informational programming on either radio or television. You generate curiosity in listeners or viewers. Then when they want to know more, you invite them to subscribe to your professional newsletter. Professional newsletters are solid and proven profit producers for consultants who use them. We'll discuss the process in further detail in Chapter 10.

Some consultants question the ethical considerations of selling information through newsletters. They are concerned that the method will, in some way, reflect negatively on them. As with articles in professional journals, the primary consideration is how transparent the self-serving aspect of the material is. If your newsletter is just an eight-page commercial for your consulting firm, most prospective clients are going to feel "taken" by their purchase. If you avoid making it a commercial, providing a newsletter service will do more to help than harm your image in every case.

SINGLE MEDIA VERSUS BLENDED APPROACH

The old adage about not putting all your eggs in one basket is good advice for any part of your business effort, and it is especially true for promotion. Depending solely on one promotional vehicle for all presentations can result in most of your prospects not having a knowledge of your services.

As an example, some prospects routinely trash any mail not directly

50 Media Selection and Emphasis: Keys to Financially Effective Promotion

related to their current operations. That includes any solicitation mail that you send them.

But don't discount the value of the media that prospects attempt to ignore. Using the direct mail example, prospects, at least minimally, recognize your name from your mailing. Then when they see or hear your promotion in another form, they remember that they've received mail from you.

Secondarily, subsequent mail that they receive from you will likely receive a bit more attention. As you keep your name within their attention span, they begin to contemplate, on a subconscious level, what services you can provide to them.

From this, you might think that a psychological war of attrition is being advocated for your promotional efforts. That's not really financially viable for most advertisers. It may be true for some of the larger corporate advertisers. Who, for example, hasn't seen the Charlie Chaplin take-off featured by IBM?

IBM has the kind of advertising dollars that makes this approach possible. Few of us can claim that much money available for promotion. Because that's a fact, we have to be more selective and more specific in our message, and more sparing in where our dollars are invested.

But the current use of promotion by IBM is indicative of one major benefit of their image growth. Few of us don't readily recognize IBM, simply from its corporate name.

Once you achieve name recognition, with prospective clients knowing who you are and what you offer, your remaining effort (as with IBM) is to reinforce your message by letting people know that you're still around—and still providing services for clients who seek your help. A positive reputation with current clients serves to augment these promotional efforts. It becomes a matter of, "Have you heard of so-and-so? Is he (or she) any good?"

Your initial efforts have to be spread out over a few different media, simply to assure that every prospective client in your market area knows that you're around. Sampling each advertising vehicle sparingly, at first, gives you a very good idea of which ones are getting prospect attention in your area.

After you've established which media are bringing the best results, you can concentrate your efforts in these areas—and discard the rest. You've established your name and the rest becomes a matter of continuing reinforcement. That's why a heavier concentration in the lower cost media is the best first advertising step to establish your presence.

The business generated from these initial efforts provides additional revenue for your advertising efforts. The most common mistake that many businesses, including consultant firms, make is to attempt too much too soon. As you read the chapters ahead, you're likely to be tempted to try all the strategies I suggest. DON'T!!!

Start slow and build up your clientele gradually. You want to succeed, not end up in bankruptcy court. Nothing is more detrimental to a prestige image than a trip to this venerable institution.

Successful promotion, like a healthy tree, starts out with a sturdy trunk from which branches can grow. Trees grow slowly over a period of years. Over a shorter time, the same principle applies to advertising. Getting the trunk and roots established is your first priority, so let's focus on selecting the media you need to establish your consulting business.

SELECTING YOUR MEDIA

As shown in Chapter 3, there is a specific stage plan for implementing marketing strategy. Selecting the media that will promote your message is central to achieving success.

Your media focus will be determined primarily by what your current business capacity is. Are you in a position to handle a fairly large volume of business? How far are you willing to personally travel to meet clients? Can you do that cost-effectively within your current fee schedule?

Answering these questions for your consulting business is an important first step in knowing whether your advertising efforts are tailored to your needs. As an example, if you are in a position to handle business within a 100-mile radius and your message is only going out in a 50-mile radius, you may be keeping your business at only half its current potential.

The general principle is to start your advertising in the newspaper and use direct mail in tandem with the newspaper effort. Each of these avenues fulfills a specific function. Newspapers serve to build name and face recognition with potential clients. They are not, however, an all-purpose method for transmitting much information to potential clients. Being informational in a newspaper advertising format could quickly create havoc on your promotional budget.

Establishing your face and name in the prospect's mind through newspaper advertising encourages receptiveness to your more detailed advertising message by direct mail. This is particularly true if you use your newspaper advertising to announce an upcoming mailing. A simple line like "Watch your mail for a special profit-building message coming next week" prepares your recipients and, at least to a small degree, creates a feeling of anticipation that makes them more receptive to your message.

As your available funding increases, turn your attention to the electronic media (radio and television). This will inevitably expand your focus from an immediate local to at least a slightly more regional focus. When you enter this arena, start with the smaller stations. Their advertising rates are less expensive and give you a chance to get acclimated to the media before taking your presentation to the more expensive stations. This is important to assure that you receive the maximum value for your advertising dollar.

The electronic media often tend to have an intoxicating effect on advertisers, causing them to overinvest in these media initially. This creates considerable disappointment when initial results do not meet expectations. Don't expect either radio or television to carry your entire promotional load.

On television, you get primary promotional value in building name, face, and voice recognition, whereas on radio you can expect voice recognition only. Don't expect to get a complex message delivered—unless you have the advertising budget to do it.

Both television and radio stations can be divided into five levels

1. Local
2. Small regional
3. Statewide
4. Large regional (several states)
5. National station or network

As you raise your sights from one level to the next higher one, the price for your efforts inevitably increases.

When you advertise on each level, start small and gradually expand your efforts as generated business justifies the expenditure. Start with 15- or 30-second commercials and expand them to programming—if results indicate that you will get a good return for your money. If you aren't getting the results, stop and adjust your approach.

Don't let anyone at the station talk you into expanding your presentation length before you've proven your approach for your market. You'll be pouring good money after bad in such an effort. Get results first and expand later.

When you've refined your presentation, assuring results at a lower level, investment in the larger markets isn't as much of a gamble. You will already have the mechanism to draw your results from a much larger area—and make your profitability soar skyward. When you start pumping six figures into an advertising effort that zeroes in on a limited-time target, you want to know that your aim is good. Otherwise, you'll be engaging in a high-stakes gamble that you could lose.

As with the print media, be certain that you're augmenting the perishable message with one that is more durable. Print media are usually less expensive, if designed right, than electronic media. Aim for authorship in regional or national publications as an intermediate step in your marketing strategy—it will make potential listeners or viewers more receptive to your message. That will build recognition and make potential clients curious about you. That feeling will be satisfied when you end up on the air.

As you expand your electronic media investment to include programming-length material, it is wise to invest a little more to advertise such programming in the print media. Your programming won't get its maximum benefit if you aren't getting listeners or viewers. At minimum, let them know that you'll be on the air, and the when and where information. This probably won't cost you that much more because this advertising is likely to be a shared-cost deal with the station. It's in *their* interest as well as yours to assure that there are viewers for your program.

If your marketing efforts reach a national level, you have gone as far as you can to project your image. The usual result of efforts on this scale is a responsive national market that generates millions of dollars in business for the beneficiary enterprise.

CLOSING THOUGHTS

Throughout this chapter, you've probably noted the emphasis on the "slow and easy" approach. There's often a temptation, especially in books like these, to give the impression that you can vault from obscurity to fame overnight. That's usually not true—and you could lose your pants in the process.

One business acquaintance told me that she spent 10 years becoming an "overnight success." While she seemingly vaulted into regional and national prominence, she spent time laying the foundation at lower levels. This gave her the resources to be ready when the opportunity arrived.

On a personal note, I can use myself as an example. I labored, in relative obscurity, for over 5 years before I gained the opportunity to reach a larger audience with my message. It took almost 8 years before I was able to touch a national audience within just one professional group.

If anyone comes to you with the idea that following their instructions will give you instant success, get ready to listen to a fairy tale. There is no substitute for rolling up your sleeves and doing some hard work to achieve success. With enough effort, you'll make it.

Be patient in the early stages. Build the foundation before you build the structure; otherwise, you'll have it falling down around you. If you follow the ideas here, you'll have laid the foundation properly. That's what this chapter, and this book, are all about.

CHAPTER
5

EFFECTIVE NEWSPAPER MARKETING TECHNIQUES

As a marketing tool on the local and small regional level, few avenues offer the message-delivery effectiveness, flexibility, and cost-effectiveness of the newspaper. Despite an age that is enamored with the marvels of electronics, most people still possess—and exercise—the ability to read.

Although there may be some question about the literacy level of the public at large, this is not a concern for our particular target audiences. Decision makers are not a passive group, given to getting their information through a form of intellectual osmosis. Given the large circulation of such major business newspapers as the *Wall Street Journal*, it's safe to assume that print media are one of the best ways to transmit information.

The major concern in reaching this audience is not whether they will be in contact with your message. There's little question about that. The central question is the memorability of your message in the large stream of materials that newspapers deal with daily.

Message memorability is the core issue in effective newspaper marketing practice. Your message has to stick in the readers' minds long enough for them to take desired action, namely, to contact you.

In this chapter, we review the essentials of newspapers to understand the underlying processes involved, the differences between daily and weekly publications, selection of the right newspaper for advertising, how newspapers calculate fees, layout design concepts, cost-effective techniques, use of press releases for supplemental promotion, writing of advertisements, pitfalls to avoid, and how to keep your prestige image in mind when preparing materials. As a final point, we discuss the "dovetail" concept, the idea that newspaper promotion can be used tangentially to augment all your other promotional efforts.

There is a common misconception that an effective newspaper marketing campaign is one-dimensional and lacking in variety. This is based on the belief that although mere message repetition, if done with sufficient frequency, will pound a message into even the thickest skull, it is not necessarily interesting. Without variety, the common result is a bored audience that will intellectually turn off your message, resulting in a gross waste of your promotional budget.

Variety is the spice that keeps your message piquant and keeps readers coming back for more, making your promotions successful and memorable. In this chapter, we'll show you how to use variety in newspaper advertising.

UNDERSTANDING NEWSPAPER PROCESSES

Although your primary interest is the effective delivery of your message, understanding newspaper processes helps you benefit from some of this media's less known qualities. Unlike many of the nonprint promotional techniques that are discussed later in the book, the newspaper plays a more central role in the functioning of most communities.

Newspapers have been forced into an evolutionary process of change by the competitive forces exerted by the electronic media, radio and television. Rather than treating a large variety of subjects superficially, newspapers have begun to fill the role of in-depth augmenters to the electronic media. You get the headlines from radio or television, but if you want the full scoop on a story, you'll read more about it in the newspaper.

Recognizing this void in the information dissemination process, newspapers are more inclined to give the details that you can't find elsewhere. Although there is a review of pertinent headline information, the focus is to move from a general review to details that other media don't touch.

This objective, however, runs into one of the most unfortunate paradoxes of our electronic age. Having been spoon-fed small doses of information through radio and television, the average attention span of the reader has suffered a marked reduction.

This poses the largest challenge for the newspaper editorially. They have to be in depth *and* in a hurry. Because the average reader's attention span is only 10 minutes, journalistic style has evolved into a crisp narrative that covers the main points, offers more detail on a dominant idea or concept within the story, and then moves on to another story.

Understanding this editorial intellectual process is a key factor in comprehending newspaper standards for what is considered newsworthy. Newspapers must serve the public interest by providing readers with advertising and editorial copy that falls within these parameters. If they fail in this objective, readers will go elsewhere—and the newspaper is out of business *fast*!

Keeping these factors in mind helps you to make your area's newspaper a valuable ally in developing your prestige image. This is where the newspaper's role becomes pivotal in your prestige building efforts. It's important to remember that prestige is more fundamentally built from what others say about you, not what you say about yourself.

DAILY VERSUS WEEKLY PUBLICATIONS

Frequency of publication is one of the first considerations in choosing a newspaper for your promotional efforts. Although there are other variations, the two most common types are daily and weekly newspapers. The daily newspaper in metropolitan areas may even come in morning and evening editions.

There are a number of arguments to be made for both types. The major advantage of dailies is their sense of immediacy to the reader. Weeklies tend to lack this quality, except for news stories that happen immediately prior to the copy deadline for each edition.

One of the major disadvantages of the daily paper is the relative perishability of its contents. After a day or two, your message may become the target for a family's new puppy—unless it's so memorable that it becomes a clipping for someone's scrapbook or file. The former fate, by any standards, is lacking in the prestige category.

By contrast, a weekly newspaper generally maintains its visibility until the next issue comes out. That provides a full week's reader exposure to your message.

This durability factor is an important consideration, especially for paid advertising. The major disadvantage of weeklies is that, with competitive daily papers in the same community, they tend to have smaller circulations. You may have your audience longer, but the audience is smaller.

When daily publications are a competitive factor, weekly newspapers tend to cover fewer stories and concentrate on greater depth in presentations. This is the editorial niche that is most logically available to them.

Greater detail of presentation poses a specific advantage for you in providing your audience with more detailed information about your services through press releases and informational articles. Because weeklies are often editorially preempted by the dailies on major news stories, they are often more open to the community human-interest story.

The weeklies' greater community orientation also has a strong effect on their basic editorial values. They focus on local news, rather than seeing a regional, state, or national focus. Recognizing this editorial viewpoint, you can present your information in this context to gain the most ready acceptance of your message.

A weekly in smaller communities may make an exception by reporting on a local person's emerging impact on the larger scene. These are those "we've got somebody famous living here" puff pieces that are more closely allied with community pride in an individual's accomplishments than with news value. At that point, however, you won't be approaching them with the story. They'll be calling you.

Daily newspapers, even in smaller communities, tend to devote most of their editorial space to hard-core news. Although local human interest stories do get some editorial space, they are generally buried inside the publication. A new office opening rarely receives front-page billing from a daily paper, but it might happen with a weekly.

The primary determining factor in choosing between dailies and weeklies, however, lies in how quickly you need to have information, either news or advertising, before the readers. Dailies will generally offer faster service and, when time is an important consideration, can give you the competitive advantage required.

SELECTING THE RIGHT NEWSPAPER

As with other media, newspapers each have their distinctive "personalities" that determine their viability for your promotional use. Because of the more intellectual orientation of print, newspapers are generally categorized by political leaning than by any other single factor. This is reflected in the editorial approach and the types of articles published.

Because, as a consultant, you deal with the promotion of ideas (as opposed to a tangible product), this distinction has a direct bearing on the usefulness of any individual newspaper in promoting your services and your views. If, as an example, your views are more conservatively oriented, a liberal newspaper is not as likely to give your story as much prominence in its pages as can be expected from a conservative newspaper.

Although journalists are trained to take their personal biases into subjection, they, like the rest of us, are only human. In expressing ourselves, our use of language is colored by our inherent prejudices. Journalists, despite care to exercise neutrality, can't totally avoid this problem.

Another important consideration is the newspaper's total size. The larger newspaper tends to be more impersonal in its appraisal of available information. Press releases and articles often are rewritten (even if rewriting isn't really required) to more closely conform to general editorial style. There is a tendency to make everything homogeneous.

Newspapers with smaller staffs generally are more open to, if they do not actively welcome, copy that is ready for their pages with little or no tampering. They need copy to fill pages. They won't reject access to a freebie if for no other reason than cost savings.

After these considerations are weighed, the most important factor in choosing a newspaper is whether your potential clientele will be exposed to your message through a particular newspaper. Secondly, will they be in sufficient numbers to warrant the investment of time, effort, and money?

As with other media, newspapers have profiles of their average audience. They know, and are acutely aware of, the people who read their pages. This is necessary to be of the best possible service to them. You can usually get this information from the editor or from the advertising department. If you use this information wisely, you can select the newspaper that gets you the best possible value for each dollar of your newspaper advertising budget.

HOW NEWSPAPERS CALCULATE ADVERTISING FEES

Your process of comparison shopping for newspaper advertising should also include the amount of advertising space that your money buys. Advertising rates are usually based on the column inch measurement.

Column inches are one column wide by one inch long. Getting a better value for your dollar is contingent on the width of columns that the newspaper features. Two newspapers of the same overall page size will present a different value to the advertiser if one has three columns per page and the other has four.

The advertising rates for the former example are likely to be somewhat higher simply because they have fewer column inches of advertising space to sell. If, however, the price differential is less than that for space, the value choice is obvious.

Although *column widths* vary, the most common for standard newspapers is two inches. This allows for six columns to be printed on an overall page width of 14 inches.

> **EXAMPLE CALCULATION**
>
> A newspaper that has a page size of 14 by 20 inches has approximately 120 column inches to offer per printed page. This assumes that the newspaper has six columns per page. Each column, from top to bottom, provides 20 column inches of space.

As with anything else, quantity purchasing tends to give a better unit pricing. Purchasing a full page (120 column inches) gives you a considerably better rate per column inch. But the final bill for a single appearance is going to be considerable for any newspaper with a larger audience. Such advertising size isn't really practical for consultants generally.

LAYOUT DESIGN CONCEPTS

Development of attractive newspaper display advertising is often considered a matter of personal taste. Examination of any individual newspaper issue easily shows how much variety is possible. Seeking the comfort of a set of rules, you quickly realize that few rules exist. They run the gamut from the heavily illustrated to just solid print.

There is, however, a general consensus that larger display advertising is more effective if some measure of illustrative balance is maintained. The balance is generally dictated by the type of business being advertised.

Advertising that is selling a specific product benefits from heavier use of illustration. Without the illustrative matter, more text is required for product description. This negates much of the space (and cost) benefit that eliminating the use of illustration creates.

By contrast, service oriented businesses such as consulting are heavily oriented to the sale of ideas and concepts. This requires a heavier dependence on text than illustration. The primary use of illustrations is to eliminate the blocky (and boring) appearance that is otherwise created.

For your purposes, illustrations can generally be limited to your consulting firm logo and/or your personal photo. Don't try to cramp too much copy into a limited space. Although the newspaper may be able to handle the assignment, the result is print that is too small to be read comfortably. Organization may be reasonably attractive, but the smallness of type will give a negative impression.

This is a primary reason why so many businesses and professionals shy away from the use of classified advertising. Classified advertising *without* the illustrative matter is an inexpensive alternative, but it lacks considerably in appearance. You aren't going to make a lasting impression using this method.

Using classified advertising is also contingent on the forum in which it appears. As an example, advertising in a major publication carries considerable weight—even if it's in classified form. The *Wall Street Journal*, for instance, is a very prestigious business publication. It's definitely not a demerit to any advertiser appearing there. In such cases, the forum gives the advertising weight that it wouldn't otherwise have.

COST-EFFECTIVE APPROACHES

Getting the most value for your advertising dollar is obviously going to be your first priority. Discounting the use of the classified advertising category, your objective will be to get the most impact in the least possible space.

Your decisions in this area will be primarily based on your specific objectives for advertising. If you simply need name identification, with no need for information dissemination, you can get good results from using nothing more than your name, address, and phone number in your advertisements. You will probably want to add your photo or consulting firm logo to enhance the reader's identification processes.

By contrast, if you seek to educate your potential clientele, you need a larger amount of space to get the job done. This should not, however, be considered for more than an initial thrust.

Get your name publicized, along with a solid idea of what services you provide. After that is accomplished, your purposes won't be served by repeating this approach too frequently.

Work to get smaller advertisements placed more frequently. This assures that potential clients continue to see your message. This repetition in the initial stages of your advertising strategy is important to build the confidence of potential clients. Using this approach for a while clearly shows that your enterprise won't fold up and slip into the night without a trace.

General display advertising is usually best accomplished through the use of two adjacent columns. Even if the advertisement isn't long, the two-column format provides better eye appeal and reduces the chance that the casual-scan reader will miss it. This is possible with the one-column advertisement.

Although the two-column advertisement may superficially seem more expensive, it's better to be noticed (and draw customers) than to be missed entirely. The little extra money involved is a sound investment. This is particularly true if your advertisement appears in the page section directly adjacent to the fold. A one-column advertisement located here could be hidden from the reader's view. That would be a total waste of your advertising dollars.

Location of the advertisement on the page is a factor, although not under your direct control. The top and bottom of a page is generally not as effective as a page midsection. Some experts contend that a location approximately one-third of the way from the top of the page is best. This is a debatable point. But it is true that the bottom of the page tends to be ignored with greater frequency. This explains why newspapers concentrate less important "filler" material in these locations.

Some newspapers vary their advertising rates depending on advertisement location within the publication. If you're willing to bury your advertising in the general area of the classifieds, you might get a better rate—even for a display ad. If your objective is name recognition through repetition, not single-appearance impact, this option is one that should be considered. You'll get the right results at a reduced total price. That isn't bad news for your advertising budget.

As noted earlier, there are very few solid rules. The greatest waste of advertising money comes when there is no clear definition of expectations. What do you want the advertising to accomplish? Do you need more than mere name identification?

If you can clearly define these expectations, you have a much better grasp of how to proceed. Specifying your objective is the best assurance that your efforts will be on target.

AUGMENTING ADVERTISING WITH PRESS RELEASES

One of the most important keys to effective promotion is to avoid total reliance on advertising. This is especially true when you want to give information to a large audience. You can never get the same results from a paid commercial in this area that you can achieve *absolutely free*. As mentioned earlier, you get greater prestige from what others say about you. That is the great value of the press release, especially if the copy is mildly laudatory.

When a business advertises in a newspaper, editors become much more inclined to grant general editorial space to news regarding the advertiser. Despite journalistic considerations, newspaper editors are sufficiently pragmatic to recognize who is paying the bills. Journalistic standards regarding news aren't applied as strictly to a regular advertiser as to a nonadvertiser.

In smaller newspapers, reporters seek out new advertisers when there's a slow news day. This eliminates your need for composing press releases. The result may not be as self-serving as you might achieve. But the article, composed by a newspaper staffer, will have greater credibility.

If you write the press release, you should be aware of the basics of the news story. For business press releases, the best method is to develop the piece from the *summary lead*: give readers a solid idea of what the article is about in the first two paragraphs, and develop the remainder from this starting point.

An important point to remember is that the material is not too blatantly self-laudatory. After all, the newspaper is providing the space free of charge. Even a very sympathetic editor won't give space for what amounts to free advertising. There has to be, at minimum, some newsworthiness built into the piece.

To understand the limits of a particular editor's sensibilities in this area, study similar articles. They will give you solid indications on how to proceed.

As an added benefit, editors who see that you're well-informed about style will be more receptive to your future efforts in this area. From a cost-effectiveness viewpoint, good copy provided by a nonstaffer in press release form (meaning a freebie for the paper) is almost always welcomed with open arms. Contingent on not abusing this privilege too frequently, you can develop a productive relationship that will give you excellent mileage for your promotional dollars.

WRITING THE ADVERTISEMENT

When we discussed designing the advertisement earlier, the primary focus was on how to organize the layout to have appealing visual impact. This alone does not constitute an effective advertisement; what you say must complement the illustrative matter you choose.

The copy, regardless of how attractively organized, must be concise. Brevity is a prized attribute in advertising, especially if brevity also afflicts your monetary supply. Don't use paid advertising as a forum for your autobiography. Keep the message brief, pack some punch into it, and conclude it.

An effective idea is to develop a business slogan that accurately reflects the image that you wish to project. Don't be too flippant. Keep your words dignified and direct.

As an example, if you're a consultant on business cost containment, you might use a slogan like, "We make your dollars go further." An investment consultant might use one like, "We get your lazy dollars back to work—for you."

Attempt to summarize the main thrust of your enterprise in a single sentence. A short phrase is even better. Advertising psychology is contingent on effective tagging of the product or service to hold it in the potential customer's mind.

Slogans, when effectively used, become as readily identifiable to consumers as the business name associated with it. Who, for example, doesn't readily recognize the major insurance company that calls itself the "good hands people"?

When this identification process is successfully implemented, it becomes an effective substitute for lengthy explanations. After consumers have identified the business enterprise behind the slogan, the slogan immediately triggers recall of this information from memory. The consumer becomes an unwitting, but active, accomplice for your advertising efforts. This is why many large corporations zealously guard their slogans and logos through the copyright law. Promotional use that constitutes a legal infringement is a direct commercial blow to the victimized company.

If you need a larger body of text to convey your information, use direct and declarative sentences. Be action-oriented. A passive tone won't sell. Keep sentence length to a minimum.

If illustrations aren't being used, place heavy emphasis on words that create mental images for the reader. Use adjectives that describe in the fewest possible words. Advertising is not the place for a rambling narrative.

To underscore the right tone, most of the sentences in the last two paragraphs were in the direct, terse tone that gets to the point quickly. They are not conversational or casual. You want the reader to respond with a specific course of action.

Ambivalency in tone displays a general lack of confidence that leads to very negative results. Confidence, when not carried to the point of open arrogance, is an important part of developing your prestige image. When effectively prepared, your advertising reflects your confidence—and gives customers the confidence in you that fosters productive, long-term business relationships.

Key Pitfalls to Avoid

- Avoid inconsistencies in your message. Potential clients might become confused by their implications.
- Avoid actively "knocking" your competition. Valid comparisons, when statistically backed up, can be used.
- Avoid hostile tones toward *any competitor* in advertising. Negative advertising usually backfires on the advertiser.
- Avoid being oblivious to the commercial climate around you. If changes occur, make necessary modifications in your approach. Flexibility usually beats intransigence in the advertising game.

COMBINING FORCES FOR PRESTIGE POWER

One of the most common promotional mistakes in business is an excessive dependence on a single facet of a promotional effort. Far too often, promotion is automatically equated to either advertising or publicity, depending on the business entity involved.

The idea of combining and correlating promotional efforts to multiply effects is not considered seriously enough. When large advertising budgets are available, there is an automatic urge to spend every allocated dime. This can be detrimental to business profitability.

By contrast, a limited budget tends to slant efforts to the other extreme. Promotion is then directed to emphasizing publicity (i.e., "free" advertising). Paid advertising efforts are not considered affordable.

When your promotional efforts complement both components, a business receives a proven double benefit. Advertising does not need to be as detailed or explanatory to gain maximum client exposure to your message. The publicity angle takes care of that, at no charge, leaving advertising's role as reinforcement for publicity's message.

Here's how one business accomplished this objective. A newspaper decided to feature a three-article series on a new investment consulting firm. Each article would detail one of the three major services that they offered.

To augment this free advertising (i.e., publicity), the consulting firm placed paid advertisements in various media calling public attention to the upcoming article series—and providing a phone number for people who had any questions about topics covered by the articles.

This consulting firm could have merely been satisfied with having the article series appear, assuming that this would be sufficient "advertising." However, these aggressive thinkers decided that the public might not feel free to approach them with questions without proper encouragement. These questions, and the answers provided, could be the seeds from which a considerable amount of new business might be generated.

Their hypothesis proved true for the consulting firm. Within two weeks of the articles' publication, the consulting firm had tabbed over three dozen new active clients. This was definitely not a bad result, considering that they operated in a small city with a population of approximately 20,000 people.

The key to why this approach was successful came from a recognition of fundamental consumer psychology. The consulting firm recognized at the outset that the article series would generate some measure of consumer intrigue. People would become curious.

This factor was encouraged, with the full recognition that a substantial number of calls would not be serious inquiries. The main point was to get these people out of an apathetic frame of mind, encourage them to take preliminary action, and convert the curious into serious service purchasers. They recognized that you cannot sell to people who never call.

THE DOVETAIL CONCEPT

Borrowed from pioneer log cabin builders, the term *dovetail* describes a special joining of two separate logs by giving them the capability to interlock with each other, making for a stronger total unit. This term accurately describes the way in which promotions from various media are used to integrate with and complement each other.

As a central player in any effective promotional program, newspaper advertising is a fulcrum around which other promotional efforts revolve. An example is the firm that decides to produce and broadcast a radio program. To assure that listeners tune in to hear the message, the firm advertises the broadcast time in the newspaper to expand public awareness.

The same technique is used in other areas as well. Suppose, as an example, that you are asked to address a major community group. Rather than rely solely on the group to publicize your speech, you sponsor advertising that benefits the group and your community-spirit image, and enhances the audience numerically when you deliver your speech.

There is an old and sage caution against "putting all your eggs in one basket." The dovetail concept is a practical application of this sound advice.

Actively search for these golden opportunities for self-promotion. Then, using skillfully placed advertisements, be certain that you're gaining the maximum mileage from each opportunity.

CLOSING THOUGHTS

Throughout this chapter our focus has been on the techniques of and major benefits from effective newspaper promotion. As you read the ideas, you may have dismissed some as being out of your current range of possibilities.

An important point to remember is that, when implemented in a coordinated and organized manner, promotional programs can be initiated in a very modest way with good results. These results in turn can serve to finance larger efforts.

A single small display advertisement can provide a beginning seed from which other efforts can grow. You don't need a full-page advertisement to deliver an advertising message effectively. In some cases, a small advertisement, when placed in a strategically advantageous location, is just as effective.

Sometimes a larger advertisement can be a negative influence on potential clients. Few people today are so totally naive as to have no idea of advertising rates. The large advertisement can easily project the image of high fees that are beyond the prospective consumer's budget. The potential customer may also feel that investment in such services includes advice for procedures that are unrealistic for anyone with a down-to-earth budget. Lavishness in advertising may alienate many potential clients. That can be a deadly mistake, along with the prospect of inflating an advertising budget beyond reasonable levels.

Advertising of any kind, whether in newspapers or other places, best contributes to a prestige image when it is maintained for longer periods. Prestige is often based on projected business stability. This is not something that one develops overnight.

Program maintenance, not a single large splash, is the key to success here. The contents of this chapter, when consistently applied, provides you with this necessary advantage to your future success.

CHAPTER

6

TARGET MARKETING THROUGH TRADE JOURNALS

Planning marketing strategy outside your immediate vicinity is, by its nature, far more difficult. In your own area, you have the automatic advantage of being a continuing member of your community. Your physical presence is, in itself, a form of advertising.

As an active member of a professional community, the same concept of continuing visibility is important. If your consulting efforts are targeted to a specific business or professional group, you must become an active member of that "community" to be thoroughly accepted by it.

Gaining this visibility is the primary value of personal and professional promotion through trade and/or professional journals. A certain amount of respect is generated for those who publish in these journals. This principle is why, in academic circles, there is an almost unwritten rule that success is contingent on publication. The cliché, "publish or perish," has more truth to it than most academicians would willingly admit.

Although you are unlikely to "perish" without publication, the benefits of publication should never be discounted. Having your opinions known within a specific professional or business group, through articles, gives prestige to those who seek to be associated with you. Although the "fame" of publishing is fleeting, especially if it's an isolated occurrence, you inevitably have a substantial sales advantage in consulting efforts through this medium. Clients often let colleagues know that they have retained the services of "that guy who was published in XYZ Journal."

In this chapter, we take a closer look at how you can gain the benefits that come from this pride of association. We look at understanding trade journal readership, gathering and using typical reader statistics, designing trade journal advertisements, using the feedback concept, enhancing image building aspects, power promoting through publication, writing editorially appealing articles as well as manuscript requirements, and avoiding the "self-service" pitfall in writing articles. This chapter shows you how to use this media to reach important professional goals.

UNDERSTANDING TRADE JOURNAL READERSHIP

One of the most common mistakes made by neophyte writers is to submit articles to periodicals without even the foggiest notion of the journal's needs. They see the name and address of a prospective journal in some marketing guide, maybe read a few lines about some general article types that the journal is interested in publishing, and falsely assume that this is sufficient information on which to proceed. With few exceptions, they face inevitable disappointment—regardless of their other qualifications.

The vast majority of editorial rejections are based on one simple fact.

The author simply never paid attention to the current needs of the journal's readers.

How does the editor know the author is out of touch with his readers? There are two indications that the author doesn't know the journal's operation. First, an author proposes an idea that is very similar to one recently published by the journal or, second, the proposed article has little or no bearing on the activities of the readers.

Most editors feel at least a little insulted if they see that you didn't care enough to even read their journal before submitting an idea or an article to them. If you read a journal, you know what types of articles are being published—and you know that a certain subject has recently been covered. To be successful, you have to be a little different from others in your approach, but still within the defined interests of your prospective readers.

Before submitting any idea or article, be sure to read at least one copy of the target journal. Even better, consider reviewing two or three recent issues to see what subject areas the journal focuses on.

Completing the picture, you should also study the advertising content within the pages. The products and services being advertised are a good indicator of reader interests. Is the journal specifically oriented toward professional performance? Or, as is the case with some journals, is there also any coverage of the personal side of the professional's life?

Effective advertisers generally choose periodicals that reflect their interests within the editorial content. This is why reviewing the content and nature of advertising is so important in determining whether your article's approach, or "slant," is really right for the publication.

As an example, a current issue of a professional journal may not have a single article about sales of professional services. However, there may be advertisers within its pages that reflect this interest. This gives you a clear clue that this could be a potential area of interest for the journal.

Doing this homework will give you an excellent cross-sectional view of the journal's readership. This definitely helps you design materials to meet those interests.

USING TYPICAL READER STATISTICS

Most periodicals, including trade and professional journals, conduct surveys among their readership to get a profile of their typical reader. Sometimes, you can find a reader profile that reads, "35-year-old male engineer," or something similar to that.

What does that mean to you? Simply put, the average reader's age is 35, the audience is predominantly male, and the reader is a college graduate in engineering. Because of this profile, you wouldn't write materials that weren't of interest to an engineer, and you also wouldn't focus on subjects slanted toward feminine issues.

If knowing reader interests is important for articles, it is even more crucial when you decide to advertise in the journal. If your advertising doesn't reflect the interests of the readers, you're clearly wasting your money—and you're not going to get any measurable response to your advertising. It really doesn't matter how effective your advertising is, or how much you spend on the effort. If readers aren't naturally interested in your services, no amount of advertising will do any good.

When a journal views you as a potential advertiser, you are in an ideal situation to get a more detailed view of their readership, including age ranges, education level, specific professional specializations, and even marital and offspring statistics. All these factors play a contributory role in their primary interests and how strongly success-oriented they are. This is particularly important knowledge for a consultant who solicits business from within a particular professional or business group.

The important thing is to translate statistics into tangible results. This is accomplished by categorizing reader information and clearly defining the characteristics of the majority. As an example, if the majority of readers are young professionals, their primary focus is on success *now*. They aren't as interested in the longer term security aspects and retirement issues as their older contemporaries are.

This does not mean to imply that the older professional isn't interested in current success. Rather, he or she sees success within the context of future security. Recognizing the contextual relationships within which your prospective clients view presented materials, you can more accurately gear your efforts to fit their psychological framework in a natural and easy way.

Every reader who sees your presentations, either articles or advertising, is a potential future client. If you demonstrate that you are in tune with their current needs, you are likely to make a favorable impression. This is how editors gear their content to meet subscriber needs. It is also the way they judge any articles or proposals that you present for their consideration. Using these same criteria in designing your advertising efforts for a journal gives you reasonable assurance that your investment will have the desired impact on the journal's readership.

DESIGNING APPEALING ADVERTISING

As you study a target journal, assess their design capabilities for advertising. For example, is the advertising strictly in one color or is there a multicolor capability? Can they reproduce color illustrations?

This knowledge puts you in a favorable position to design your advertising for the best effect with the smallest investment. That balance, impact per invested dollar, is very important to the profitability of your advertising effort.

Advertising that is strictly on a text basis tends to be boring—and won't command attention. There has to be some feature of the presentation to command attention. That may be as simple as headlining in larger lettering or adding some line art or a photo. Variation is the key to commanding attention.

Another consideration is the width of columns available in the journal. Column inch rates, as a strict criteria for comparison, are somewhat misleading. Narrow column widths force you to design advertising over two column widths to get desired impact. As a result, your advertising fees end up being doubled.

Wider columns are a better value for your advertising dollar. You don't need as many column inches to deliver an effective advertising message.

Measure the size of a common advertising display currently featured in the journal. Pay special attention to the size of the advertisements that effectively captured *your* attention. Those advertisements will tell you how much you actually have to invest to get desired results.

With this information, you are in an excellent position to deal with the journal's advertising director. Don't let that person talk you into a larger advertisement than you initially planned. Although most of them are on salary, there's almost always an incentive to sell more space.

Don't cramp advertising copy into a space that is too small to deliver your message effectively. Journal design departments often offer considerable amounts of copy in a reduced space. But the end result is print too small to read. That surely won't create a positive impression on potential clients.

After you've chosen a basic design concept, gear the text to reader interests, as discussed earlier in this chapter. If you established your identity in other ways within the journal, you won't have too much difficulty reinforcing that identification with a relatively simple advertising format. Your name, address, and possibly a phone number is sufficient to get at least limited results from your advertising. You can also offer some type of incentive to encourage response. (This feedback concept is discussed later in the chapter.)

As a final note, don't try to outshine other advertisers in the journal. Although advertisers reflect personal conservatism in their presentations, the designs may also reflect what journal readers consider is "good taste" in promotion. Going beyond these limits may do more to offend, rather than attract, potential clients. This is an easy pitfall to avoid.

USING THE FEEDBACK CONCEPT

When you advertise in media that isn't on the local level, you may wonder if your message is reaching its intended target audience. Without some way to measure advertising effectiveness, there is reason to wonder about your advertising investment.

This is why a growing number of advertisers use a reply-coupon design to encourage responses from potential customers. Rather than writing a letter or making a phone call, the respondent simply fills in name, address, and possibly a phone number on the coupon and sends for further information. This allows you to direct more specific information only to those readers who show an interest—rather than invest more money to deliver your entire message to potentially disinterested consumers. That could be a severe waste of your advertising budget.

Trade and professional journal advertising is particularly good if you have a specific printed product to offer for sale, as in marketing an informational newsletter. (See Chapter 10 for more detail on this combination product/marketing vehicle for your consulting business.) Having readers order a sample copy, for a price, is an excellent marketing hook to get readers to purchase your consulting services.

Finally, to get the best results from trade and professional journal advertising, be prepared for a fast response from potential clients. Respondents may forget that they contacted you if they have to wait too long for requested materials. That can send your materials, inadvertently, into the nearest wastebasket. That won't do you any good at all.

USING JOURNALS AS IMAGE BUILDERS

Although it's possible to build image strictly through advertising, it won't be as cost-effective as a varied approach. As mentioned earlier, writing articles provides considerable benefits toward building a prestige image. Best of all, you might even get paid for achieving your own goals.

As with everything else, reliance on one particular journal isn't a good idea. This is especially true if there are several journals serving the interests of a particular business or professional group. When this is so, it is unrealistic to assume that one journal assures coverage of all members within the group. This is true even if the journal has a national scope and orientation.

Being published in only one journal also gives readers the impression that you can only make the grade with one individual editor. Broadening the scope of your approach increases your exposure within the professional group.

As a practical matter, editors have to limit the amount that they publish from any individual author. If they don't, they give the appearance of unwarranted favoritism.

The major exception is if you are a regular columnist for the journal. These columnists often are featured on the journal's masthead, being listed as contributing editors. This gives your name continuing exposure, even when your writing isn't featured in one particular issue of the periodical.

Writing regularly before a trade or professional group, not just a one-shot deal, keeps adding to your prestige within the group. Unlike advertising, which is perishable, the appearance of articles has a cumulative impact on readers. Regularly contributing authors can often build a "fan club" for themselves among subscribers. This group can form an excellent core constituency for any product or service that you offer, if you use this opportunity.

SPECIAL HINT ON POWER PROMOTION THROUGH AUTHORED ARTICLES

When you've established an identity base through authored articles, you can use this to add special power to your advertising efforts. These people already know you a little. That's an asset that you can't afford to overlook.

Use your article authorship as the asset it is. Within your advertising, don't hesitate to let potential clients know that you're the one who is the "noted author featured in XYZ Journal" or that you're a "contributing editor"—whatever is true in your case.

You don't have to brag unnecessarily in your advertising. Just state facts and let them speak for themselves. They will have plenty of impact without need for exaggeration.

This type of advertising calls attention to your writings, directing potential clients to an opportunity to personally review your skills and knowledge. There is considerable reciprocal value in using this approach.

Another thing to consider is the value of the "bio notes" commonly included with each article printed in trade or professional journals. These notes give a very brief profile of the author. In your profile, include the fact that you're top man of your own consulting company. That includes using your business name.

On a local and small regional level, this type of publicity can have quite an impact. In smaller areas where newspapers are starved for local notables to report on, published writings on a national scale are often considered newsworthy. That presents an opportunity for additional exposure within the author's own area—publicity that has no cost, but has almost limitless value in the development of a solid prestige image.

This same principle, to a lesser degree, applies in metropolitan markets. Because there is more news available to newspapers in these markets, there may be fewer opportunities for such exposure in metropolitan papers. Also, there is a greater sophistication among metropolitan readers. They aren't as easily impressed by these achievements, simply because they are more common in these areas. There are more people and therefore more talent available. The achievements have to be greater to be newsworthy.

Whether you promote your business through advertising or publicity, don't indulge in excessive humility. If people don't know of your accomplishments, they won't know if you're good, or good for them.

PREPARING EDITORIALLY APPEALING COPY

Although manuscript mechanics, the way in which your material is organized on a page, is of some importance, the more critical aspect of marketable material surrounds what you say and how you say it. It's important to note how this was just expressed.

All too often, people who sit down to write an article, book, report, and so on shift gears and assume a literary pretense that gives no indication of the author's personality. If we make the false assumption that such pretense is necessary, we allow this to get in the way of our natural writing talent and make the writing process unnecessarily difficult. It's important to note that the only difference between written and verbal communication is the method of delivery to an audience.

The most successful magazine and book authors write in the same style as they speak. If we ever were to talk to each other, you would find that the words on these pages accurately reflect the way I speak.

Failure to observe this reality is one of the primary causes of "writer's block." You can't set your personality aside when you take a pen in hand or sit down at a keyboard to write. If you try to do that, you can suffer a severe intellectual blockage that is very difficult to overcome. Being totally comfortable with who and what you are is essential to allowing this natural talent to emerge.

Writing with blockage results in communications that are stiff and artificial. Sometimes when you sit down to write, you can be confronted with a case of literary "stage fright." You find yourself focusing on the idea that there may be thousands of readers who will see what you've written. If you lack basic confidence in what you are trying to communicate, this can be a considerable source of trepidation.

Don't place your intellectual focus on that larger audience. You are reaching your readers individually. Talk to *one* person. Imagine that the person is sitting across a coffee table from you. Tell them what you feel they should know, explain the important points of your message (as you would in verbal communication), and when you're done with your message, simply shut up.

At this point, you're probably thinking, "It's not that simple." The important thing to know is that it really *is* that simple. If you have a solid vocabulary and can express yourself effectively in verbal communication, there is absolutely no reason why you can't transfer these skills to the written word. That, more than anything else, is the predominant secret to writing editorially appealing copy that will find its way into journal pages.

Incidentally, this is also the secret to seemingly awesome writing productivity. If you view writing as a painful, even agonizing exercise, you won't look forward to doing it. Some people have the same attitude toward writing as to having their teeth pulled out without novocaine. They agonize over each individual word—and the final product shows it. There is no smooth flow, coherency, or natural quality to it at all.

Wearing the pretentious royal mantle of "writer" is the surest way to crush your creativity. Throw pretensions into the nearest wastebasket, sit down, and simply write. Before you begin, clearly think through what you want to communicate, say it, and you're done. There are no great secrets here. You're just transferring verbal communication into words on paper.

As a final note, don't consider writing courses as an instant panacea on your route to publication. This is particularly true if you take a course in the university environment. Acedemia is usually far more interested in form than substance, fails to teach true communication skills, and usually puts student creativity in communications into an intellectual straitjacket.

Samuel Clemens, better known as Mark Twain, once commented that he never allowed his education to get in the way of his learning. That statement is particularly true of your ability to communicate. Courses may teach you general form. You have to learn the rules—to know when to break them for maximum effectiveness.

You would never have considered consulting as a vocational choice if you weren't reasonably confident of your general communication skills. Don't let the written form intimidate you. No one is asking you to be another George Bernard Shaw. Simply be yourself. Who knows? You may end up being just as famous.

MANUSCRIPT REQUIREMENTS

Although we've just reviewed how to throw the rules away, there arc a few rules that you would be well-advised to observe. These are the format rules that should be used when submitting materials to editors. They are strictly for the smooth operation of the journal publishing process.

Your first manuscript page is the most important. In the upper lefthand corner, remember to include your name, address, possibly your phone number, and your social security number. In the upper righthand corner, indicate what rights you are offering to the journal (see the Special Hint on Magazine Rights), the approximate length of your article (number of words), and the page number. Subsequent pages only need your last name in the upper lefthand corner and the page number in the upper righthand corner.

Article content should be double-spaced. Editors generally like to tinker at least a little bit with almost every manuscript, even if it's only a minor correction. They need double-spacing to give them room for copyediting. Avoidance of stingy margins on both sides of the page will also help the editor. A minimum 10 spaces on both left and right margins is recommended. Editors generally prefer pica type to elite. It's larger and is less likely to cause eyestrain from lengthy reading sessions.

Also, use plain white typewriter bond. Colored paper, regardless of its color, is more difficult to read than white paper. Editors also prefer the standard 20-pound bond to lighter papers, but they won't scream very much if you use paper that's one grade lighter in weight. Just don't succumb to the temptation of raiding the office onionskin supply for your manuscript. It is very difficult for editors to handle efficiently and drives them crazy. That surely won't create a favorable impression.

SPECIAL HINT ABOUT MAGAZINE RIGHTS

Generally, you can publish the same article in a number of different journals—with one condition. Circulation should not be competitive among the journals.

This is why your preliminary article marketing effort should emphasize that you're offering *first* rights to the material. Even those journals that claim to acquire all rights will reassign remaining rights to the author after publication, but you won't get them reassigned unless you specifically ask.

When you submit previously published material, indicate that you are offering *reprint rights*. Although some journals won't consider previously published articles, most welcome them. You can get extra mileage from your writing efforts if you thoroughly explore this avenue to reach your audience.

AVOIDING THE SELF-SERVICE PITFALL

As noted before, journal editors take a dim view of articles that are little more than prolonged advertisements for the author. This can be a particularly tricky proposition for some professional authors.

There's a very fine line between discussing your experiences in your work and "tooting your own horn." The best way to get around this problem is to emphasize experiences and techniques that others have used successfully. In this way you serve also as a reporter, and you are not merely performing an exercise in ego-inflation.

If you base your writing on your own experience, simply state what techniques were used and the results obtained. Let the readers decide whether they consider the results successful. Avoid editorializing by saying that your results were spectacular. Your readers may not share your opinion—and would consider such commentary boastful and unwarranted. Let your facts speak for themselves. If they are spectacular, your readers will know it.

Reader empathy is an important asset in communication. You sacrifice it whenever you put yourself on an elevated perch, seemingly above the reader who you're trying to reach. One of the best ways to achieve it is to share mistakes that you have made—and the steps you took to correct them. Your readers will find themselves thinking, "I screwed up like that once." Instantly, you've developed a rapport that commands the reader's attention.

The prestige image is not based on what you say about yourself. It is based on what others say about you. Remembering this is the surest way to avoid the self-service pitfall in preparing materials for your target audience.

CLOSING THOUGHTS

One of the most important distinctions to make to be successful in this marketing media is to differentiate between the trade and the professional journal. They often contrast in both content and stylistic approach.

By publishing-industry definition, trade journals are those journals that focus on larger business or industrial groups. For example, if you are an automotive consultant, you won't be able to interest a journal that concentrates on batteries in an article on brake systems. Yes, these journals do get that specialized.

Trade journals often focus on practical applications, the nuts and bolts of a profession's operation. By contrast, professional journals deal more with theoretical materials. They want wider brush strokes of the picture, rather than a microscopic review of a single spot.

In studying your target markets, consult a good marketing reference. Two good ones are *Literary Marketplace* and *Writer's Market*. The latter is an annual publication of Writer's Digest Books. In both sources, you'll receive a breakdown of journals based on subject categories. For the neophyte in the writing business, the number of subcategories can be surprising.

Some journals pay handsomely for articles, often rivaling hourly fees paid in other professional areas. In others, the remuneration amounts to little more than public relations exposure to the target group. In either case, particularly if you're not going to make your living as a writer, recompense won't be of major concern. You will be mainly interested in the exposure value of publication.

As a final note to this chapter, I recommend that you closely study publications regarding how serious their orientation is. Some journals have no objection to authors sprinkling a little humor within their presentations. This is particularly true if it's self-deprecating humor. Taking yourself too seriously makes you seem unapproachable—a definite "sin" for the consultant seeking to gain business.

Humor, applied sparingly, is the leavening that holds our lives together. It provides a breathing space that allows pages of serious material to be absorbed without intellectual stress.

Although it is important to get a positive reaction from a journal's editor, the most important reaction for your success is that coming from the reader of the journal. This chapter helps you achieve the rapport with both editor and reader that contributes to your ultimate success.

CHAPTER 7

POWER PROMOTION THROUGH RADIO ADVERTISING

As one of the older forms of advertising, radio promotion has become a somewhat neglected element of many promotional programs. Yet it can represent a unique creative challenge. Radio advertising provides an excellent—and lower cost—entry point in communicating with prospective clients.

In this chapter, we take a closer look at radio advertising, examining how we can make the most effective use of this media. We cover the basics of radio promotion, listener demographic surveys and how to use them, target market selection, costs of effective radio advertising, setting the advertising tone, and writing effective radio advertisement.

We also examine various elements of the production process, seeing how they affect the way in which your advertisement is written. We review sound mixing principles, musical backgrounds, and effective use of sound effects.

Finally, we discuss timing of radio commercials and correlation of radio promotion with your other efforts to make this media a solid contributor to your total marketing package. When effectively used, radio promotion is an adjunct to the advertising arsenal of any business.

RADIO BASICS

To establish a firm foundation for subsequent discussion in this chapter, we will review and define some of the basic terminology of the radio advertising industry here. You won't feel like I'm speaking a foreign language.

Let's run through a quick list of the most common terms.

Radio spot. A *spot* is the most common term used to describe a commercial.

Boom mike. In a larger radio recording studio, this is a microphone that is attached to a long metal arm, allowing the mike to be at a considerable distance from the main control panel.

Electronic squeal. An ear-piercing shriek resulting from not having the volume setting correctly tuned to the tone and volume of the person delivering the advertising message. Few people who record their own commercials are able to avoid this experience at least once.

Sound mixing. The blending of recordings from two or more separate sources. When the text of a commercial is being spoken, it is usually recorded alone. Afterward other elements are added, including music, sound effects, and so on from other sources. This blending process is defined as *mixing*.

Sound effects. The mechanical reproduction of familiar sounds, such as running feet, racing horses, creaking door hinges, and so on. The variety is only limited by one's imagination.

One of the primary challenges of using radio as an advertising media is that it forces us to change our primarily visual frame of reference. Being a television-oriented society for so long, we tend to measure our perceptions by what we see. We have to learn how to "think with our ears."

The most effective radio advertising creates a visual illusion by making the listener an ally through the imagination. This was the magic that was so effectively used in old-time radio programming. When you understand how to create visual illusions, you can recreate this "magic" for your advertising.

LISTENER DEMOGRAPHIC SURVEYS AND HOW TO USE THEM

As with other media, understanding the type, size, and general philosophical slant of your proposed audience is an important part of selecting and using radio advertising effectively. You can't sell to people who aren't listening to you.

The unique aspect of radio is that most broadcasting stations appeal to a much wider range of interests than other media can. They do it by offering various types of programming at different times of the day. This variation reflects itself in the listener demographic survey for the station.

In conducting their market studies, stations knows what type of audience is listening to them at various times during each day. They key their programming accordingly.

This is an important consideration in determining when you want your advertising to be heard. Many radio stations will offer special program sponsorships to area business establishments. If a program has a proven large audience delivery, it can be a powerful way to reach consumers.

When you sit down to talk business with the radio station advertising salesperson, tell him or her who your proposed market includes. As an example, the demographic study indicates that a large number of prospective clients are listening in their autos as they commute to their offices or commercial establishments. You want to place your advertising messages into this time frame. The morning and afternoon traffic rush hours is the best time to reach these people.

This information also helps you to accurately assess the best tone for your advertising message. As an example, the jangled nerves of people commuting in the afternoon rush hour surely won't welcome a blaring bugle in an advertising message. You won't get many favorable reviews that way.

Radio demographic surveys generally do a breakdown of the day by the hour or by the programming being featured. The results can sometimes be as detailed as percentages within each given age-group, professional or vocational choices, gender, peripheral interests, and so on.

Your most important statistic is the estimated total audience. Knowing the estimated total audience, along with the estimated percentage that represents your target market, you can easily calculate whether your message is being delivered cost-effectively to prospective clients.

COMPARATIVE STATION ANALYSIS

Because most areas have a number of radio stations to choose from, don't succumb to the temptation of investing your money too quickly. Study all the stations before making your choice.

Unless cost is the single overriding consideration for you, don't automatically buy commercial time from the least expensive station. The advertising rates may be lower for one very important reason. The station doesn't have a provable audience delivery. Why waste your money that way?

Closely examine the strong points in each station's broadcasting schedule. As an example, a station has a strong morning audience—and is practically dead after lunch. Another station is the prime choice for afternoon listeners. If your prospective clientele follow this trend, you will find it profitable to advertise on more than one radio station, gaining maximum benefit from a natural audience shift.

The final factor in the selection process is to carefully consider the image that each station projects to the community. As an example, if your primary market is conservative, you won't get many positive results if you advertise on a radio station that features hard rock music. Your prospective clients won't be listening to hear your message.

Take the time to personally listen to a radio station. Are you comfortable with their methods? Does the station project an image that is compatible with your marketing objective? If your answer is no to either or both of these questions, don't actively consider using these stations—regardless of how attractive their advertising rates are.

CHOOSING YOUR TARGET MARKET

Just as you want to project a certain image, so do radio stations. For this reason, there is less tendency for radio stations to be homogeneous in their broadcasting approach. Specialization is the surest way for them to maintain their marketing focus.

For lack of a better method, radio stations classify themselves by the type of music that they broadcast to their listeners. This can be anything, including country and western, rock and roll, easy listening, classical, and hard rock. Each of these types has specific groups attracted to it.

The central issue in choosing a radio station is not the image that you want to project. Rather, it is a determination of where your specific potential customers are most likely to be listening.

If you leave the design of your advertising to the radio station, the station's musical focus tends to be reflected in the tone of advertising that is created for you. Country and western and rock and roll radio stations are very informal in their advertising tone.

As an example, a funeral director in cattle country winced when he heard the commercial created for him by a country music station. His advertisement began with the words, "If you're headed for your last round-up, there's only one place to consider as your final corral." Obviously, this wasn't the dignified approach that he wanted. Incidentally, he cancelled his advertising agreement with the station.

This caution does *not* imply that you can't advertise on stations that differ philosophically with your approach, but it does indicate that, in these circumstances, you have to take greater personal control over advertising contents and style of presentation. If in doubt, don't delegate this important function to the station.

As a guideline, you can generally target the age demographic of a given station by the tempo of the music. The faster and more raucous music appeals to a more youthful market. As the music tempo and style become more sedate, the median age of the listener increases.

As a practical matter, your greater concentration of potential customers is likely to be in the latter area. Executive decision makers are most likely to be middle age. This group is also more intellectually open to the possibility of personal and professional improvement.

As far as older groups are concerned, there is a tendency to feel that the "school of experience" has lessened their need for new information. Although you may receive some business from the older sector, they may not be as favorable as clients. Their slightly younger contemporaries bring more favorable results for your consulting efforts.

There is, however, one cautionary note here. Avoid psychological stereotyping of potential clients. As an example, there is a considerable number of "baby boomers," people who were in their formative years during the hard-rock rebellion period of the sixties. Although they may have formed their musical preferences during these years, they may now be as conservative as their slightly older contemporaries.

This is the primary argument against advertising on the more offbeat radio stations. Although musical preferences may still be influenced by his or her youth, the listener is not as receptive to less dignity in business solicitation. This comes from age-acquired conservatism.

I am an excellent case in point for this phenomenon. Having spent my formative years with the echoes of Elvis Presley's music ringing in my ears, I still find myself drawn to that musical style, along with some of the newer country and western artists. This is in stark contrast with a solidly conservative viewpoint on almost everything else, including economics and politics.

An advertising approach that effectively contrasts with the station's musical approach is probably the most successful in reaching—and delivering—the radio audience to your office door. The contrast commands attention because the advertising doesn't blend in with its surroundings.

COSTS OF THE RADIO APPROACH

The two prime factors to consider in designing your radio advertising program are length of commercial and frequency of its airing. The length of each commercial and how often it is heard by listeners determines your total cost per advertising day.

Generally radio stations, like other electronic media, calculate their fees on a per-advertising-minute basis. This is for each time that the commercial goes on the air. If you go for a commercial that is less than a minute in length, you can expect to pay a slightly higher fee on the per-minute basis.

As an example, one station charges approximately $10 for a one-minute airing of a commercial. However, for the single airing of a 30-second spot, the fee is around $6.50. This example is not, however, typical of all radio stations.

Fees charged for commercials are affected by two additional factors. They are the approximate number of listeners who will be exposed to your message and the total number of times that you agree to have your commercial aired. If you agree to a larger number of airings, you are likely to receive (or can easily negotiate) a lower per-airing fee. This is especially true of shorter commercials. The production costs of making the original recording is spread over a larger number of airings.

Let's take our earlier fee example and extrapolate that into a sample radio advertising budget for one station. We agree to buy a 30-second commercial and air it four times per day for five business days.

Your first discount is likely to come from calculating your advertising rate on the full minute, rather than half-minute, basis. That would reduce your per day cost from $26 to $20. This represents a week's savings of $30. By committing yourself to a week of advertising, you will probably receive an additional discount, sometimes 10 percent or more of the week's fee.

Comparative advertising rates among radio stations, as with any other media, are determined by whether they have a local, regional, or national range. The high-output "superstations" have comparable superrates.

The example rates included in our earlier calculations are in the median range for local stations in small and medium-size cities. This can escalate to $100 or more per advertising minute for large metropolitan and regional stations. An intensive advertising campaign on these larger stations is likely to be in excess of the resources available to an average consultant. A relatively low-level advertising campaign, as used in our example calculations, could top $50,000 per year on one station.

If you do have this amount of money available for radio advertising, the situation becomes a basic judgment call for you. There is, however, the old axiom "Don't put all your eggs in one basket" to consider. Will the station totally serve your radio advertising needs? Will you reach all the people that you want to reach with just one station? If your answers to these two questions are both yes, you *might* consider this possibility. But I strongly advise caution before you make this type of investment.

AN ALTERNATIVE OPTION

Rather than put your advertising dollars into one station, consider the use of the overlapping radius principle to gain a larger broadcasting range from smaller stations. Let's assume that you have two radio stations, each with a broadcasting radius of 75 miles, available for your advertising. If they are about 140 miles apart, your message would only overlap in an area of approximately 10 miles. Two small stations would cover a total circle that's almost 300 miles wide.

Another possibility is to use a broadcasting peculiarity of AM (amplitude modulation) radio. If the station wattage is sufficiently high, the late evening hours can expand the station's broadcasting range enormously. An AM station may have a range of only 100 miles during the day. But, at night, this range may expand to approximately 1,000 miles, depending on weather conditions.

One Midwestern organization has capitalized on this idea, choosing a non-prime-time slot to broadcast their message. They have a 15-minute program once a week on a metropolitan radio station. The cost for the 15-minute program: $100 a week.

SETTING THE ADVERTISING TONE

As in our discussion of the general tone of a radio station, radio advertising is also based strongly on the tone that is projected. An important point to remember is that in radio, unlike other media, there can be no reliance on your audience's visual perception abilities.

If it is important for your listener to visualize something, your commercial must describe it in words. This is the thrust you should pursue to be successful.

Radio commercials are divided into two general categories: musical and nonmusical. Radio advertisements that rely strictly on verbal communication, with no other background considerations incorporated into the production, work reasonably well if they *contrast* with the programming that surrounds them.

As an example, a nonmusical advertisement works well if it interrupts a program that is predominantly musical. That sets it apart from the general format.

By contrast, if your commercial airs during a talk show or within a news program, advertising with a musical background achieves the same objective. The difference serves as a "frame" for your message.

Similarly, your choice of music can have a framing effect for your message—if it contrasts with the general music format of the radio station. As an example, during one political campaign, I wrote a commercial for one candidate using the *William Tell Overture* ("The Lone Ranger" theme) as background music. It truly fit the image for this law and order candidate.

Both words and music can serve to set the tone for your advertising. Direct and commanding statements project a take-charge image. If this is suitable for your projected audience, it is extremely effective. Coupled with music that conveys regimentation, the words make an effective combination.

As an example, I chose the *El Capitan March* for one advertiser, conveying the image that a parade was forming to their door. The advertisement was so effective that it initiated a trend at radio stations in the area. There were countless "copycat" commercials that aired in subsequent months.

If you choose, by contrast, the more relaxed image, slower and softer music is more appropriate. Choice of musical instrument is also a factor in setting the mood. Electric guitars, as an example, set a considerably different tone than the classical Spanish guitar. Organs tend to be more mellow than pianos. The list goes on and on.

Your awareness of this factor helps you to choose just the right tone for your particular message. Tone and message, blended effectively, have a lasting effect on the listeners you're trying to reach.

WRITING EFFECTIVE ADVERTISING COPY

Writing advertising copy for radio is an essentially direct task. You do not have the luxury of a convoluted presentation. Get to the point, make it, wrap it up, and stop.

To keep your advertising economical, you should keep your message to one minute or less. A short message, delivered with greater frequency, often has more impact than a longer one.

Four elements are generally considered mandatory for an effective radio commercial. They are

1. Name recognition
2. Definition of consumer need
3. Highlighting of specific difference between advertiser and competition
4. How to contact advertiser

Accomplishing all four points within a minute, and also setting an advertising tone, can be a considerable challenge. For the sake of discussion, let's assume that you are an architectural design consultant seeking new customers. You will consider assignments of any size. Let's set up an advertisement.

Sample Commercial

(Open with 15 seconds of music, the lyrics from "Over the Rainbow" from The Wizard of Oz, *concluding with the words, "the dreams that you dream will always be coming true.")*

WHETHER YOUR DREAM IS A NEW HOME OR A HIGH-RISE OFFICE BUILDING, B & B ARCHITECTURAL DESIGN CONSULTANTS IS THE ONE STOP THAT PUTS YOU ON THE YELLOW BRICK ROAD TO YOUR SPECIAL DREAM. WE HAVE THE EXPERIENCE TO TURN YOUR DREAM INTO A REALITY. WE'VE DONE IT FOR COUNTLESS OTHERS IN THE PAST 10 YEARS.

CALL B & B ARCHITECTURAL DESIGN CONSULTANTS TODAY AT 555-9000. THE REALITY OF YOUR DREAM IS A PHONE CALL AWAY.

This commercial, somewhat more elaborate than an average presentation, has a running air time of less than 45 seconds. That's not a bad deal. The combination of music and words implies the fulfillment of a listener's fantasy or dream. In this case, it is the starting point for a consumer's need for the advertiser's services.

When you prepare your commercial, choose a specific theme to communicate to your listener. In the above sample, it was the prospect of dream fulfillment.

Examine your current customer files. Try to ascertain the dominant reason why these customers chose to patronize your company. Look for this reason along with a secondary one, and capitalize on it in your advertising. When you write your commercial around this objective, you have the necessary ingredients for successful advertising for your consulting business.

PRINCIPLES OF SOUND MIXING

Sound mixing is a technique by which two or more sound tracks are blended together for unique results. The preceding sample advertisement used the technique of sound mixing for results.

Most radio stations have the technological capacity to accomplish effective sound mixing in the production process. This provides a smoother blend in the final product than is possible if the music is being played at the same time as the commercial's text is being read for the recording.

With effective blending, the music or sound effects are placed at lower volume in the background of the words being spoken. This uses the subliminal message psychology of advertising. The music is not commanding the listener's primary attention, but it has its effect nonetheless.

To accomplish sound mixing effectively from two separate sound tracks, three separate units are required. Two of the units have the master recordings. The third contains the blank recording that receives the blended result. A pure blended recording, with no undesirable peripheral noise, is achieved through the use of recording jacks that connect the two sending units with the receiving unit through direct wire. This blocks out any external noises, unlike the external microphones used in standard recording.

By adjusting the volume settings of the sending units, you can achieve a variety of special effects in the finished product. With the appropriate equipment and a little practice, many of these same results can be obtained by anyone. Generally, though, it is advisable to leave this process to established professionals in the field to assure the best results.

MUSICAL BACKGROUNDS

Discussed earlier in this chapter, the use of musical backgrounds has special considerations in the production process. Before you design your commercial, ask the radio station about their music library.

Most stations own a considerable variety of music, even though they specialize in a particular area. Don't assume that, just because a station predominantly broadcasts one type of music, nothing else is available for commercial use. As an example, the *El Capitan March* was available at a rock music station. Talk about contrast!

You can achieve many effects with music that are not possible otherwise. Some experimentation is required to get the best result, but it can be accomplished.

> **SPECIAL NOTE ON MUSIC**
>
> If a major portion of a piece of music is used for commercial purposes, there is generally a royalty that you must pay for its use. Whenever this is a factor, the station customarily includes this charge as part of your total advertising fee. You won't usually pay it separately. To be safe, though, you should ask about a royalty fee.

USING SOUND EFFECTS

As mentioned earlier, the major challenge of the radio media is achieving visual effects without the aid of pictures. One of the pioneer techniques for getting the visual illusion is the use of sound effects.

If you ever listened to old-time radio shows, you undoubtedly noticed that all sorts of special sounds were incorporated into their presentations. Through mechanical reproduction, sounds ranging from doors slamming and hinges creaking to the clattering noise of running horses was accurately reproduced for radio audiences.

Properly integrated into advertising, the use of sound effects adds considerable appeal to the message being presented. This is limited only by the station's sound effects library and the advertiser's imagination.

As with the directional note on the music in the sample commercial script, sound effects and their timing must be specified within the script format. You include this instruction in parentheses.

Examine the radio station's sound effects collection before preparing your advertising. You'll be surprised at the wide variety of options available to you.

I should sound a note of caution here. There is a tendency, particularly among copywriters first discovering the sound effects library, to use this feature excessively. Sound effects, like spices in cooking, should be used sparingly. Used well, they provide a distinctive difference that drives home an advertising message effectively.

TIMING COMMERCIAL AIRINGS FOR EFFECTIVENESS

One of the trickiest elements of planning a radio advertising campaign is in timing the airings of your commercials. Most radio advertising people urge you to air your commercial frequently, arguing that having your message on often increases your business name recognition.

To a point, they are correct, but there is a point at which too much of a good thing can be bad news for both consumer receptiveness and your advertising budget. If potential consumers begin reacting with the idea, "Oh, no! Not him again!", you're in big trouble. You might even end up with backlash from your advertising efforts.

The natural question, then, is, "How much is too much?" Although there is no simple answer because of variations in personal taste and tolerance to advertising, it probably isn't wise to have your commercials aired every 5 or 10 minutes. That's almost a sure bet to weary even the most patient listener.

A general rule is not to air a commercial more than every 15 minutes during the peak period for your target market. Intervals of 20 to 30 minutes are well within the acceptable range. Because most radio listeners tend to listen (with attention) one hour continuously, advertising of lesser frequency means that some segments of your target market may not hear your advertising at all.

After your peak period is over, don't advertise during other times. It doesn't make a lot of sense to advertise all day long—if your prospects won't be around to hear your message. Don't let any station advertising salesperson talk you into airing your radio spots during these "dead zone" periods.

Because you will most likely be dealing with the business community, their intrinsic habits should be an effective guide for your advertising efforts. Most of your potential clients are occupied during the course of the business day. Although they may have a radio on, they are probably only listening with half an ear. It's turned on for background noise, and little else.

For these people, the best times will usually be during the early morning hours (seven to nine AM) and the lunch hour. After that, the only remaining period (though usually not as effective) is immediately after quitting time. Quitting time is not as effective because these listeners are physically and intellectually tired from their work. This fatigue factor reduces their receptivity and concentration. Their thoughts are directed to going home and settling down to a nice dinner and an evening of well-earned relaxation with their family.

As a final note, you may reach some potential clients during the late night period (after 11 PM). Some people do have insomnia because of their problems, turn the radio on, and may be ripe for a suggestion for solving their problems. Another benefit of this time period, as mentioned earlier, is the expanded broadcasting range with some stations. Although your concentration of listeners is not as high, the increase in range makes up for this loss in your station's immediate vicinity, which amounts to a regionalized delivery on a local advertising budget.

TYING IN RADIO WITH OTHER PROMOTIONS

When you have successfully built name recognition in your area through radio advertising, you can use this effort to tie in other promotional elements. One popular technique is identification with special events or activities within the community.

One consultant has been very successful helping to sponsor local high school athletic event broadcasts. He has tied in that effort with a public relations coup of providing a small annual scholarship for the school athlete's Most Valuable Player. Every year, he gets free media coverage—and considerable community goodwill—when he personally presents the award at the school's Athletic Booster Club banquet.

Although this idea may not work for everyone, it does show that innovative thinking can create favorable results. With some imagination, you can gain considerable public exposure beyond the limits of your advertising. Your advertising does, however, set the stage for these additional efforts—and makes them effective.

Many businesses gain valuable exposure by combining appearances at major public events with their media advertising. One consultant annually sets up a business information booth at a county fair—and advertises her presence on the radio station, along with urging listeners to attend and enjoy the fair.

Don't overlook these special opportunities. Many previously unidentified prospective clients have been uncovered by using innovative thought in planning and coordinating promotion efforts. Shouldn't your consulting efforts receive the benefits of this expanded clientele?

CLOSING THOUGHTS

Throughout this chapter, we've taken a close look at the basics to achieving success in radio advertising. Consulting is unique among professional endeavors because of its specific marketing challenge. The lack of an immediately tangible product makes any marketing effort tricky.

Advertising on radio poses the special challenge of maintaining the delicate balance between compelling, interest-generating content and the distinct risk of being overbearing and obnoxious. The line of distinction can, in some cases, seem almost invisible.

This is particularly true if your consulting efforts are directed to groups that have a tight ethical restraint on their promotional activities. Any promotional effort, beyond the most rudimentary basics, can create feelings of envy that block their receptivity to your message. These listeners may get the feeling, from the tone of your advertising, you don't understand the restraints under which they must live.

Even in these circumstances, though, you can gain valuable benefits through advertising. Observing the cautions mentioned earlier in this chapter, and capitalizing on some of the key elements presented, you should be well on your way to planning an effective radio promotional campaign.

The key factor is to keep radio advertising in its proper perspective. Don't expect it to do the entire promotional job for you. Coordinate it with other efforts to get the best results. If you do this, you can develop a balanced advertising approach that yields the solid dividends that your efforts deserve.

CHAPTER

8

TELEVISION ADVERTISING AND PROMOTION: THE CRITICAL EDGE IN IMAGERY

In a visually oriented society, few media can rival the psychology match of television. Combining the benefits of the print media and radio, television adds action to a presentation that can only be duplicated in person and it does it without the inherent limitations of the one-to-one approach.

Although television is the most expensive of the media per advertising unit, it has a proven track record for effectiveness in customer delivery. Not having the limitations imposed by other media television is a dream come true for those who seek creative advertising or promotional programming.

In this chapter, we explore the basics of production for television advertising, examining visual impact, options to consider, and the cost factors involved. Further, we learn how to set up the "shooting script" (the written text and instructions) for commercials and programming, a glossary of script terminology, camera angle considerations, and how to expand the short advertising format.

Beyond the mechanics of television production, the chapter also explores scriptwriting of commercials and public service programming. The discussion also includes understanding the station psychology behind public service programming, using television as an educational forum, and the influence of television in building your prestige image.

This chapter shows you how to use television and tie it in effectively with other promotional media for a solid total package. This is the key to making cost-effective use of this creative media.

PRODUCTION PRINCIPLES OF TELEVISION ADVERTISING

With the development of videocassette recorder systems and cameras that general consumers can afford, the amateur's ability to produce television advertising and programming has revolutionized this medium. Given this alternative to professional handling of all aspects of production, there has been considerable growth in amateur productions.

Certain standards of acceptability and quality are essential, however, to have amateur productions used on commercial television. Knowing the production principles of television advertising is helpful if you produce your own videotape, but this information is also useful if you let a commercial studio or a television station handle production. You'll be an ally, rather than a hindrance, to the process.

Although many advertisers and television advertising programmers use studio facilities, a growing number are going to the "on location" option. They use the business location and personnel of the client in producing the advertising or program.

This approach may save the cost of studio facility rental, but the drawbacks make this "savings" counterproductive.

Basic production principles include three important factors: (1) background, (2) lighting, and (3) general environment. Having each element up to professional production standards assures the best result. Let's examine each factor in more detail.

Background

Professional videotaping studios and television stations often have one characteristic common to their production systems, the dominant use of light colors for the background where the taping is done. This is for a specific reason.

Light colors require less light to be photographed effectively. Although videotape is, in many ways, more sensitive than ordinary film, it has limitations. Dark colors absorb more light. A predominance of dark colors in a shooting background requires higher intensity lighting to get good results.

Gloss enamels and similar paints for background surfaces are not recommended. They tend to reflect light too readily. At certain lighting angles, they create a glare that only becomes evident when you view the final product.

You should remember this factor if you do your videotaping in your office or business facility. Some videotape cameras feature on-unit monitors that allow you to check the image being taped. This is a useful tool to assure professional results—or to check out any special effects that you want to create.

Another point is to avoid walls that have too much variation in color or design. An example is wallpaper with a printed design. This gives the background a cluttered appearance that detracts from the production. You want viewers to remember your message, not the appearance of your walls.

Lighting

Another important factor in getting professional results is the availability of adequate lighting. A single 100-watt bulb or a fluorescent lamp for a light source, for example, is not adequate to get good videotaping results.

Concentrated, rather than diffused, lighting is important to get a good videotape. Diffused lighting tends to minimize contrasts, which are critical in getting clear images.

Diffused lighting serves a purpose in the videotaping process, softening visual effects where desired. However, it would be a mistake to place reliance on it.

Concentrated lighting used in combination with diffused lighting assures good results. If you eliminate the diffused lighting, you can create a spotlighting effect that gives dramatic impact. The shortcoming is that if you do not get the correct lighting for an entire screen width, the image broadcasted will be improperly framed.

General Environment

One major challenge of videotaping or filming on location is that the environment has so many distractions. The "busy" surroundings clutter the image.

This is particularly true of business offices generally. Very few desktops are neat enough to avoid being a distracting influence.

Outdoor videotaping, especially in metropolitan areas, is not a better bet. Background sights and sounds can't be easily controlled, leaving much videotape wasted. Without sophisticated videotape editing equipment, available only in professional studios or television stations, you end up shooting a production several times to eliminate imperfections.

Lighting in the outdoor environment also poses a special challenge. You may not always be fortunate enough to have sunlight.

Because you are not working in the confined space of a studio, you have the problem of extensive light diffusion. The sky, or darkness at night, makes for considerable lighting problems. You have to check your lighting meters carefully to be sure that you have enough illumination. If you don't, any taping or filming is a wasted effort.

SPECIAL HINT ON VIDEOTAPE VERSUS FILM

Because of the relative complexity of videotape, some first-time producers tend to work better with film. Editing film requires less sophisticated equipment than videotape.

The drawback, however, is that most commercial television stations have videotape-based operations. Many do not own any film equipment, and this makes them unable to broadcast film productions.

Unless you're planning to make extensive use of videotaping, it isn't cost-effective to buy the sophisticated editing equipment needed for videotaping. Let those in the business handle your production.

UNDERSTANDING VISUAL IMPACT

Because of the high cost of television advertising, you have to get the most value for your dollar. This is especially true for the short television commercial. You have to command viewer attention to get results.

Understanding Visual Impact 99

A striking example of visual impact in television advertising is the commercial using animated raisins singing the pop rock hit, "I Heard it Through the Grapevine." Although one could argue that the approach is rather nonsensical, the commercial definitely achieves its primary objective: it commands viewer attention.

Another example is the import car commercial that features a notorious liar as its on-screen spokesperson. In one version, his mother is struck by lightning because he didn't tell the truth about the product.

Although this second example is of questionable taste, it, like the first example, gets viewer attention. We may laugh at the commercial (or at least chuckle), but we're listening and watching. That's what the advertiser wants us to do—after which we're supposed to go out and buy the product.

In a world deluged with commercials, these two examples show the fundamental point of visual impact. You have to be different from the crowd to get results. Of course, you don't have to violate the standards of good taste to accomplish this objective.

Advertising for consultants requires a considerable toning down of this approach. Some consultants may choose to do a bit of grandstanding to gain attention, but even this has to be subdued to maintain an image of integrity within the business community.

Television is particularly well suited to the extensive use of graphic art. Charts, graphs, and other illustrations can be put on the screen with adequate speed and in sufficient variety to hold viewer attention. This is an important advantage when you're working with a 30-second or one minute commercial.

This is where television has a clear advantage over radio. Using visual imagery, you can cut down on the number of spoken words to deliver your message.

Further, you can combine visuals and words in the same image if you wish. A favorite technique is to lead off with an image. After the viewer has had a chance to gain an impression from it, the image is placed slightly out of focus and words are superimposed on the image to reinforce the visual message.

Mixing these elements effectively helps you create visual impact. It also allows you to deliver a more complex message in a shorter time frame—a definite advantage from a cost viewpoint.

As a general rule, don't change images at intervals shorter than five seconds. You create a dizzying effect that keeps viewers from absorbing any of your message. They may even tune you out completely if the pacing is too frantic.

The only acceptable alternative to this would be to animate your graphics. As an example, show a business graph as the profit line is continually being drawn upward. That is an excellent way to reinforce an advertising message promising continuous growth.

Because television is so versatile, you can become as innovative as your imagination—and your advertising budget—allows. The one guiding principle is to maintain viewer attention. If you can keep them watching, your pursuit of visual impact has been successful.

SETTING UP THE SHOOTING SCRIPT

The television *shooting script* is a detailed set of instructions that includes camera angle, sound effects, dialogue, and the total scenario for a visual presentation. There are a few basic rules to remember in setting up the script, making it fit the television format. They help to assure production efficiency, making the experience more beneficial and enjoyable for you.

Your primary emphasis in setting up the script is on who will appear before the camera, what the person will say, and what action will occur within each sequence. Every script is set up on a scene basis. If the camera angle and/or its location changes, it demands a separate scene designation. Some commercials and programs are set up from a single-camera angle, but this tends to mark the production as amateurish.

To assist you, here are a few of the important format rules to remember. Following these rules, you'll be presenting a slick package which will show your professionalism and understanding of the medium. These rules are in accordance with standard teleplay practice used in filming for network programming—including all of your favorite television shows.

Standard Script Rules

1. Use narrow preliminary left margins with each individual camera angle numbered.
2. Type the primary information for scene setting in capital letters.
    Example: STAGE SET WITH PODIUM IN CENTRAL LOCATION.
3. Details of setting are indented right by five spaces (minimum) and presented in standard capital/small letter format.
4. Speaker name or designation centered on page.
    Example:
                    ANNOUNCER
5. All spoken words should be sufficiently indented (in addition to spaces allotted to setting details) to readily identify them as "dialogue."
6. All sound instructions are presented in CAPITAL LETTERS.

7. All continuous instructions and dialogue exceeding one line on a page are single-spaced.
8. Use double-spacing to separate individual instructions and dialogue from each other.

Finally, there is a general consensus that scripts translate into a minute of air time per page. This may vary somewhat, depending on how elaborately detailed the peripheral instructions become. The rule does, however, give some idea of how long a commercial or program script should run while you're preparing it.

The following is a brief excerpt from a typical script.

Sample Shooting Script

ESTABLISHING SHOT
(Scene includes podium with microphone and two charts on easels)

PLAY FIFTEEN SECONDS OF SELECTED THEME MUSIC

VOICE-OVER

Welcome to the Arthur T. Consultant Show, where your questions on financial matters are always welcome. And now, here's our host, Arthur Consultant.

ANGLE ON Consultant walking on set. Camera follow to podium.

CONSULTANT

Good evening, ladies and gentlemen. Thank you for tuning in to another edition of our popular financial program. Tonight's special topic will be on the important aspects of estate planning.

ANGLE ON charts on Easels

CONSULTANT

As you can see, I've provided some important charts here to help simplify some of the more complex aspects of this subject.

CLOSE ON Consultant

CONSULTANT

By the time we leave you this evening, you'll have the necessary information to make the first important decisions you face in planning your estate. You'll leave a larger legacy to those you love and reduce the taxman's painful bite on the inheritance.

INTRODUCTION TO SCRIPT TERMINOLOGY

The preceding discussion on format represents half of the task for writing professional-looking television scripts. The other half involves understanding script terminology. A short list of common terms follows that is readily picked up by anyone interested in writing television advertising. These terms give your script a smooth appearance. Let's review the most common terms.

Glossary of Common Script Terms

FADE IN. Designates the opening of a script. An equivalent is the raising of the curtain in a stage play. FADE OUT is the equivalent term designating the end of the script.

ANGLE ON. What the camera shows, the focus of the shot.

FAVOR. In a camera shot involving more than one person or thing, this term instructs the camera to give one part preference (or FAVOR) in the camera's view.

TIGHT ON. Instructs camera to go in for a close-up.

CUT TO. Camera shooting and editorial direction to abruptly end a scene or specific angle and move to another immediately. This technique is not possible with the use of only one camera.

CLOSE ON. Similar to TIGHT ON, except that it usually implies a camera shot that is slightly less close.

VO. Abbreviation for VOICE OVER. This instructs a voice to be heard without an apparent source on screen. It is similar to an off-screen announcer or film narrator.

DISSOLVE TO. A technical camera and editing trick that allows one scene to fade out as a new one comes into focus.

ESTABLISHING SHOT. An opening camera shot in a script that sets the location. An example is the picture of the outside of the White House that often precedes televised Presidential news conferences.

MOVING SHOT. Instructs camera to follow action as it happens in a program. For example, if you move from a podium to a group of charts displayed on easels, this is a MOVING SHOT.

INT AND EXT. Abbreviations for INTERIOR and EXTERIOR respectively.

CAMERA ANGLES IN SCRIPT DESIGN

One of the greatest difficulties that first-time scriptwriters face is the ability to think visually. This particularly applies to the angles from which any given setting is being shot.

A common mistake is the failure to transpose left and right in viewing a scene. When you're facing a camera, you automatically know what is to *your* left and right. But that is *not* how the camera sees it. The camera sees it in reverse.

Anything that is to your right, facing the camera, is considered "camera left" for the photographing lens. Remembering this helps you to keep script directions accurate and keep the camera focused where you want it.

Another important camera-angle consideration is the appearance of the person or material being filmed or taped. Most of us have a side that is more photogenic than other angles. You can capitalize on this by having the camera favor your best side.

One of the peculiarities of television is that it tends to add pounds to a person's appearance. This explains the inordinate preoccupation of many television and movie stars with dieting.

I am a prime example of having a previously poor appearance on a television screen. Prior to a 30-pound weight loss, I looked a lot like a beached whale on a television monitor. When I saw myself the first time, I vowed that I had two choices: (1) lose weight or (2) never appear on television again. I chose the first option.

Although I still have a few extra pounds on me, my appearance on a television screen is no longer a personal embarrassment. If you are more than 10 pounds over your ideal weight, seeing yourself on a television screen will be a surprise.

To avoid looking heavier, place considerable emphasis on straight front filming. Avoid any angles that are from an elevated position. This highlights figure flaws and ruins image projection. In exaggerated cases, it can even make a slimmer person appear like a beanbag. The camera angle isn't very flattering unless you know how to use it.

EXPANDING THE ADVERTISING FORMAT

As company growth allows, many consultants and other businesses set their sights on a longer advertising program as a way to deliver a more detailed message to their consumers. The most common program is the half-hour format.

Many television stations, particularly local network affiliates, welcome these programs as "fillers" in their schedule. A common programming gap for these stations is the period between the local news segments and the beginning of the network's prime time evening schedule. Many stations have either a half-hour or an hour to fill each evening.

Although many stations rely on syndicated programs, including game shows, some use this time to broadcast locally produced programming that is of public interest. The key words are "public interest." The program has to be perceived as being of general public interest or it won't have a chance of being produced.

If your program fits this criterion, you can usually find a station to broadcast it. The only real question is airing time. You don't, as an example, want to have your program buried in the broadcasting "graveyard period" between two and four in the morning. This doesn't yield much for your advertising dollar. The rates are much cheaper in this time period, but the reduced response rate negates any benefits.

Once you have established an advertising program on a station with shorter commercials, you can often use the themes from these efforts to develop longer programs. Expand on the information that the public currently knows about your services—with the possibility of answering viewer questions about your particular field. This helps to build the "public service" angle of your program, making it more acceptable to the station. In some cases, incorporating this idea into a program's format can make it qualify as legitimate public service programming. That can dramatically reduce your broadcasting costs.

Cooperation with a station's news department can cement your image further. One company in my area has capitalized on this aspect by presenting programs that inform the public about its activities—and the benefits of its presence in the community.

As you plan your program expansion efforts, check all possibilities. You can sometimes receive a surprising amount of cooperation if the station considers your efforts newsworthy. They use the same general criteria as we discussed in Chapter 5 for newspapers. If you qualify in this area, you can receive a considerable amount of air time for a surprisingly nominal cost.

WRITING THE SHORT COMMERCIAL SCRIPT

Writing the short commercial script for television is a challenge equivalent to preparing a radio commercial. In this format, you have to get in, say what you want, get it done smoothly—and get out fast. That's not an easy assignment.

As indicated earlier in this chapter, you should rely on the visual aspect of the media to deliver your message. It also reduces air time.

Your message commands the most audience attention if it contrasts in tone with the programming that surrounds it. One advertiser who sponsors news programs has an extremely raucous commercial with a spokesman running around and yelling like an escapee from an asylum. This contrast really separates the commercial from the programming that it interrupts.

I don't mean to imply that you should follow the lead of this advertiser. That approach isn't consistent with the dignified image that a consultant wants to present.

The commercial does, however, illustrate the basic concept involved. You're doing the same thing here as you would in a radio commercial. You can use different background techniques, including the use of music. Play off these potential contrasts for the best results.

One effective trick is to use a combination of print and graphics for the majority of the commercial's air time—without any voice over. This causes viewers to check if something went wrong with their televisions. Then, at the end of the commercial, you tell viewers that you don't have to yell about your services. Your reputation speaks for itself.

As a general rule, these short commercials are complete in one script page or less (see the format described earlier). Although you will want some speech in the commercial, this inevitably expands your air time. Most television stations particularly welcome 30-second commercials. They fit into tight programming schedules very well, often following station indentification breaks mandated by the Federal Communications Commission.

Before approaching any television station about advertising, spend some time viewing the station's programming and general context of presentation. Pay special attention to the commercials currently being aired. They will give you the best idea of the station's advertising tone.

WRITING THE PUBLIC SERVICE PROGRAM SCRIPT

When you begin to develop a public service program, you should be aware of the production operations of your target station. The general rule is that the average half-hour program involves 22 minutes of actual air time; the remaining 8 minutes are devoted to commercial time or station breaks.

This means that scripts must be designed to incorporate these breaks into the natural flow of the program. Every 5 to 10 minutes there has to be some natural break in the program text to prevent choppiness of presentation. Even if you don't put the breaks into the script, they will happen. It's the inherent nature of the business.

One useful approach is to develop separate commercials for your business to fold into the programming format. This keeps the flow of your message relatively uninterrupted and allows you to focus informationally, rather than promotionally, in your main program.

In the script itself, make these divisions at 8- to 10-page intervals. This is a fairly accurate method, based on running time averages. The station generally won't quibble about a minute one way or the other in scheduling breaks. But these breaks absolutely must be in the program.

The key to keeping your audience through the break periods is to develop several peak points in your script. One technique is commonly referred to as the "teaser."

A teaser is a planted sequence that is interrupted for the commercial. One form involves asking a question important to viewers. Then, you tell them that you'll reveal the answer right after these important messages. That is the lead-in for the commercials. Of course, when the program returns, you fulfill your promise and answer the question.

This is a technique that is well executed on some prime-time drama programs. The station wants to get back to the program. The commercials are often seen as rude interruptions to the enjoyment of the program. The audience eagerly waits to find out what comes next.

Using these ideas, coupled with the technical aspects described earlier, you can develop a program that will hold the viewer's attention. Keep the flow of information steady and visually interesting. You are appealing to two senses, vision and hearing. Address both in your programs to get your message across.

SPECIAL DEMANDS OF PUBLIC SERVICE PROGRAMMING

Many consultants and other businesses that regularly advertise with commercials falsely assume that graduation to a long program is an easy matter. Anyone who has experienced the hot lights of a television studio for long hours has been effectively weaned from that notion.

The experience of taping a program is entirely different than speaking before a live audience. You don't get the feedback to allow you to make adjustments as you go. Your only audience is a few camera personnel, a director, and a few staffers at a control panel away from your view. You are center stage, at times feeling as though you were talking to yourself.

Unless you're taping one of your seminar lectures for broadcast, you won't have the benefit of an audience. Some speakers prefer to go this route, but this poses its own set of hazards.

No audience is responsive to the demands of production. This poses problems that can only be addressed in the tape editing process. Without the editing, you end up with a discordant mass that is not acceptable for quality television.

Larger television studios have accommodations for a live audience. In this method, studio personnel brief the studio audience on the limitations involved, requesting their cooperation in the process. This could be a workable compromise for you. The presence of the studio audience adds to your credibility with television viewers. They can see you holding an audience's attention. Viewers won't feel alone with your message.

The greatest challenge, however, is the balance between content that is of common interest and content that is predominantly self-serving. If your program is inherently of the latter character, your efforts will not be considered "public service."

This becomes a basic business decision for you. You are paying for the air time to broadcast the program—unless some other sponsors get into the act. If you choose to make an extra-length commercial, you should have some way to measure audience response to your efforts.

This is a plausible explanation for the large number of such programs that offer publications for sale to viewers. They are in any one of several forms: books, magazines, tapes, and so on. Regardless of form, they allow the program creator to judge whether similar future efforts are worthwhile. Additionally, these sales help to make the program more profitable.

Caution should be exercised in this type of promotion. Don't weave such promotion into the program itself. If you do, you automatically forfeit any semblance of being a public service program. Keep such promotions as totally separate commercials—with sufficient dividers to distinguish them from the program.

TELEVISION AS AN EDUCATIONAL FORUM

Today's television, the product of an evolutionary process spanning over a quarter century, has achieved a balance between being informative and entertaining. This balance should be considered when you decide the content of your program.

Most American adults are television viewers, and even our leading educators concede that reaching school-age students effectively requires a greater use of television. Average viewership today is often more than six hours per day. With an ever-increasing array of programming to choose from, there is an intense competition for viewer attention.

The day of major network monopoly of programming structure and content appears to be gone. Cable and pay-TV services have carved a substantial bite out of that monopoly, leaving an ever-shrinking pie for the Big Three networks to share among themselves.

Working within this environment, there is a growing trend to blend education with entertainment for the best results. This trend can even be seen in the religious broadcasting systems. The prevailing theory is that viewer attention can't be held without a liberal dash of fanfare.

The major challenge of this approach is to avoid losing important educational messages in the need to entertain. This challenge is being met by children's educational programmers. As examples, we could cite "Sesame Street" and "Mr. Rogers' Neighborhood," both on PBS, as leading innovators of this blending process for children.

Although the approach for a consultant should be more mature, the blending techniques used by these programs show that education need not take a secondary role to entertainment. They can coexist effectively for the benefit of the viewer.

The secret of blending education and entertainment is to tie in practical elements that viewers identify with. This identification process allows viewers to assimilate information without even being consciously aware of the learning process.

Getting the attention of a passive television audience demands the avoidance of lecturing. The audience tunes out even if the television remains on and your program is running.

One of the best methods to achieve this balance is the use of the educational documentary. Viewers won't be overexposed to your personal appearance. You can narrate scenes that viewers see, using this approach to give them necessary information. This also avoids even the appearance of a formal lecture.

As I already noted, this approach is commonly used in children's and young adult's programming. Although the age-group may be different, the approach is equally valid for an older audience. The subject matter, not the approach, is the primary difference.

As you review your program subject matter, look for opportunities to incorporate these principles into your programming. They help you to capture a greater share of the viewing audience—and offer more information to your prospective clientele.

TELEVISION AS AN IMAGE BUILDER

Regardless of the programming format, there is little question that television rapidly gives a person public visibility. This impact is directly related to the type of audience that sees the program.

Who, for example, hasn't heard of Louis Rukeyser, the moderator of Wall Street Week? Another example is Adam Smith of Money World. Both of these men have developed a national following through their television programs.

A single appearance on even a local television station can elevate a person to a mini-celebrity status. The person can gain in visibility very quickly and significantly.

With this in mind, it's extremely important that every televised appearance that you make captitalizes on this public visibility factor. Even a short news interview should be viewed as a serious opportunity to further your business image.

The three important factors to remember in each television appearance are

1. Your appearance
2. What you say on television
3. How you say it

The second and third factors are the most important ones to attend to. Even if you have the world's best appearance, it has little value if what you say and how you say it reflect negatively on you.

If you're being interviewed, watch out for questions that won't put you in the best light. When such questions pop up, move the discussion to other areas without being too transparent about it. Give only the most cursory answers to these questions, saving detail for those areas that will further your objectives.

Many notables beg off a question that is not to their liking, saying that they need time to study the matter before answering. This approach is effective for persistent journalists, but should be used only sparingly. Too much coyness gives the appearance of ignorance, which won't boost anyone's confidence in your qualifications and abilities.

Most of us won't get into this situation during the early stages of our image building efforts. This usually happens after you have achieved a measure of fame. There is an idiosyncrasy about the press that likes to tear down people who are at the top. It has nothing to do with a person's professional qualifications and conduct. Scandal sells copies and boosts ratings. In the competitive environment of television, no ground is considered sacred—including individual privacy.

This caution shouldn't scare you away from television. Rather, it is given for your awareness, to help you avoid any nasty pitfalls that might be lurking to dismantle your prior image building efforts.

COORDINATING TELEVISION WITH OTHER PROMOTION

Whenever you invest in television broadcast use, especially the program format, it makes business sense to assure the largest possible audience for your message. That's what you're buying for your money.

To get a large viewing audience you should make some promotional efforts in other media for a coordinated strategy. As an example, if you're scheduling to air a program, you can get excellent results by running a small reminder advertisement in a newspaper. This advertising serves to arouse the curiosity of potential viewers, increasing the likelihood that they will tune in to your program.

As you develop your total promotional program, try to maintain a similarity of theme between your television efforts and those in other media. Thematic considerations, like a company trademark, increases public identification of you and the services you're offering.

If you vary these themes too much among different media, you will have considerable difficulty in establishing your identity in the market. You could end up wasting your advertising budget in extensive efforts that lead nowhere.

An excellent way to use television is as a prelude to a personal appearance in an area. This idea is used quite effectively by those who conduct seminars. They grant interviews with local television media people—and sometimes feature programming on the stations. This serves to get people acquainted with them before their arrival. This familiarity can only help to give their presence more attention and their business greater profitability.

CLOSING THOUGHTS

Of all the major media, television has the highest advertising costs. Except for the smallest television stations, costs will be, at minimum, two to three times that of radio advertising for the same amount of time.

This extra cost factor is more than recovered by the level of audience response that television generates. Local and small regional television stations usually have a base rate of $100 to $200 per broadcasting minute, depending on how much total on-air time your contract is for.

As you get to the larger stations, particularly on the national level, this rate can escalate rapidly. On highly rated programs nationally, this rate can go over $500,000 per minute. In one instance, an advertiser going for the audience offered by a Super Bowl football extravaganza shelled out over $700,000 for the privilege of airing a one-minute commercial.

That is no small outlay. This cost factor is the primary reason why effective use of air time has been stressed so heavily in this chapter. Television time does *not* come cheaply.

As you move to the program format, your per minute costs decline dramatically. Still you can't realistically expect to air a 30-minute program on any television station for much less than $3,000 on a for cash basis.

The principal variant to this approach is when stations offer air time on a commission basis. This applies when a program specifically offers a tangible product for sale to the audience. The station offers air time for a specific percentage of the proceeds of product sales.

This approach offers significant reductions in costs, keeping them in direct proportion to your audience response. If your program draws considerable popular response, however, commission costs could exceed those of the traditional route. This is a gamble that both you and the television station undertake mutually. The television station is betting that it will be the winner.

The idea isn't all negative, even if the station does come out ahead monetarily. You'll have gained some profitability from the effort—and you'll have an accurate picture of the scope of your audience-drawing capability.

Regardless of which method you use, television is an advanced promotional technique for your consulting business. Build your initial base in the less expensive media before coming here.

When you are ready for the move to television promotion you'll be equipped. The information offered in this chapter helps to assure that you get the best value for your media dollar. This helps you to gain the maximum profits that your efforts deserve.

CHAPTER

9

CABLE TELEVISION AND SATELLITE SYSTEMS: EXPANDING TO THE NATIONAL FOCUS

In the last chapter we discussed the specifics of developing commercials and programs for general television. We focused on the special demands of traditional commercial television on your promotional efforts.

Although the same technical aspects of advertising and program development apply when using cable and satellite television stations, the marketing aspects are different. Marketing strategy is different because most cable and satellite television stations are more specialized in their fields of interest. As a result, your programming is more closely geared to audience interests.

Cable television, because of technological limitations, is inherently a regional medium in its purest application. Some metropolitan areas have cable television stations that are equivalent to closed circuit operations and do not go beyond city limits. These stations are fed directly into the cable systems with no true airwave broadcasting (as from an antenna).

A strong interrelationship between satellite television and its cable counterpart exists in many areas, although it has been weakened by the wider use of privately owned satellite dish antennas. In the satellite-cable relationship, satellite transmissions are picked up by cable service providers and fed into the cable system for their subscribers. The cable systems generally have a financial arrangement with the broadcasters for the rights to receive and transmit these satellite signals within their subscriber radius.

Any television station that is arranged only for cable access suffers from a limited reception range. This range is controlled by factors other than the station's construction and management. This limitation is, however, offset by substantial cost reductions during the initial station setup phase.

In this chapter, we take a closer look at cable and satellite television operations, showing how they differ from more traditional television broadcasting operations. Although we discuss their technology, the greater focus is on the changes in marketing strategy that these stations necessitate. These changes dramatically affect both the tone and content of your productions on these media. This chapter shows you how to make these changes for your maximum benefit.

BASICS OF CABLE TELEVISION

Since its period of infancy in the late 1950s and early 1960s, cable television has become a substantial force in the broadcasting industry today. The major commercial networks have begun to watch nervously as these special-interest broadcasting entities have developed a voracious appetite for attracting the audiences of the broadcasting giants.

Originally founded as CATV (standing for community antenna television), the primary purpose of these outlets was to augment broadcast coverage for areas where environmental factors reduced television reception. They operated in cooperation, not in competition, with the major broadcasting networks.

As both the infant medium of television and its audience became more sophisticated, the demands for special interest programming increased. The major networks, operating under the mass market mentality, chose not to respond to this demand. Smaller stations, in direct cooperation with cable broadcasting companies, stepped in to fill this important market niche. This sowed the first seeds for the intense rivalry that we witness today.

Special-interest broadcasting is particularly beneficial to programmers who don't specifically fit the commercial entertainment modes that are preferred by the major networks and their affiliates. Programming that is primarily educational in intent and focus falls into this category. Because your promotional efforts are essentially educational, your programming is more welcome to these special interest broadcasters.

The 1980s has witnessed a dramatic proliferation of these special-interest broadcasters, ranging from rock music networks like MTV to CBN (the Christian Broadcasting Network). Each sector has its prevailing philosophy. With less competition for air time in these channels, there are greater opportunities for new voices, but your programming has to fit into the general schematic of the group involved. As an example, a program on positive business ethics corresponds to the tone espoused by CBN.

Independent television stations offer even greater opportunities for the nontraditional programmer. Without formal network affiliation, they are more dependent on locally generated productions. This includes educational programs.

Although special-interest stations don't directly compete with the more commercial broadcasting entities, this does *not* mean that they accept bad programming. Many of the same production principles discussed in Chapter 8 apply equally in this arena.

The primary advantage of these stations can also be their greatest drawback. Although their audience is more specialized, it is also considerably smaller than general television's. This is especially true if the station is purely a cable-feed operation. Later in the chapter, I will show how this factor affects your programming and marketing efforts on these stations.

The best system for your promotional campaign is a station that has a satellite-feed system to broadcast signals outside the station's immediate geographical area. You enjoy the special-interest programming base, but have an expanded audience potential. Some stations offer a combination of direct cable feed and satellite broadcasting capability.

AUDIENCE REACH AND ITS IMPACT

Although our first consideration is always keeping costs reasonable, there is a clearly defined trade-off to be made in using cable television. This is primarily true for stations that are locally oriented and have a limited broadcasting range.

Your advertising and programming charges are considerably lower in these low-budget operations. However, you face two drawbacks. First, the low-budget operation generally produces a televised product of lesser quality. Second, you are not as likely to reach as large an audience with these stations.

On the positive side, your broadcasts are more directly attuned to a larger percentage of your audience. This translates into less stringent ties to "entertainment value" in programming on these stations. Your audience is already interested in your message. You won't have to be as concerned about inflicting boredom on John Q. Public.

This doesn't, however, give you license to create inferior programming; you should not, as the chameleon does, change color to fit into the surroundings. Placing a quality programming product on a low-budget station creates a greater impact because of the contrast involved.

With standard commercial stations, you are lucky to get one or two percent of your audience for clients. Although your specialized audience is smaller, your percentage of delivery is likely to be much higher. These small stations attract viewers who are sufficiently interested in the subject area to actively search out these stations. Larger commercial stations attract "couch potatoes" who are watching because they can't think of anything more productive to do, not because they have any particular interest in the programming being offered.

Numerical program ratings are sometimes very deceptive. A station may receive high numbers in the ratings, but suffer in terms of audience quality. Keeping this factor in mind helps you to assess the situation more accurately—and base your decisions accordingly.

CABLE TELEVISION'S IMPACT ON PROMOTIONAL STRATEGY

As mentioned earlier, one of the major benefits of cable television is a sharper definition of audience interests. This applies most to the smaller stations. With larger, and more general-interest stations, the same general rules apply as for general television, discussed in Chapter 8. You are addressing similar audiences, except over a larger geographical area. There are no specific limitations imposed by broadcasting variables such as weather or stratospheric conditions. The only substantial limitation is in the number of areas that are served by the cable system involved.

With an expanded geographical format, your promotional emphasis, by necessity, changes from providing personalized services to promoting nonpersonal applications of your skills. This assumes that you are either unwilling or unable to meet personally with potential clients who might be a thousand or more miles from your company.

As a promotional alternative to the Big Three commercial networks, national cable and satellite television channels offer larger potential audiences at a somewhat lower price. This can be a productive detour on your way to promotion on the major networks.

An important fact to remember is that promotional and programming rates are always determined by the proven audience delivery of the station involved. As with everything else, you get what you pay for—or can afford. The purchasing decision here is comparable to the choice between a Lincoln Continental and a Cadillac in automobiles. Both are quality products. They differ in the price and the measure of status imparted to their owners.

The key to success here is a clear definition of marketing objectives. How far do you want your message to reach? What geographical areas are you prepared to handle?

Don't gamble on trying to gain national status if you aren't prepared to handle business on that scope. You'll be opening yourself to serious problems that can backfire on you.

Very few one-person consulting operations should even consider going national. To reach this level, you require, at minimum, an auxiliary staff to handle the extra paperwork load.

Pure cable stations are generally local or small regional in their orientation. They are most often found in major metropolitan areas such as New York City. They do not reach far beyond the metropolitan boundaries in broadcasting range.

This orientation creates a programming emphasis that is decisively different from stations with a larger coverage area. Programming for these strictly local stations is geared predominantly to the concerns of their immediate vicinity. National issues, when they are used in programming, must have a strong local tie to be successful.

Later in this chapter, we will review satellite stations and their focus. Although most of these stations broadcast their programming over cable antenna systems in various areas of the country, they are, by strict definition, not pure cable stations. Because their focus is not limited to their immediate vicinity, they seek programming and advertising that is of national relevance. This difference is mentioned here to distinguish them from pure cable stations.

Successful programming and advertising on the pure cable stations, as with local radio, requires a clear identification of the concerns that are predominant in the immediate service area. Programming is less general in focus than it is on the national level.

As an example, suppose that you're a consultant in New York City. You are designing a program for a metropolitan cable channel. In this effort, you want to focus your attention on problems and solutions from the metropolitan New York area. Some solutions that work in New York might not work in a city like Seattle or Detroit. You focus on the uniqueness of your immediate environment for this localized station.

By contrast, you want to feature solutions from these other areas if your program is reaching a national audience. Recognizing, and capitalizing on, this difference gives you the best opportunity to aim your marketing strategy correctly and gain the best value for your promotional and programming investments.

COST FACTORS OF CABLE TELEVISION

From the cost viewpoint, the pure cable television station falls in the intermediate range between radio and the small regional noncable television station. Because these cable channels are not burdened by the costs of larger and more sophisticated broadcasting and transmission facilities, they do not have the high overhead that results in higher advertising and programming rates. In some cases, their rates compare favorably with radio—and you get the added video component for your promotional message.

Cable stations are a stepping-stone from radio to general television. They are an excellent place to refine your television programming and advertising skills before applying them to larger—and more expensive—television stations.

On the average, you can expect to spend approximately 10 to 20 percent more per advertising or programming minute at these localized cable stations than you would with radio. In some cases, the rates are less than radio, but you should have a healthy skepticism if the rates appear *too* attractive. The station may have such a small viewership that they are a waste of your promotional investment.

CONTRASTS WITH GENERAL TELEVISION

Because of the low-budget orientation of pure cable stations, the greatest noticeable contrast is in some technical areas. Studios are not as elaborate. This inevitably reflects itself in the programming being produced there.

In many ways, localized cable stations recall the pioneering days of commercial television. Some of these stations offer live, rather than videotaped, programming. Except for local and national news broadcasts, regular commercial stations rely exclusively on videotape.

Although live broadcasts offer some cost advantages, you have the disadvantage of not being able to cover up your mistakes. You're in front of the camera. If you goof, the entire broadcasting radius sees it. More than one outrageous broadcast blooper has been committed in these circumstances. Unless you have a solid sense of humor and the ability to laugh away your own mistakes, you are well advised to stay away from this particular mode of promotion.

Without the editing capability of videotape, you must make an extremely disciplined presentation. You may indulge in a bit of rambling monologue on videotape, knowing that you can edit it later. In a live broadcast, you don't have that luxury.

A live broadcast, without editing capability, also reduces your ability to use graphic art in your presentation. This situation is similar to giving a live seminar.

Videotape editing can provide some very sophisticated programming qualities that simply can't be duplicated in a live presentation. You can provide a tape sequence recorded outside the studio and include it in a live program, as news programs do. But this leaves breaks in the programming that add choppiness to the final product.

If you can live with these limitations, you can get programming and promotion at a reduced rate on pure cable stations. But you must recognize the risks to your image that results from an unpolished presentation.

Organized presentations give the best results in any circumstances. To achieve satisfactory results from these low-budget operations, solid organization skills are mandatory. If you are adequately prepared, you can minimize the disruptive effects that these limitations create.

CAPITALIZING ON THE CABLE ADVANTAGE

In graduating from radio to television, there is a natural temptation to expand presentations to a longer format. With general television stations, costs are prohibitively high and preclude a longer presentation. That's where the localized cable television station fills a major role in the development of your total marketing program.

Many businesses find that the 30-second to 1-minute commercial is totally inadequate to communicate the complexities of their operations to potential consumers. However, cost factors of standard commercial television restrict them to short commercials.

If you and a cable television station share an audience objective, you have a golden opportunity to go beyond the limited short format without totally wrecking your promotional budget. As an example, you can develop a 15-minute "public service" style program to be aired on the cable station. Many of these stations have a crying need for filler programs to fit into their sometimes erratic schedules. They may even have occasions when there is *no* programming for a particular time spot. Their only alternative is a blank screen.

In such emergencies, some stations rebroadcast these public service programs free of charge to the producer. They keep these programs on file for just such occasions. You are a lifesaver for the station—and the free airing is a sure way of showing their appreciation.

These budget stretchers should not, however, be counted on in your marketing plan. They're a nice bonus when they happen, but most stations are sufficiently organized to make these occasions relatively rare.

You can, however, stretch your budget through the authorized and paid rebroadcast of your program. After the initial production costs are met, these additional broadcasts are a profit bonanza for the station—even at a reduced rate.

Although you can get considerable benefit from these local cable stations, your primary objective is to set the stage for other efforts from this launching pad. As mentioned earlier, cable stations are an excellent proving ground before moving to the larger stations.

Use cable stations to refine your television marketing strategy. If you make some mistakes initially, they won't be as financially catastrophic. Become accustomed to the larger programming format that a cable station offers. With some practice here, you will be more comfortable with television promotion. It makes your future efforts at more expensive television stations smoother and more effective in gaining your desired results.

MOVING TO SATELLITE SYSTEMS

After you have refined your television skills, you may decide that the large regional and national markets are a desirable objective. For all but the larger corporations, national television promotion through the major commercial networks is prohibitively expensive. Short commercials are the only viable choice here, even for the corporate giants. Longer programs are virtually impossible financially—and generally aren't accepted because they lack entertainment value.

This is the important void that is filled by the satellite television network system. Giving a national audience to ideas that would not fit in the major network mold, they make national broadcasting of programming a viable option for larger companies that want to present a more detailed message.

The primary difference in moving to satellite television is in basic production values for programming. Programming for these channels is often equivalent in slickness with those found on the major networks. You won't see an amateurish effort in the entire lot.

Programming focus is also different than in most other media. Generally this sector can be characterized as a hybrid between standard commercial stations and the small cable stations that we just discussed. You are required to incorporate some entertainment value into programming—as the commercial networks do, but your programming can be more specialized than on general television.

There is a remarkable similarity between this sector and that of the Public Broadcasting System. The difference is that they prefer a lighter tone in programming. Some PBS programming can be as somber as an embalming seminar.

Because satellite television stations operate in a competitive environment that includes the major commercial networks, there is a tendency to balance the need for being different with a natural "cloning instinct" that restricts innovation in television. Everyone wants to be different—but not *too* different.

Even when you pay to air a program, a satellite television station's main concern is to maintain, or improve, its ratings in the market. If a program can't keep viewership, it won't serve as a sufficient quality lead-in for the program that follows it.

The dominant principle of competitive television is to get you to tune in—and stay tuned in—to the station for hours at a time. They want to keep you from turning channels, or turning the television off, for the entire day if possible.

You won't face the same problem if you restrict yourself to the shorter commercial format. Your message then is not a major influence on the station's ratings. You're just a meal ticket for the main programming fare being offered.

If there is some concern that your programming can't achieve sufficient ratings, you are given a non-prime-time scheduling slot (a time other than the 8:00 PM to 11:00 PM Eastern Time period). The prime time schedule is of greatest concern to television stations because it determines network and station ratings, which also decide a station's advertising rates.

If your program can't draw the audience ratings, long-term costs for the station will be far greater in lost revenue than they can ever hope to recoup from charging you for the airing. This, incidentally, is the primary reason why you almost never see any religious programming (like those featuring evangelists) during prime time on commercial stations.

Study the station carefully before approaching their management with a programming concept. A key indicator to watch for is their level of reliance on advertising within the programming format. If advertising is heavily used, there is a corresponding increase in concern for ratings. The high operating budgets that are indicated by this concern can't be supported if ratings take a substantial beating.

If you can fill this unique niche with your programming efforts, you can make a substantial impact on the national scene. Although we may dream of becoming instant "stars," we should temper this with a dose of realism. Unless your established reputation on a local or regional basis lends itself to national promotion, you can't expect to get on the air nationally except in the short commercial format during prime time.

Although this airing timing is the most advantageous for promotion, the costs are also much higher. You have to be reasonably sure that your target audience is viewing programming then to give your gamble a clear chance of paying off.

SATELLITE SYSTEMS AND MARKETING STRATEGY

In moving from a regional to a national marketing strategy, you have to coordinate both promotional and logistical factors. As mentioned earlier, you have to be prepared to handle the potentially large business influx that can result from national promotion.

Moving to satellite stations that have a potential national and international broadcasting range necessitates a definitive change in marketing strategy compared with the more locally oriented pure cable and small regional standard broadcasting stations. The key difference is the need to be more general in focus. Although every business or professional group has concerns that are specifically regional, your focus should be directed toward those areas that apply without regional distinctions.

As with any other broadcasting source, understanding a satellite television station's dominant philosophy helps you to develop your marketing thrust to correspond with it. Every commercially oriented television station defines its image in terms of its dominant audience.

Citing an example of this, Turner Broadcasting System, one of the better known satellite-style operations in the United States, capitalizes on the nostalgia element in their programming. The network has even acquired broadcasting rights to some of the best known cinematic productions from the Golden Age of the movies, including *Gone With The Wind*. They perceive their market as yearning for a return to the values and times of the past.

This market definition has a clear impact on what tone is most effective in promotion. You must take into account this psychological frame of reference in your advertising.

A clearly defined audience distinguishes satellite operations from the commercial operations of the Big Three television networks. The major networks see a truly mass market mind in programming and advertising. Although the increasing popularity of alternative networks has caused some redefining of strategy at the major networks, they still do not direct their efforts at specific marketing niches as much as satellite television stations do.

If you can successfully identify the market segment that is being addressed in each case, coupled with an approach that is psychologically compatible with it, you can sell effectively on a satellite television station. Although market segmentation seems to restrict creativity in advertising to a greater degree than in standard commercial stations, your first concern is to avoid alienating the audience.

This is particularly true with essentially conservative audiences. You can alienate a conservative audience with an outlandish and liberal tone. Not surprisingly, there is less danger of turning off a more liberally oriented audience with a conservative tone. You may not get anyone excited, but you won't drive them away either. Liberal audiences are more tolerant of the nonconformist in their presence.

Keeping these factors in mind helps you to gear your promotional efforts accordingly. You are paying to reach these people. You won't be successful if you alienate the audience. Avoiding this assures that your message reaches its intended target.

COST FACTORS FOR SATELLITE TELEVISION

As a general rule, satellite television stations should be considered intermediate in cost between the regional standard television station and the commercial networks. This cost escalation is based on the number of households being reached by each broadcast.

Station size and broadcast output power have a direct bearing on costs as well. By technological necessity, most satellite stations require a greater broadcasting power than their conventional counterparts (a factor to be discussed in the next section). This overhead factor inevitably escalates promotional costs to, at minimum, 10 to 15 percent above what you pay for air time at a network-affiliated standard television station.

The larger and better-known operations have advertising rates that are closer to those of the major networks, but the smaller operations won't hit you with equivalent rates because they can't justify such fees based on audience statistics.

Until satellite systems become as powerful as the major networks (a distinct possibility by predictions of some prominent media analysts), you can reasonably expect to save at least 15 to 20 percent on advertising that provides national coverage for your promotional message. You won't achieve the audience density in each given market area that you do with the major networks, but the financial gamble of "going national" won't be as large either.

STATION OWNERSHIP FOR THE PROMOTER

One of the fastest growing trends in broadcasting today is the growth of satellite broadcasting systems. Because there is considerable room for expansion based on satellite capacity, it seems that anyone with appropriate Federal Communications Commission (FCC) authorization and a spare million dollars or so for equipment can get on the airwaves this way. A clear example is the considerable growth of religious broadcasting in the satellite spectrum. This sector represents a wide variety of religious beliefs that cannot receive air time on other commercial channels.

The key to organizing your own operation is to have a clearly defined broadcasting philosophy and a reasonably firm broadcasting schedule to adhere for general operations. Provided that broadcasting content is not blatantly pornographic, almost any viewpoint is licensable by the Federal Communications Commission. Even the lines defining pornography are blurred in today's broadcasting climate. At this writing, the U.S. Supreme Court is moving to a conservative ideological outlook. This may have a dramatic bearing on what is acceptable here and in other media as well.

With a license from the Federal Communications Commission you get direct control over two areas of station operation. They are broadcast frequency (assigning which channel you use for broadcast) and broadcasting power, both video and audio.

As a practical matter, the financial health of a television station depends on gaining funding from advertising sources. Although you may wish to maintain total control of air time as a station owner, the financial obligations are usually beyond the resources of a single commercial organization without outside advertising revenue. Broadcasting is a business enterprise. The costs of operation have to be obtained somewhere.

This requires that the programming appeals to its designated audience. I strongly recommend that you do *not* consider station ownership for promotion until you have acquired considerable television experience. Without this experience, the combined challenge of station management and the production of quality programming may prove beyond your current resources.

Religious broadcasters have been able to survive in this medium through donations and by maintaining the appearance of being a noncommercial broadcasting entity. On closer analysis, however, it becomes clear that they must also respond to market forces. The more successful broadcasters in this genre seem to mix as much entertainment and showmanship as they do religious content. This provides the visual and listening appeal that draws financial support for their programming.

As a station owner, you are a service provider both to your viewers and to potential advertisers. Ownership gives you the dominant voice in programming content and helps all programming, at least tangentially, benefit your cause.

Although you have the autonomy of ownership, you still have some constraints on your programming philosophy if you intend to draw financial backers for your programming. This is directly affected by the policy decisions of day-to-day management, but it should be addressed in the organizational phase. If you don't have the financial resources to operate the station without outside advertising or other sources of revenue, you have to address this question early.

Logistically, a television station can be a considerable challenge. At minimum, your operation requires the services of four people. This barebones operation includes a general manager of station operations, an executive producer in charge of the coordinating control panel to monitor video quality, an audio quality control monitor, and a person to operate one camera. With additional cameras, the staff expands accordingly.

Because of equipment complexity, there is no way that a staff smaller than this can achieve production smoothness and quality. Placing too many responsibilities on one staffer creates a comedy of errors that is far from funny.

During this organizational phase, retain the services of a person having a strong technical background in television operations. This person will assure that your station's equipment is adequate and organized in a way to give you the best operational system for the dollars invested.

COST BENEFITS OF STATION OWNERSHIP

The cost-benefit ratio of television station ownership can be debated at considerable length. Extensive marketing programs on television are an expensive proposition through regular commercial channels.

Planning extensive marketing programs is the main reason to become an independent station owner. Your advertising budget has to be sufficiently large, though, to assure a basic operational base for station operations. If you're only an occasional television advertiser, the viability of this option isn't even an issue. It would not be a practical choice.

Significant cost reductions are based on your marketing ability to draw other advertisers to your station. On this basis, regardless of how educational your programming focus is, you are operating a commercial television station.

Although there are no firm guidelines for privately operated stations, a good goal is to acquire outside advertising to cover at least two-thirds of your station's operating budget. This gives you plenty of air time to present your message while, at the same time, keep your costs at a nominal level.

Annual operating budgets for television stations are usually upward of a half-million dollars. This doesn't provide for many frills, but it does give a forum for limited-scale operations. Full-service all-day stations can expect operating budgets in the million dollar-plus range annually.

If your station's marketing program provides sufficient revenue to cover operating costs, your advertising cost-benefit ratio can be considerable. Excluding your initial investment for equipment, your own advertising is technically free.

Ideally, you should plan for a multiyear operating scheme. This spreads your initial investment over a longer period. If you can make the station self-sustaining from advertising revenues, you can easily justify the million dollar-plus investment for equipment if you currently have a measurable advertising effort on a national level. But be prepared to make a long-term commitment to this media. It is the only way to make your investment pay off in a way that rapidly expands your total business profits.

MANAGING THE PROMOTIONAL STATION

Although the daily management of the station is delegated to someone else, your first priority is to set basic policy for station operations. As the owner, it is your responsibility, in consultation with the staff you've assembled, to clearly focus your broadcasting objectives.

As mentioned earlier, if you don't have to rely on outside funding sources, you face few limitations except for the boundaries of good taste and common sense. Few of us, however, are *that* affluent and will need extra funding from advertising revenues.

In the initial chapters of this book, we discussed the basics of image building. Many of these same principles apply to managing a television station. The station has to have a perceived image with the viewer and you have to decide what that image will be.

As station management unfolds on a daily basis, every programming and advertising decision should coordinate with the basic policy decisions that were made initially. This involves a detailed analysis of the projected viewership market for your station. Understanding your viewers is an essential part of meeting their needs.

In some cases, initial policy decisions may not have been quite on target. Don't assume that your initial policy is engraved in stone. Maintain sufficient intellectual flexibility in the process to assure that you don't lose an established viewership base. If that happens, your investment yields less dividends than if you were advertising on someone else's facility.

As a general rule, allow six months to a year minimally to give your station time to get established. This is a period of experimentation and change as your station attempts to identify and capitalize on its market niche.

After this period, review your situation in a more detailed fashion. You should have a solid idea of what your market needs—and make necessary changes to meet them.

When needed changes are made, you can expect more stability in operations. Your sense of direction is established. After that point, your direct hands-on management can gradually decline, leaving the daily operations to the skills of staffers who are more technically oriented to general operations.

CLOSING THOUGHTS

In this chapter we reviewed one of the fastest growing areas of broadcasting. As alternatives to traditional commercial channels, defined by the three major networks, these stations provide a forum for opinions and ideas that do not fit into the programming philosophies of mainstream commercial operations.

Some of the materials covered have been technically complex by nature and we discussed only enough to give you a preliminary picture of what to expect.

Our focus here, as in the entire book, is on the marketing considerations of the media. Although there are considerable similarities here with the principles discussed for general television (see Chapter 8), cable and satellite television stations have more specialized viewerships and call for a different marketing strategy.

To successfully fit into this sector of the television medium, you have to focus on the essential differences in audience and what appeals to them. This knowledge gives you the necessary edge to market effectively to the groups involved.

As noted in Chapter 8, television is definitely not a minor league investment, but the potential payoff is considerable.

In the last two chapters, you've learned how to develop television marketing skills. Success lies in practicing the art to perfection. Although this requires the expenditure of time, effort, and money, television's impact on your financial future makes this investment a worthwhile consideration for any consultant who wishes to do more than dream about a well-known professional practice.

Television is the medium of the future. The information contained here gives you the tools to make it your key to the brightest possible future.

CHAPTER
10

ORGANIZING THE PROMOTIONAL NEWSLETTER

Most consultants, and businesses generally, view the publication of newsletters as a business cost—not as the creation of a marketable product in its own right. Although this may be true for many other businesses, consultants are in a unique position. Because the primary product of consultants is information, the newsletter is a natural adjunct to this process and therefore a marketable product.

In this chapter, we take a closer look at newsletters and how you can use them to further your business objectives. The chapter focuses on the elements that make the newsletter a marketable product, how to start the organizational process, how to organize newsletter articles, and how to gear article length to the newsletter format. Further, we look at design ideas for mastheads (the newsletter logos), attention-grabbing headlines, illustration-copy balance, and layout procedures.

After everything has been designed, we examine the final steps before printing, selecting the right printer, the page proof review process, and getting the final product. Finally, we look at how to distribute your newsletter effectively. Although the same process applies to both the free-distribution newsletter and the marketed product, the difference lies in using the newsletter as a marketing tool or a product for sale. This chapter shows you how to use newsletters in both ways.

SPECIAL OBJECTIVES OF NEWSLETTERS

There is a tendency to greatly underestimate the power of newsletters as a marketing tool, much less as a marketable product. The key to making the newsletter a marketable product is to remove the self-serving aspect of this medium and concentrate largely on its use as a vehicle for information dissemination.

An important bonus is its value as a tool to promote other products or services offered by the newsletter's sponsor. One consultant uses separately printed inserts with the newsletter to market books and videotapes that are related to the reader's interests. Even better, he collects subscription fees for the newsletters themselves. That's a special double bonus. He gets paid to advertise his products to a proven interested audience. Who could ask for anything better?

The key here is *not* to put promotion for other products in the newsletter itself. The newsletter is devoted *strictly* to providing information. This is the way to avoid the appearance of selling an "advertising rag" to your customers.

The information contained in the newsletter can, however, communicate the value of other goods and services that you offer. You don't want to be extremely overt about it in your presentation, though. See Figure 10-1, issues of the People's Dental Association newsletter, for an example. This is an information and marketing vehicle for Oramedics International and, tangentially, for the large family dental practice of Dr. Robert Nara and his son, William, also a dentist. This is one of the most peculiar marketing strategies ever conceived. They tell their readers *not* to visit dentists while, at the same time, encourage them to do so. What could be stranger than that?

Strange as it seems, the fact is that the strategy works. They receive a vast amount of business from a national clientele that seeks an alternative to the usual dental practice.

Why is this information valuable for you? Quite simply, they have shown uniqueness in a crowded field. They used the newsletter media to deliver that message. You can accomplish the same thing for your consulting business.

Beyond these considerations, the newsletter serves as an excellent method for building professional contacts. It can be used as a way to start a business relationship with an influential person by granting special favor or recognition. Some consultants successfully court influential people by providing them with complimentary subscriptions (though of very short duration) as a form of thanks or as a special personal favor. Because the recipient knows that other readers had to pay for their newsletters, this has an inevitably positive effect on the recipient. This can be a bankable asset if a professional favor serves to expedite an important business deal.

This is especially useful when, because of ethical considerations, other forms of reward are not appropriate. Few people construe a few issues of a newsletter as a kickback or bribe. This avoids appearing indelicate, while still achieving useful business objectives.

> **SPECIAL HINT**
>
> Don't throw away extra copies of back newsletter issues. You can get special advertising mileage out of them. When you advertise consulting services, you can offer a "Free Report" to persons responding to your advertising. The free report is a back issue of your newsletter, along with information on how to purchase more issues, as well as on other services that you offer.
>
> Although the semantic significance may seem quibbling, it's important to call it a "Free Report"—as opposed to offering free information. The word "report" tends to generate a more positive response within many target markets.

PDA NETWORK NEWS

The People's Dental Association

Fall 1985 Issue No. 7

How To Eliminate The Dentist From Your LIFE... Using Self- Help Methods

"Enjoy" Healthy Teeth For Life... With No Pain, No Expensive Dental work, No Fear

Life's most valuable asset is health... and yet in today's world it is frequently valued only after it is lost. Very few people today have escaped the problems of dental cavities and gum infection. The few who are totally free of any dental disease, no cavities, no fillings, and no gum problems all enjoy common ingredients in their health picture. Good nutrition is a key factor among the group who enjoy freedom from any dental problems. Teeth, like bones, are made up of primarily calcium and phosphorus. Individuals who at any time in their lives have been shortchanged of these two valuable elements in their diet will most likely suffer adverse dental effects... soft teeth, weak bone support for the roots, etc. The saliva that is produced for us by glands in and around the mouth contains calcium and phosphorus in solution, along with various enzymes. The calcium and phosphorus ions help to keep teeth strong by depositing themselves in the outer layers of the teeth. Therefore under the "right conditions", teeth are constantly being hardened or mineralized. This condition is a factor enjoyed by all "decay immune" people. Those experiencing decay can, if they so choose, reverse the decay process (demineralization) and bring about remineralization, thereby eliminating the need for drilling and filling, or pulling of the teeth.

THRU - THE - MAIL ORAMEDICS PROGRAM

SELF—HELP PROGRAM TO ELIMINATE THE DENTIST FROM YOUR LIFE!

Sound too good to be true? Not really if you possess the proper KNOWLEDGE, and are willing to take ACTION.

Many people simply do not know exactly how teeth and gums get into trouble, so if one lacks knowledge it's impossible to take corrective action.

> SOLUTIONS do not come to those who do not understand the problem.

Teeth and supportive jawbones are weakened by improper nutrition, or by toxic waste products produced by bacterial colonies collecting within the mouth. The toxic waste products raise havoc with the calcium and phosphorus of the teeth and they cause inflammation of the gums. Cavities appear in areas of greater concentrations of the acid-like waste products and if inflammation of the gums is allowed to persist for any length of time it leads to infection of the gums. Loose puffy gums that tend to bleed easily is the next step in the deterioration process. Prolonged loosening, flabby gums, destroy the connective fibers that hold our gums tight to teeth and bone. Then a space develops between the neck of the tooth and encircling gum tissue. This "abnormal" space is commonly called a pocket. As the space (pocket) deepens, it then erodes away the bone that holds the teeth in place. This is com-

continued on page two

Figure 10-1(a) PDA Network News, Fall 1985, Issue No. 7. Reprinted Courtesy of Oramedics, International.

Eliminate The Dentist

Continued from page one

monly referred to as pyorrhea. More teeth are lost due to pyorrhea than due to decay. About 98% of all Americans have at least some areas of diseased gum tissue in their mouths, over half of these are also experiencing a progressive "bone loss".

> Fortunately, cavities and pyorrhea (gum disease and bone loss) are both 100% preventible and both are reversible.

Most health oriented people these days know a good diet from a bad one. The so called "secrets of nutrition" are really NOT secret at all to the nutrition conscious individuals who care about themselves and their minds and bodies. The building blocks of all body tissues are similar. A diet lacking in essential elements will suffer consequences throughout the body, not just in one organ or tissue. The building blocks of both teeth and bone are calcium and phosphorus, but shortages of these two ingredients will cause other problems as well.

Those who enjoy good nutrition but still suffer dental problems are generally suffering the ravages of toxic waste products stemming from an overabundance of bacterial colonies within the mouth. For many people brushing and flossing is not enough to completely control dental problems, especially those who have already developed pockets at the necks of the teeth. Conventional cleaning is simply not enough to rid the mouth of the toxic waste products responsible for all the trouble.

For years dentists and gum tissue specialists have recommended gum and bone surgery to cut away loose flabby gums and infected bone. Supposedly after healing, the mouth can then be "again" kept clean by brushing and flossing. This is seldom the case, however, and most people wind up in the same condition in a short time and are told that surgery is necessary again, and again. The reason for this is that the real "cause" of the problem is not being attacked. A "cut job" is not the solution to the problem. The solution is hidden in a common sense approach to eliminating the toxic waste products; a solution, by the way, recommended by Dr. Levi S. Parmly in a book; "A Practical Guide to the Management of the Teeth", published in 1819! Most schools of thought today give Dr. Parmly credit for being the first dentist (scientist?) to discover and report the real cause of cavities and gum infection. The majority of the American public lack this KNOWLEDGE, therefore cannot take ACTION.

Once pockets form (98% of Americans have early, moderate, or severe pocket formation), brushing and flossing alone cannot remove toxic waste products from these "below the gum line spaces". The only way known to accomplish this flushing away of the disease producing toxins is by use of an oral irrigator, i.e. Water Pik™. If the pockets are shallow, the regular Water Pik Tip is adequate. If the pockets have become moderate (even in limited areas), then a "Special Tip" or elongated-directional tip is necessary.

> NOTE: This "Special Tip" is available thru Oramedics International, 200 E. Montezuma, Houghton, MI 49931 (906) 482-1419

When the toxic waste products that are being trapped in "below the gum line spaces" are flushed out daily with warm salt water, the body's normal reparative processes set in and heal the diseased gum tissue. In most cases, once the gum tissue begins to heal, the bone follows suit, growing back new bone where it's been lost and tightening up loose wobbly teeth (self-help healing of pyorrhea).

In mouths where bacterial toxins run high, the decay process is also represented, so by eliminating the bacterial waste products from the teeth and gums the decay process stops as well as gums and bone healing.

The saliva can then return to it's God-intended condition of healing fluid rather than a sewage-transmission fluid. Only when this "healing fluid" state is achieved can cavities harden (remineralize). When toxic waste products abound, everything gets worse, not better. The human body normally produces approximately one quart of saliva each day. When this saliva exists under such environmental conditions to be in the "healing fluid" state, then and only then will:

1. cavities heal (remineralize)
2. gums heal (rejuvenate)
3. bone heals (tightening up loose teeth)

Note:

When the saliva is of "healing fluid ability" an interesting phenomenon occurs: the calculus or tartar that builds up on teeth (deposited) is slowly dissolved, eliminating the need for painful and expensive scraping of the teeth by the dentist or dental hygienist.

Purifying the saliva and mouth can be speeded up today with new "state of the art" products. A rinse of a solution of highly concentrated calcium and phosphorus ions (with a remineralizing catalyst) has recently been developed by a biochemical company here in this country. To combat the build-up of bacterial colonies (producers of toxic waste products) a new teeth cleaning substance has been developed to retard the bacterial colonies from growing in the first place. Yet another rinse is available to kill off high concentrations of bacteria when a saliva test has shown them to be excessively high. It is important to note here that the 2% of the public who are immune to cavities and gum problems, do not need these products, and diligent and effective removal of all bacterial colonies will, in time, produce the same beneficial effects. These products are only intended to hasten the process in cases where conditions are considered moderate to severe.

Figure 10-1(a) *Continued*

Editor's Note

Dr. Nara will be speaking at a health meeting - Pasadena Convention Center - January 17th - 19th, 1986. For more information contact PDA.

We here at Oramedics International feel very strongly that the public is desperately in need of help that they seldom or never get from the dental profession. To emphasize the extent of this problem we are printing the following letter.

Dear Dr. Nara,

I have a history of family dental problems. My brother has gum disease - serious. I always have tried to have good hygiene and dental care. I had no proper instruction for cleaning teeth and gums ever. I have receding gum problems around dental work, bad breath at times. I value my teeth and smile!

I feel dentists could do much, much more to help patients prevent serious dental problems but purposely do not for their own selfish gain. I've recently learned this in more than one instance: I was informed of a root resorption taking place on a front tooth - until it had to be pulled! I've seen at least six different dentists during the time it takes to get to that point. And NOT ONE informed me! Even though I've been told that it is rare and not preventable - just knowing would have eased the trauma of losing the tooth.

Secondly - after having huge cavities refilled and going on to crowns - I now have gum problems caused by ill-fitting dental work and even decay under one crown. I've complained to one dentist about a sore-bothersome gum area and was told "No problem, nothing wrong." Another dentist said "We don't get excited about gum problems until they reach a certain point and then we tell the patient to have the proper procedures done." This smells like more money in the dentist's and surgeon's pockets to me! I've also had a periodontist write a letter saying my gums were infected due to "dental neglect." However, in his office he said the pockets were caused by dental crowns that did not fit. Sounds like he won't back up the truth on paper.

The conventional dentists and their methods are no longer of interest to me. I do not trust dentists any longer. I feel I have been taken down the sorry path of expensive and painful fillings, re-fills, and crowns, and led on to gum problems. I sincerely want to do all I can in proper hygiene, diet, etc., to get back on the "healthy road of a healthy mouth".

I await your reponse. Thank you.
Sincerely,
J.L., Montana

Dear J.L.,

We receive thousands of similar letters every month. Yours is a complicated problem which has developed over a period of time.

Your best course of action is: Put your trust in a doctor who helps you to become self-reliant... Do not trust any doctor who causes you to become doctor dependent . . . And, never lose the most important factor . . . TRUST IN YOURSELF. Enclosed are 3 pamphlets that will explain things in greater detail.

Sincerely,
Robert O. Nara, D.D.S.

Dr. Nara answers thousands of questions each year about healing cavities and dissolving tartar.

The following are his answers to the most frequently asked questions.

Question: What are the special oral conditions that are necessary for cavities to heal and for gums to rejuvenate and bone to grow back, tightening up painful wobbly teeth?

Answer: The mouth must be in a state of "biological balance", and conditions are as follows:
1. good nutrition
2. saliva that is rich in calcium and phosphorus ions
3. blood that is rich in calcium and phosphorus ions
4. low oral bacterial count (write for free pamphlet . . . Why Have an Oramedics Saliva Test?)
5. Ph of mouth about neutral
6. low oral acid production
7. minimal toxic waste products
8. outward hydraulic fluid flow of all individual teeth

Question: What steps are necessary to accomplish this biological balance?

Answer: In simple terms:
1. Soft debris must be removed → brushing.
2. Bacterial colonies "controlled" → irrigation, i.e. Water Pik™ with Oramedics Special Tip, anti-bacterial rinse.
3. Calcified deposits → dissolved by the use of anti-deposit gel, special floss, i.e. Clean-Between™.

Question: What toothpaste do you recommend?

Answer: Stay away from all toothpastes that foam and/or tingle - (toxic effect on gums). The only toothpaste I suggest for those who have gum problems is chlorophyll toothpaste. Research at Boy's Town in Nebraska show it

continued on page four

Figure 10-1(a) *Continued*

Questions And Answers
Continued from page three

to be effective in reducing inflammation of gums.

Question: It seems from what you're saying, Dr. Nara, that there is no one factor or one product that does it all, in helping cavities to heal and dissolving the calcified deposits?

Answer: That is correct, achieving biologic balance in the mouth may sound difficult but it's not really - once you know how. We find most people anxious to take action once they understand the problem. Unfortunately, almost all dentists offer fillings, extractions, etc. This is not hard to understand when you consider the fact that research studies show across the board that dentists suffer more dental problems than the average man on the street.

Question: A 34 year old woman wrote from California, "Now that I understand how to heal cavities and dissolve calcified deposits off of my teeth how can I best gain these benefits for myself when your material says that all people's mouths are different?

Answer: It's true that no two people's conditions are exactly alike. However, you can determine some personal generalities that will lead you in the right direction. For example, have you experienced a lot of cavities in your lifetime? Have you experienced previous gum problems, or do you now have receding gums, etc? All of these factors and others indicate what's been going wrong. That is why we include an extensive past medical and dental health questionnaire at the same time we do a bacteriologic test of the saliva and also acid production test of the mouth.

Question: I've asked six or seven dentists about calculus and/or tartar dissolving. They all seem to indicate it's not possible to dissolve it.

Answer: Dentists are not trained to think there's any other way to solve periodontal problems without "doctor treatment". I believed that myself for many years until the self-reliant people developed biological balance within their mouths. It was eye-opening to me to have discovered this is really possible. I was taught by the public that it is possible to dissolve calcified deposits but only under the right conditions.

Question: Where can I find a dentist in my area who's thinking is the same as yours?

Answer: I doubt that you can . . . almost all dentists are mechanically oriented and money motivated. This approach requires a "scientist" not a mechanic. But . . . not to worry, you can learn all you need to know (knowledge) through the mail. Then use self-help (action) to stop the decay process, stop gum problems (infection), heal cavities, rejuvenate gums, etc.

Therefore, the only reason to "need" a dentist is for mechanical care . . . I can probably refer you to a good (technically good) dentist . . . or you can find a good mechanic by word of mouth . . . neighbors, friends, etc., or come to Houghton, Michigan and my son and I will advise and/or treat you.

From The Doctor

Following the cleaning and scraping of the teeth, every human being has experienced pain for several days, sometimes weeks or months. This pain is caused by damage to the roots and cutting of the gums by the instruments used to scrape off calcium deposits called scalers. It is much healthier to dissolve these calcified deposits rather than exposing one's self to the damage and pain of the scraping. The only known method today to dissolve tartar of calculus is through the Oramedics program. As it says on the front page of this newsletter, the necessary knowledge to do this can be handled through the mail.

The four pages of this Newsletter are only a synopsis of the Oramedics process. An expanded version is available on tape. Dr. Nara presented two lectures at the World Health Expo in Anaheim, California, September 7th and 8th, 1985. The titles of these two lectures were "Eliminating Dentists From Your Life, Part 1", and "Eliminating Dentists From Your Life, Part 2". These two tapes are available from Womack Enterprises at $6.50 each. The same two lectures have been consolidated on one tape available through Oramedics International at $6.50 (plus $1.50 postage and handling).

The preceding information is intended to only represent an overview of healing cavities and stopping gum problems by self-help methods and products. Any reader who wishes to take advantage of these methods and products should gain more detailed individualized information. This is available from the organizer and founder of Oramedics International:

Dr. Robert O. Nara
Chief Dental Consultant to
The People's Dental Assoc.
200 East Montezuma Avenue
Houghton, MI 49931
(906) 482-1419

Exclusive phone number
for members of
The People's Dental Assoc.
(906) 482-3530

Figure 10-1(a) *Continued*

PDA NETWORK NEWS

The People's Dental Association

Issue No. 9

The Gum Disease Conspiracy

In a recent report published by the dental profession, the blame for so much gum disease was placed squarely on the country's dentists. The headline of the report is: "Periodontal Disease in America: a Personal and National Tragedy."

This recently published dental bulletin clearly states that, "almost **all Americans**, except the millions who already wear false teeth, have gum disease!"

The price tag for this disease is in the billions...mostly for extractions and false teeth. A 1980 survey by the U.S. Department of Health and Human Services concluded that only 5% of dentists' time is spent in attempting to treat gum disease and yet the majority of all teeth that are pulled (or fall out) are lost due totally to gum disease!

A study conducted by dental authorities in North Carolina states that: Gum disease in America is "rampant" and in the last 14 years gum problems have "significantly worsened!"

Dr. John Ingle, a government dentist in Washington, stated at a 1975 health conference that: the insidious and painless nature of gum disease is "a personal and national tragedy". The report goes on to say: "The general dental practitioners should be regarded as the pivotal elements in the broad scheme of preventive and therapeutic periodontal programming." By programming it would appear to mean teaching and or doing...However, in a survey done by Dr. A.B. Wade he reports in this same publication that: "plaque scores and plaque control of dentists themselves were worse than those of patients."

After learning this information a member of The People's Dental Association recently wrote..."It was interesting...particularly the part dealing with the fact that the "professionals" have more problems than the public does...so how can they help us???"

—Keith Moses, Pasadena, Calif.

Periodontal Disease in America: a Personal and National Tragedy

A position paper prepared for the American Association of Public Health Dentists by the AAPHD Subcommittee on Preventive Periodontics, October 24, 1981

The crying shame of the entire 8 page report is that it's conclusion offers no viable solution to the problem...so the national tragedy goes on...and on...and on... A copy of this report - "Periodontal Disease in America: a Personal and National Tragedy", can be obtained from The People's Dental Association. Send $5.00 to cover handling. Send to:

The People's Dental Association
200 East Montezuma Avenue
Houghton, MI 49931

It becomes very obvious that the only way to solve this major health problem is for individuals to learn about the cause of this disease and to take action to stop or treat it themselves...dentists will never be able to do anything about it if they can't stop gum disease in their own mouths!

Webster's Dictionary defines con-spire: to join in a secret agreement to do an unlawful or wrongful act, or scheme, to plot.

The current "National Tragedy" as the profession calls it, is sufficient proof that: dentists' are simply failing the public...Miserably!

The obvious conclusion is that a conspiracy does exist...the thing speaks for itself.

The astronomical increase in the costs of health care and the rapid rise of malpractice suits against doctors in this country and worldwide is further proof that something is wrong. The system is not working...subsequent pages of this report will delve into the real problem and the **only** solution possible.

The diagnosis of the problem and it's predictable solution is based on over 30 years of study, research, and private practice, of Dr. Robert O. Nara. Dr. Nara is the founder of Oramedics International, the world's only group dedicated to helping people AVOID disease rather than treating the results of the disease process with needles, knives, drugs, drilling, pulling and **false teeth!**

The dentists are to blame.

Figure 10-1(b) PDA Network News, Issue No. 9. Reprinted Courtesy of Oramedics, International.

The Problem...

When any human being is faced with a problem, the first consideration in attempting to find a solution... is to thoroughly understand the problem. The biggest reason that gum disease is so widespread is that no one seems to understand the problem. The dentists certainly don't, so how can the public be expected to know? The answer to that is self-education.

HERE ARE THE FACTS:

Carefully examine Fig. 1. It shows a cross section of a tooth. The spongy looking material is the supportive bone that holds our teeth in place. The bone on the left of the tooth is shown as normal, on the right side it has deteriorated because of gum disease. The gum tissue covers the bone and a thin layer of tissue fibers surround the tooth and attach the tooth to the bone (a velcro-like attachment).

Early in life, when the teeth first grow into our mouths a small crevis exists between the tooth and the gum tissue. In the healthy condition this crevis is about one millimeter deep. Figure 1 shows an instrument called a pocket marker, inserted into the left side crevis. The crevis on this side shows to be two to three millimeters deep. This condition is already unhealthy because bacterial waste products are causing inflammation of the tissue. This leads to infection and deep bone deterioration . . . this condition is shown on the right side of the tooth in Fig. 1. The depth of the crevis or pocket on this side is seven or eight millimeters. This depth of pocket formation and bone loss is very severe, and if not arrested very soon will undoubtedly cause the tooth to be lost.

For many years dentists have been telling the public to brush twice a day, floss once a day, see them for scraping of the teeth every six months and everything will be all right. Millions of Americans have been following these orders, only to be told after a few years that . . . NOW they have gum disease and need to see a gum specialist for surgery. This means cutting away the diseased gums so the process can start all over again. This is a painful, expensive, merry-go-round that leads

———Fig. 1———

to false teeth. This whole "personal and national" tragedy continues for only one reason: It's very profitable to the dental profession. A well known Michigan gum specialist has bragged for years that he makes over a million dollars a year on gum surgery and related treatments. Since the automobile industry has instigated such elaborate dental insurance, his "take" must have doubled or tripled by now!

The irony of the whole situation is that, if armed with the right knowledge, and if motivated to take action, with the proper instruments anyone can simply rid the mouth of the offending microscopic little bastards. An enthusiastic user of the methods recently wrote: "They told me my pockets would have to be cut out, but they healed up by themselves."
—Bob Pike, Box 1260, Arleta, GA 91331

It's very simple, the mouth routinely harbors about 300 different varieties of bacteria, however it has been scientifically proven that the troublemakers are spirochetes, motile rods, and cocci. Reduce these "nasty" bugs below certain levels and:

THE BODY HEALS ITSELF!

Once a person realizes how easy it is to understand the cause of gum disease, a little additional thinking then allows one to understand the decay process . . . the same mechanism applies here, only here it's the acid part of the toxic waste products that eats holes in the teeth. The notches that many people have at the necks of some teeth are almost always caused by a build-up of toxic waste products below the gum line "before" the gums receed. Dentists always want to blame the patients for improper tooth brushing . . . That's not true. The notches and the receeding gums are both caused by the same problem. All doctors are alike, dentists, medical doctors, etc. When there are good results taking place they immediately take all of the credit. When bad results are happening they blame the patient!

If you need further help in understanding the problems of gum disease, or other dental problems, help is available from: Dr. Robert O. Nara (exclusive direct line for members of the People's Dental Association) (906) 482-3530. Or write: Dr. Robert O. Nara, Chief Consultant c/o PDA.

* * *

When searching for an Answer, while the origin of the problem is unknown, <u>ALL</u> potential solutions are at best . . . Guess Work.

Figure 10-1(b)   Continued

137

...The Solution

The bottom line on the problem of gum disease is simply that the neck-of-the-tooth is not given proper attention. Dentists are directly to blame because they concentrate all of their efforts on the crowns of the teeth...they fill them, inlay them, bridge them, etc. That's where the big money is! Therefore the public never learns that the main "trouble spot" is the crevis at the neck of the tooth. The solution lies in cleansing this crevis of the toxic waste products from harmful bacteria.

Early in life this can be accomplished with a tooth brush and Clean-Between, plus...a device to flush out the crevis. Figure 2 on this page shows a diagram of how this is easily accomplished. If some gum disease has set in so the crevis is rapidly becoming a crevasse then a "Special Tip" is required...the Special Tip squirts a stream of salt water that is much more directional than the ordinary tips. If the disease is even more advanced, then more sophisticated tips and methods, and therapeutic rinses, may be necessary. These stages of the disease and the corresponding treatment tips are illustrated in Figures 3 and 4. An enlarged view of the side-port tip is shown in Figure 5.

These self-help methods of controlling gum disease have been used successfully for over 20 years. The reason that the results are so dramatic is that this approach is aimed at stopping the cause of the problem . . . other methods are an attempt to control the symptoms.

One should be cautious however, in his thinking about these methods. The more severe the gum disease the more difficult these methods become. It may be necessary to retain the help of a dentist who has been specifically trained in helping people to help themselves. Doctor-dependent-treatment such as gum surgery is rapidly being replaced with self-help methods aimed at eliminating the cause.

INTRINSIC FACTOR

As a final consideration in understanding the etiology of gum disease, it is well to keep in mind that no two human beings are exactly alike. There is a wide variation of people's resistive ability when it comes to fighting off gum disease.

In a large sample of people who's general health would be considered good, a few would have such strong resistance that their gums and supportive bone stays healthy even if they were very neglectful of oral hygiene, eating habits, etc. Another small group would be highly prone to gum deterioration even if they were very conscientious. A large group in the middle would suffer what might be called typical gum disease.

Also a certain number of people will suffer from what could be called "magnified" gum problems. Gum disease can be exacerbated by many conditions, including immunosupression, malnutrition, or other general debility, endocrine abnormalities, etc. Therefore anyone who has been using all the right methods of eliminating the cause of gum disease but still having problems, should analyze the possibility of some **Intrinsic Factor** that might be complicating the overall health picture.

Being treated medically for a variety of problems can also have side effects complicating the gum disease situation. For example, about 500 different commercially prepared drugs have side effects that can cause a reduction in the amount of saliva flow. Reduced salivary flow can have an extremely damaging effect on the gums and supportive bone. Some of the most common drugs that produce the dry mouth syndrome are:

Actifed	Librax
Benedryl	Ornade
Chlortrimeton	Sudafed
Compazine	Thorazine
Dimetane	Valium
Donnatal	

One cannot be too careful when it comes to good nutrition. This is probably more important than any single factor. A 25 year empirical study has lead the staff at the People's Dental Association to a determination of certain basic nutritional needs. It seems that

Cont. on page 4...

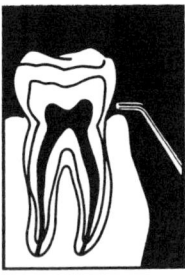

———Fig. 2——— 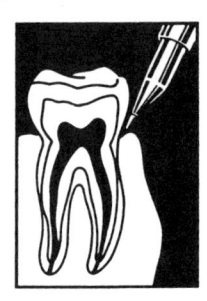 ———Fig. 3——— 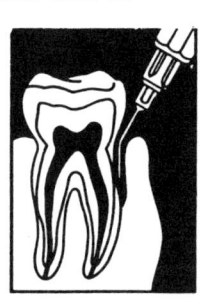 ———Fig. 4——— 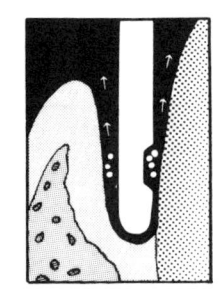 ———Fig. 5———

Figure 10-1(b) *Continued*

Beneficial Rinses

Our American forefathers cured meat by soaking it in brine and hanging it up to dry. The primary function of the brine was to kill bacteria. Millions of people have helped to cure oral abscesses, gum boils, etc., by simply rinsing several times a day with warm salt water. The warm water along with the salt helps to pull "fluid" out of the gum tissue, therefore reducing swelling, aleviating pain, and killing harmful bacteria. Warm salt water in an irrigating device means sudden death to millions of hostile bacteria ...in gum line crevices and periodontal pockets! Brushing and flossing is simply not enough to stop gum disease...that's why so many people who followed their dentists advice still wound up with gum disease (infection).

For many years...almost 300 years, it was falsely believed that gum disease was caused by plaque in general. Therefore people who didn't clean well could expect gum disease and those who cleaned well were protected...Wrong! So is it any wonder that we have so many disillusioned people suffering an unwanted disease today?

About 10 years ago the light at the end of the tunnel began to appear. Research studies by Socransky at Forsyth Dental School in Boston, and by Loesche at the University of Michigan began to indicate that the cause of gum disease was much more "specific" than the old plaque theory. In fact, the new technology described at least five different types of gum disease based on the specific nasty bugs involved in the infectious process. This new evidence is probably best understood by thinking of an old disease we all know and understand..."strep throat". A reddened throat, inflamed, and infected by betahemolytic streptococci, and you have..."strep throat". This is a very specific disease, with a very specific cause, and needs very specific treatment. So it is with gum disease, seen in light of today's knowledge. Gum disease is a very specific disease, with a specific cause, and needs specific treatment. The presence of plaque and tartar are only insidently related...they are NOT THE CAUSE!

Healthy gums: gram-positive faculative rods and cocci-predominately Actinomyces species and streptococci.

Sick gums: gram- negative anaerobic rods primarily Bacteroids and Fusobacteria.

GI-aids

GI-aids: a diseased condition of the gum tissue characterized by lowering or reduction of the strength of the immune system to resist bacterial invasion of the gums, further manifested by an allergic-like reaction of the supportive jawbone to the toxic waste products produced by the bacteria. This progressive deterioration of supportive bone is a very insidious disease. This disintegration of the bone results in such a sea of pus and infection that it encapsulates the teeth and destroys them.

As previously mentioned warm salt water used in an irrigating device is probably the best all around protection when one wants to rinse away toxic waste products produced by harmful bacteria. It cannot be stressed enough that brushing and flossing are not enough!

For situations where the gum disease is more advanced the therapeutic rinse of choice is sanguanaria extract (SaE). For many centuries various herbs have been used to help create oral health. Sanguinaria, a herbal extract, is an example of a beneficial rinse used for centuries by native cultures. It is a well recognized homeopathic remedy. The extract is principally a mixture of benzophenathridine alkaloids, the chief constituent alkaloid being sanguinarine (Sa).

It seems very strange that in many cases native cultures using herbal methods were able to accomplish a much higher degree of health than so called Modern Medicine. The reader has probably learned of many other - personal examples in their own lives.

The only significant factor in todays world are the irrigating devices...These undoubtedly have a beneficial effect in delivering the salt water or Sanguinaria extract to the right spot...the neck of the tooth, namely the gum crevis around the neck of the tooth. This no-man's-land of trouble, the neck of the tooth must be brought to the public's attention so that they...the people can take over and solve this problem. Those who are waiting for dentists to "carry the banner"...will have a long wait. Most teeth won't last that long. Now is the time for people to take charge of their own dental destiny.

... The Solution cont.

those who's gum tissue and bone stay healthy have been eating well and adding additional nutrients included in a "Defense Mechanism Formula". This 25 year emperical study has found that when lacking any of the nutrients in the "basic" ... Defense Mechanism Formula, almost everyone will suffer some degree of gum and bone disease. Some people need a few additional nutrients over and above the Defense Mechanism Formula, which is a matter that requires individual investigation and decision. As with all dental nutritional and health matters, personal consul can be obtained by phone or otherwise from the People's Dental Association.

The People's Dental Association
200 East Montezuma Avenue
Houghton, MI 49931
(906) 482-3530

HEAR DR. ROBERT O. NARA
AT THE NHF
NATURAL HEALTH CONVENTION
August 9th & 10th, 1986
Holiday Inn
O'Hare Kennedy
Call or Write to PDA For More Information

Figure 10–1(b) *Continued*

STARTING POINT FOR NEWSLETTER ORGANIZATION

Although our preceding discussion focused on a specialized area of consumer interest, the same idea can be applied successfully to communication with a professional audience. The approach is more sophisticated than that displayed in the People's Dental Association example, but the general idea remains the same.

Your first objective in newsletter organization is to define a theme. What types of information do you want to offer to your readers? Where do their interests lie? How are you going to address these interests and concerns and at the same time retain their attention for more than one issue of your publication?

One of the intriguing benefits of a newsletter is that it can have very narrowly defined interests. Some consultants with a wide area of expertise publish several different newsletters and are able to market them effectively. This may reduce the number of potential subscribers for each publication (and have some effect on overall profitability) but it reaches considerably more total readers. You can attract more subscribers to an interest-specific publication than to a more general vehicle.

If you've been in business for some time and know the concerns of your clientele, you've encountered plenty of subjects that prospective readers need information and help on. This is your starting point.

Your next consideration is the size of your publication. Most newsletters are between four and eight pages. The most common size for a professional newsletter is four pages (approximately 8½ by 11 inches).

The third consideration is frequency of publication. Most professional newsletters are either monthlies or bimonthlies. Since annual subscription rates are often well over a hundred dollars, publication at less frequent intervals puts the newsletter at a distinct disadvantage in drawing readers and customers.

When you answer these questions, you have defined the general parameters of a newsletter that you can produce to benefit your consulting business. This preliminary information serves you well as a guide for the beginning, and the future, of your publication.

FINE POINTS OF ARTICLE ORGANIZATION

One of the primary challenges of writing articles to fit the newsletter format is the absolute necessity for brevity. This can't be overemphasized. Most readers are disappointed if each newsletter contained only one article. In a four-page format, you don't really have time to get chatty. You must get right to the point, say it, and stop.

In the four-page format, you are confined to articles that are around four double-spaced manuscript pages (about 1,000 words). This size gives you the opportunity to feature two articles in a single four-page issue of your newsletter.

For this reason, your subjects can't be very large in scope. Focus on small aspects of larger subjects. This serves two very useful purposes. It allows sufficient detail of the aspect to make the article useful to your reader. Second, it enhances reader interest in the larger subject area. This often triggers business for the consultant-author of the newsletter. Readers want to know more. Who is a better source of information than the author of the original article?

To illustrate the tight constraints of the newsletter format, the writing contained in this section represents approximately one fourth to one third of the *total* length for one newsletter article. If a newsletter makes reasonable use of graphic arts (a subject covered later in this chapter), this could represent as much as half of a total article.

Length varies somewhat, depending on the size of typeface that is used to print the newsletter. However, it is not advisable to reduce type size too much in an effort to stuff more copy into a single newsletter issue. You end up with a product that is difficult to read and unappealing to your target clientele.

Beyond this, newsletter articles are more direct from a stylistic viewpoint. This allows greater information dissemination in fewer words, a necessity to observe within limited space.

This is one reason why many professional newsletters use a six-page format. It allows for more detail and gives more value for the reader's money. Of course, this does translate into increased production costs. But, considering the general profit margin available on marketable professional newsletters, this is not as great a consideration. (It is, however, a concern for any publication that is distributed free.)

When you organize and write articles for your newsletter, you should be constantly aware of the fine line involved in reader perceptions. You don't want to tell them too much, but you must give them enough—to make them want to come back for more.

As you progress with your newsletter, take your readers along in shorter steps, not giant leaps. A favorite technique is to offer a series of articles on a single subject. The series is spread over several issues of the newsletter. This keeps your readers coming back for future issues, wanting to get the total picture offered by the series of articles. When you develop ideas, look for this possibility in larger subject areas.

One pitfall to avoid, however, is not to use the "to be continued" gimmick too extensively. Give a complete article in each issue. Readers resent a serialized approach, if it is too blatant. If you do use an article series, don't go beyond three issues. Doing this virtually guarantees an aggravated readership.

As an adjunct marketing idea, an article series can be published as a Special Report, giving you twice as much mileage for the same writing effort. This is directed toward potential clients not currently subscribing to your newsletter service. The target information whets their appetite for more of the same—and draws them into your special circle of loyal customers.

Always remember that your underlying message to your reader is to emphasize the value of your consulting expertise. The information provided in your newsletter articles, clearly directed and concise, is effective in delivering that message to your consumer.

MASTHEAD OR BANNER DESIGN HINTS

One of the first things that your reader notices on receiving your newsletter is the masthead or banner design. This is the area at the top of your newsletter that names your publication.

Newsletters are designed in a similar fashion to general newspapers, but in an abbreviated form. The banner serves the same purpose as the cover of a magazine. It projects an image to your reader. This is one very important reason to devote some thought and energy to it. Rightly or wrongly, the reader is going to judge your publication by this first impression.

In Figure 10-2 I've shown some banner ideas that are based on a system called integrated computer graphics design. This is a combination of graphics and print generated through computer software.

At least one of the designs, "Bull Market" showed a whimsical approach. The others are more conservative. The major feature of them all is visual appeal. A combination of graphics and print is the best way to add a distinctive flavor, a sense of individuality, to your product. The banner serves to set it apart from similar products in the competitive marketplace. It's the printed identification by which your efforts are recognized.

One of the most common mistakes in developing a marketable newsletter is to design too conservative a banner. Some newsletters project an image of total boredom. There is nothing really exciting about them.

The publication's contents may offer considerable material of benefit to the reader, but the design, beginning with the banner, sometimes blocks readers' absorption of what is being delivered. Although you shouldn't

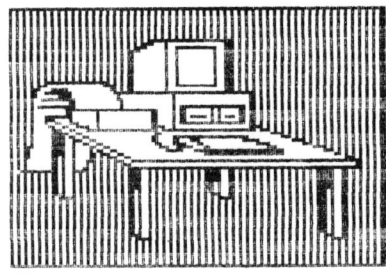

Figure 10.2 (a) Business computers; (b) bull market; (c) practical investments; (d) national management issues and answers.

judge a book by its cover, human nature tends to go against this logic. We do it much of the time, whether we realize it or not. Your banner presentation will be judged by the visual impression it makes so you should make certain it is appealing.

The four banners in Figure 10-2, all created for this book, show some of the basic principles of banner design. Let's examine them briefly.

The "Business Computers" example shows shaded art graphics. This is created by taking a basic line art graphic of the computer unit, putting a box around it, and putting some background shading within the box outline. This is a common approach that is used successfully by many newsletter publications.

The use of the Old English typestyle for the newsletter title was not accidental. This typestyle projects an image of a strong link to tradition. It is in direct contrast to the modernistic idea of computers themselves—and primarily designed to encourage tradition-bound readers to give computers a good try.

"Bull Market," the whimsical example, shows straight line art graphics. The picture of the bull is a standard line art piece, with no extra embellishments added. There are no line dividers or any other decorative features. It is sparse, direct, and reinforcing of the newsletter's title.

If you do decide to use the tongue-in-cheek approach, you must show the connection between your banner illustration and the title. Otherwise, it shows a lack of purpose—and reflects negatively on the total product.

"Practical Investments" shows an extensive use of line dividers, shading, and other variations to set off areas within the banner. This is often preferable to jamming copy together without dividing lines. The result is usually more attractive.

"National Management Issues and Answers" uses a block right banner copy, with the rest of the banner area being solid graphics presentation, either through illustration or shading. This principle is effective if the only information that you want to present in the banner is the newsletter's title. This helps you to avoid an excessive amount of empty area that can sometimes detract from the overall appeal of your finished product.

Although you may consider these designs lacking in conservatism, the underlying idea of the banner shouldn't be compromised by lack of innovation. This is especially true if your newsletter is entering a market already containing a competitive product. Even in a totally monopolistic market, your leadership role can quickly be usurped by a bolder presentation.

The absolute minimum requirement for the banner is the publication's name. Other optional information includes frequency of publication, date of issue, and organization responsible for publishing the newsletter. Some newsletters also indicate copyright status in this area. That, however, can be indicated elsewhere in the publication and may detract from banner appearance in some cases.

> **SPECIAL HINT**
>
> If you have access to a personal computer and the appropriate software, you can make the designing process for banners a breeze. The four banner illustrations contained here were all designed and printed out on a computer printer in slightly over two hours. With the right software, the process seems more like fun than work. Don't overlook this possibility. You don't need an ultrafancy computer to get the job done. These were done on a Commodore C-64 unit that is within almost anyone's budget.

ATTENTION GRABBING HEADLINES

After your banner presentation, the material contained within your newsletter's pages is going to be judged by the article titles and headlining techniques used to draw reader attention. They set a basic tone that either intrigues or bores your readers. If they are bored, they won't bother to read the article.

A common pitfall of professional publications is that they often seek to project a scholarly appearance. It doesn't take long to feel that masochism is a prerequisite to reading them. Article titles are ponderous, clumsy, verbose. They totally fail to intrigue the reader.

Imagine seeing an article title like, "Migration Flight Patterns of Canadian Geese." The title sounds scholarly. Unless you're extremely interested in the subject, you won't consider reading it.

By contrast, consider the title, "Wings of Destiny: Canada Welcomes Its Geese." You get the same information, but there isn't a heavy-handed tone to it. You don't feel that reading the article will be a form of cruel and unusual punishment—even if the subject isn't a predominant interest of yours.

Writing appealing headlines is one of the keys to making your newsletter readable. You want your readers to go through your entire newsletter. Make it a reasonably enjoyable process. This begins with the tone of your headlines.

The appearance of your headlines is also important to the total package. Two of the most common headline type styles are the serif and sans serif typefaces. These two styles were used in designing the banner for our "Bull Market" example. The larger print is the sans serif type style. Both serif and sans serif styles come in large and small versions. Headlines naturally use the larger version. The smaller versions are primarily used for the text of the articles in the newsletter.

An all capital letter format is preferred for headline copy. Some newsletters vary this for special effect, but the basic idea is to make headlines easily readable. The type style used for the title on the "Business Computers" banner, Old English, is *not* recommended for headline copy use.

THE ILLUSTRATION-COPY BALANCE

The development of an effective illustration-copy balance for a newsletter is often a matter of personal taste, both for you and for your prospective readers. Assuming that your projected audience is a reasonably sophisticated group, you won't need to rely as heavily on illustrative matter for relaying important material to them.

Illustrations serve as a complementary element to any article, but they are particularly crucial on the *first* page of your newsletter. Having a solid block of copy facing your reader initially gives a very boring appearance.

Consumer publications generally devote at least 25 percent of their space to illustration. The preferred ratio is one-third illustration to two-thirds copy.

That much illustration isn't necessary in professional newsletters, but you shouldn't go much below 15 percent on illustrative matter. Try to put a bit more on the first page to give a more appealing "cover" appearance and devote subsequent pages more extensively to copy.

This is *not,* however, a recommendation to totally forego illustrations on other pages. Many professional newsletters fall into the trap of being so boring in appearance that only the most devoted reader takes the time to even look at them. This boredom comes from the lack of illustration.

This chapter has been extensively illustrated to show you the contrast between it and those that are almost entirely straight copy. Where applicable in other chapters, Special Hint sections have been used. These serve a similar function to artwork. The basic idea, however, is to break up longer material by some method to add interest and sparkle. Reading any book or publication should not be total drudgery.

EFFECTIVE LAYOUT TECHNIQUES

Unlike other publication efforts, the restrictive length of the average newsletter places a premium on effective layout skills. From an editorial viewpoint, the first page is the most critical.

One of the most common failures of professional newsletters is a blandness in appearance. Often devoid of illustration, they have the appearance of a piece of correspondence—without the benefit of a decent letterhead. When there is a colorful banner, it is often the only feature that is attractive about the entire package.

This is where layout enters the picture. When you achieve a balance between text and illustration, you get a better result.

Often there is a temptation to use larger illustrations in smaller quantity. Although this achieves some balance, a more attractive alternative is found by decreasing the size of illustrations and increasing their quantity. This offers the benefit of breaking up large blocks of print into smaller intellectual bites.

Effective layout involves knowing what is visually appealing in a printed product. Illustrations placed near applicable text within an article, give the reader information along with an improvement in appearance. That's a solid benefit.

Another common feature of professional newsletters is a one-column design. You don't find that often in a more consumer-oriented publication. Why is a professional audience any different? They're people (consumers) too.

There's a limit to the number of columns that can be made on an 8½ by 11 inch sheet, but two columns can be easily accommodated. If the newsletter format size is wider than 8½ inches, you can easily consider three columns. The standard typewriter sheet size is the most popular, however, because it can be folded and inserted into a standard size 10 business envelope for mailing. This eliminates the need to put a mailing label directly on the publication itself.

Another helpful technique is to use special box design areas. These areas can be all text, but they still serve the same function as an illustration. The box design adds visual variety to the page that keeps a reader's attention.

You can also minimize a boring text appearance by varying the size of paragraphs within your newsletter articles. As you've probably noted in reading this book, there is an almost constant changing of paragraph sizes throughout the text. This gives some variety and is necessary to avoid reader fatigue.

Whenever possible, avoid large blocks of text that lack variety. You won't be winning any friends if you write a one-paragraph article—and it covers an entire page. If you don't have illustrations (or the capability to print them), you can, at minimum, put in some lines or asterisks to note important points along the way and to lighten the appearance. This is possible, even if you've dug up an antique mimeograph system and pressed it into service. There is no legitimate excuse for boredom in a newsletter presentation.

FINAL STEPS BEFORE PRINTING

After you've gathered your articles and illustrations and designed your general layout, your last assignment is to check for errors. Even if you're very careful, errors have a way of slipping into a printed product. Total elimination of errors with a complex product such as a newsletter is almost impossible. Humans aren't perfect, but you can keep errors to an absolute minimum.

Before you send your work to the printer, check out typographical errors, spelling mistakes, and common errors in punctuation. Don't place commas where periods belong. If a word doesn't look right to you, check it. Keep a dictionary handy just in case you need it.

Also, be sure to double-check your layout. Most printers offer page proofs (a sample of completed work) before doing a larger run on the presses. This is the time to pick up errors that the printer has made, but it is *not* the time to redo everything because you're not satisfied with your own work. Changing your layout now dramatically escalates costs.

If you use a pasteup technique (actually pasting illustrations to a layout sheet), be certain that the illustrations are securely in place. If they come loose, the printer may not know where they belong, switch their locations, and inadvertently create a fiasco in the final production process. This can be avoided with a little caution.

Many printers, as part of their total package, offer a detailed layout service. If you have little or no experience in this area, let the professionals handle this part of the job, at least initially. After you become more acquainted with the layout process, you may want to exercise greater creative control over the final product by, at minimum, setting up a sheet of directions for the printer to follow in doing the final layout. This comes as you gain experience.

Most consultants have busy schedules, so delegating this responsibility to the printer makes sound fiscal sense. The most important thing is to keep your position as final arbiter over quality control. You're paying the bill and you deserve the best product that your money is purchasing.

SELECTING THE RIGHT PRINTER

Most businesspeople view printers in an adjunct function only. When contact is limited to acquisition of letterheads, envelopes, and business forms, this may be true, but this changes when discussion turns to the production of a newsletter, especially if it is to be a regularly published periodical.

Selecting the right printer becomes a critical consideration. Although quality is of prime importance, you must also be able to work in a congenial fashion with the printer's staff. Continuous acrimony removes all pleasantness from the process and impedes your creativity and productivity. Who wants to get a newsletter issue completed if the next step is that unpleasant?

Finding a printer who is located close to your business is an important consideration. This cuts down the amount of lead time required to get each issue out to your prospective readers.

When you have narrowed down your field of candidates, your next step is to check the quality of the printer's completed product. Be a stern critic, although you don't have to tell the printer about it. Look for errors in printing, problems in print quality, and so on. Ask yourself one important question: If the sample belonged to you, would you be satisfied with the final result?

Your final consideration is printer's costs. You can expect to pay for several levels of service in the total process.

The first point of comparison is in the setup charge to have the type set for your newsletter. Even if the printing is done by photo-offset, eliminating the actual typesetting process, you still have a setup charge. For photo-offset printers, the charge is for making your layout camera ready.

"Camera ready" is a term used to define copy that needs no alteration and is of sufficient clarity and sharpness to be photographed easily. The photograph replaces the press plate in the printing process.

After this setup charge, there is a per copy cost for the actual printing. You can really cut your per copy costs if you have a larger circulation. Most printers have a minimum quantity that they will print. It is better to go at least one step up from this minimum on the quantity price scale. This alone can cut your per copy printing cost by as much as 30 percent. This is in addition to spreading your setup costs over a larger number of copies. Setup costs remain the same regardless of how many—or how few—copies you order.

Although costs are an important consideration, don't be too stingy with your production. The subscription fees of professional newsletters are high. Many charge between $150 and $200 for a subscription of 12 monthly issues. If your readers are paying that much, they have a right to expect quality, even in production.

If your newsletter is going to be distributed free, the cost factor is much more important. But, if what you have to say is important (and paid for) when it's delivered personally, why shouldn't the recipient pay for it in print?

If all factors are equal between two printers, choose the one who offers you the most comfortable working relationship. This can be a very important asset to you, especially if you expect to have reasonable longevity for your publication.

PAGE PROOF REVIEW

When you receive the page proofs for your newsletter issue, you're almost done with the publishing process. Simply check for basic errors. Don't try to rewrite now. Delays and cost overruns are common when neophyte newsletter publishers get overzealous at this point.

If you do find apparent errors in the page proof, compare the page proof with the copy that you submitted to the printer. When you've done your preliminary work thoroughly, the error may have originated with the printer. Any mistakes that are made by the printer can be corrected with no additional costs to you. That is their responsibility in providing this printing service to you.

When errors are the printer's fault, you can usually ask for a second page proof at no additional cost. If errors happen in the early stage of your working relationship, you may want to ask for this service, even with the delay involved, simply to be sure that the corrections have been made.

As your working relationship progresses, you will probably dispense with a second page proof. Most printers are sufficiently good at their work to avoid repetition of the same error in a follow-up effort. Corrections, provided they don't cause shifts in page content, won't cause major disruptions in the production schedule. Your initial experiences help you to accurately assess production times and make the necessary allowances for corrections.

Whenever possible, avoid compromising quality because of time considerations. This, if repeated too frequently, reflects badly on your operations and your image, and erodes the profitability and impact of *any* newsletter operation you pursue.

RECEIVING THE COMPLETED PRODUCT

The big day has finally arrived. Your first issue is hot off the presses. They have arrived in your office. What's next?

After indulging in self-congratulations, you should check this final product one last time. Be certain that you have the quantity that you ordered, the paper stock that you ordered, and so on. Generally there won't be a problem, but it doesn't hurt to check.

When that's completed, place the copies in a convenient location to prepare for distribution. It's important to set aside a small area in your office for this function. This eliminates inefficiencies that can result if you plan to make newsletter distribution a regularly scheduled part of your operations.

DISTRIBUTION

The most common method of newsletter distribution is a subscription list. For cost reasons, it is an important consideration. You don't want to have a press overrun, resulting in copies that have no destination.

An important element in the distribution process is how your initial marketing effort for the newsletter was conducted. If it was treated as a single product, your schedules must be kept fairly rigid to keep customers satisfied.

One technique that is used effectively to keep a newsletter operation from becoming burdensome is to tie this product to another. One way is to make the newsletter a part of a total package. Small "associations" can be formed for your clients. Clients pay a membership fee that covers the newsletter and other support services you offer.

This is totally ethical and legal, securing clients for a regular program of help and advice from your consulting practice. The newsletter becomes a part of the total package.

The advantage of this technique is that a newsletter, if not promised on a precise and set schedule, can be a few days late without having your office phone lines jammed by irate subscribers. Using this technique gets you away from a rigid monthly publication schedule, maybe even reducing the schedule to bimonthly or quarterly without negative public relations repercussions.

You should not, however, use this technique as a cover for irresponsible management practices. This puts you at a serious competitive disadvantage if another consultant begins to court the same market.

CLOSING THOUGHTS

Throughout this chapter, we focused on the procedural aspects of publishing a newsletter. One question remains. What's in it for you?

The answer is a considerable amount of cash money for your consulting business if you manage the operation properly. Consider the fact that an annual subscription for a professional newsletter runs between $150 and

$200 per year—and sometimes more. You won't need a large newsletter operation to add substantially to your consulting practice income.

One Midwestern consultant started out modestly with a circulation of 450 subscribers. It quickly grew to a 2,000-copy monthly output. This newsletter, priced at $175 per year is earning about $350,000 annually for this consultant. That's not chicken feed.

There are numerous examples that can be cited of successful newsletter operations, some more modest than others, that have added substantially to consulting income. The important thing is to conduct the operation properly to be profitable. The information in this chapter helps you to start publishing a newsletter that will be both an income booster and an image builder for your consulting practice.

– CHAPTER –
11

SPEECHES: KEY TO EFFECTIVE PUBLIC RELATIONS

Maintaining a high public profile is one of the most important keys to achieving a solid prestige image. In previous chapters, we looked at numerous methods of image building, but the main shortcoming of most of these ideas is that they cost *you* money.

This is one of the great advantages of using the speech delivery forum to accomplish important public relations objectives. You don't have to pay for the privilege of getting your message to interested listeners. They pay you to advertise before them.

I should, at this point, qualify the word advertise. You are placing your knowledge and communication skills on public display. They, when shown off effectively, speak favorably for you on their own merits.

In this chapter, we take a closer look at the speech forum, why consultants are wise to accept speaking engagements, speech secrets of top consultants, simple rules for effective speech writing, how to grab audience attention right away, connecting the opening with the middle of the speech, pulling together the loose ends for an effective speech closing, and special secrets of delivery that hold audience attention effectively. Putting all these elements together is the key to making a lasting impression on an audience. We learn in this chapter how it's done.

WHY CONSULTANTS ACCEPT SPEAKING ENGAGEMENTS

Successful consultants are in heavy demand for speeches before business and academic groups. If you're a successful consultant and a good public speaker, you may find yourself with so many demands for speaking engagements that you'll have to turn many of them away.

One of the reasons why top consultants don't turn down the best opportunities is because every speech plants important seeds of influence that germinate in the future. One consultant addressed a professional convention—and received over a half dozen new clients from *one* speech. This brought in thousands of dollars in new business, in addition to the top dollar fee that he received for delivering the speech.

Depending on the budget of the group or event, speaking fees can range from several hundred dollars to several thousand dollars (sometimes even more). Some well-known speakers easily generate annual incomes of six figures just from speaking and lecture fees. Few of us can afford to ignore that kind of money.

The benefits of a speech aren't limited to the immediate audience listening to you, however. Top consultants realize that the impact extends outward from the colleagues among their listeners through word-of-mouth advertising. Comments like, "You should have heard So-and-So last night. He was pretty good" are solid contributions to the speaker's publicity efforts.

An opportunity to address an important event also brings publicity through newspaper coverage—and possibly radio and television. These bonuses can spread the benefits over hundreds of miles beyond the confines of the original audience.

A single speech, favorably reviewed, can generate several additional speaking opportunities. There's almost a pyramid effect to the entire process. One marketing and personnel motivation consultant I know spends almost as much time on the lecture and speaking circuit as she spends in active consulting. Her popular speaking style keeps her in almost constant demand. She said that she turns down almost half of the requests made—or she'd be a full-time speaker and not an active one-on-one consultant at all. Her several cars and several homes, all well-appointed, are a good indicator, though, that she isn't suffering a financial sacrifice from her speaking efforts.

SPEECH SECRETS OF TOP CONSULTANTS

One of the primary reasons why most of us aren't anxious to accept speaking opportunities is that we aren't psychologically prepared to face a group of people who are physically in front of us. Having a few hundred eyes staring at us as we begin speaking is not a comfortable feeling.

When you're called upon to deliver a speech, you face the pressure to say something "significant." Looking out into an audience, you can sense their expectation. They've come to hear you say something important, to learn from you, and to "get their money's worth" from this invitation extended to you.

One of the primary secrets of the top speakers is to "turn the tables" on their audience. They use some mechanism early in their speeches to defuse the air of tension, get their audiences into a relaxed frame of mind, and make them even more receptive to their message. A favorite technique is the sparing use of humor.

One speaker, facing an audience of over one thousand, received a very glowing introduction from the master of ceremonies. After the customary applause, the speaker saw this expectancy in his audience. He began his speech with the following statement:

I'm the fellow who was just so glowingly introduced. Who gave our emcee that shot of truth serum?

That opening comment brought a few moments of laughter from the audience and set the stage to put his audience into an empathetic mood. The speaker launched into his message—and he was very relaxed and animated until the conclusion of his presentation.

Another secret of top speakers is: Never operate with a fixed microphone. You don't want to spend the entire speech glued to a podium. By detaching the microphone from its stand, the speaker can move around a little bit (within the limitations of the cord, if a cordless remote isn't being used). This gives the speaker the illusion of being part of the group, not the center of attention. The speaker is still the center of attention, but, in moving around a little, he or she won't feel the psychological pressure that this attention can create.

Some successful speakers go, with microphone in hand, right out into the audience. This allows the speaker to more effectively use the one-on-one, rather than group, focus for speech delivery. This technique further defuses the tension of speaking before a group.

The best speeches are those that are conversational in tone. This won't happen if the speaker relies strictly on verbatim reading of the presentation, which results in a flat monotone that ends up boring the audience to sleep. This is the one pitfall that top speakers avoid.

Instead of reading from a verbatim text, the best speakers have a general outline and a thorough command of the information to be presented. This is the same principle that I used to write this book. This entire section is being written from a single line in an outline that reads "top consultants' secrets for effective use of the forum." This serves to remind me that this information belongs at this location in this chapter.

Everything else here is the result of extemporaneous flow, coupled with a general idea of how much space should be devoted to this subject in the book. With experience, you can develop this same ability in delivering speeches. You can deliver an effective speech with the entire contents on a single 3 by 5 inch index card, maybe two or three of them at most.

Some top speakers go into a speech with a text fully prepared, but they are also sensitive to the moods of their audience. Their best secret is that they aren't afraid to depart from prepared text, delivering totally off-the-cuff remarks when they seem appropriate. This reactive ability, also a result of experience, can turn an average speech into a memorable event.

SIMPLE RULES FOR EFFECTIVE SPEECH WRITING

In Chapter 6 we discussed at length the importance of writing in the same style as we speak. This, to a degree, is one of the most common sources of difficulty in preparing speeches. Writing that appears to be getting your message across may not be attention-getting enough when it is delivered as a speech to an audience.

Most of us have heard that old speechwriter's axiom: "Tell 'em what you're going to tell 'em, tell 'em, then tell 'em what you told 'em." If you read some of the chapters in this book in their entirety, you probably recognize the strong influence of this statement in the design of the chapters. Almost all of the chapters in this book are speeches in writing.

Although this old axiom is a useful guide for you in writing speeches, it is an oversimplification because the summary lead-in isn't the *only* way to write a speech. It is one of the most effective ways to do it, but it isn't always the best way.

Let's quickly put together a thumbnail sketch of the points you'll need to observe in preparing a speech, divided into the natural sections of a speech: the opening, the middle, and the closing.

The Opening

- Present a single dominant theme.
- Establish two or more elements to connect this theme.
- Establish a final objective.

The Middle

- Focus on each connecting element individually for closer review.
- Tie in important facts to illustrate your viewpoint.
- Establish the relationship between the individual elements in listeners' minds.

The Closing

- Relate the individual elements with the final objective.
- Summarize the main points.
- End your speech.

These rules provide a general framework to write any type of speech. You may not be able to expound on your theme if you have only 10 minutes to deliver your speech. In a short speech you have to condense your remarks.

When you are under a time constraint, your primary sacrifice is the number of connecting elements that you can introduce and develop. That's why speeches must have a sharply defined content to be successful. The most common pitfall, which leads to disaster, is to attempt to cover too much in a short speech. You end up teasing an audience with the promise of more information—and disappointing them with a lack of substance.

For very short speeches, state your theme and develop one connecting element to satisfy your audience. No one, not even the superfast talker on those television commercials, can stuff the history of Europe into a 10- or 15-minute speech. An interesting aspect of a subject, especially a little-known one, makes an excellent basis for a speech. Never count on more than 30 minutes (an average speech). Forty-five minutes or more is a bonus length allocation.

These guidelines provide a supporting structure for a speech. The next step is to begin writing an attention-grabbing opening.

WRITING THE ATTENTION-GRABBING OPENING

Grabbing the attention of an audience of more than two people is one of the most difficult assignments you can face. Although you assume that you have a receptive audience, particularly if the group has requested (and possibly paid for) your presence, you can't automatically assume you have the license to bore the audience to death. This is one reason why almost every speaker uses a prepared text for at least the opening remarks.

A speaker generally has between one and two minutes of polite attention from an audience. After that, the speech has to make it on its own merit. To keep audience attention you have to grab more than polite attentiveness in the first minute or two.

The most effective speech opening is telling the most interesting or exciting aspect of your subject. For the sake of discussion, let's assume that you're a consultant for fund-raising functions. You have been contacted by a civic organization to deliver a keynote speech in your community to get a fund-raising project rolling. The regional news media will be present to cover the event. You want to get the job done—and make your speech as memorable as possible. How do you get their attention? Here's a sample idea.

> *According to a designer's estimate, the new auditorium being planned for this community will cost about $750,000. Tonight, I'll show you how, in six short weeks, you'll have that money in hand and ready to go.*

In two sentences, and approximately 20 seconds of delivery time, the speaker has set the stage for a speech on how $750,000 will be raised in a six-week period and on the reason for raising the money. Two sentences emphasizing the audience's obvious interest at the start is the key to getting past the "polite" attention period.

The primary problem in speech openings, common to far too many speakers, is a tendency to ramble. The opening has to define the scope of your subject, even if you don't spell out each element. Developing expectancy in your audience is the key to keeping their attention. Do this immediately. Don't tell them about the time you and the emcee got tipsy celebrating an early career success. Save anecdotes for later in the speech, when you're developing a point. That's where they belong, not in your opening.

Be direct with your statements. Short sentences pack considerable punch. They jab at the listener early. Later in the speech, you have the luxury to vary your approach, but, initially, you have to get their attention.

A preacher that I know gave some very pithy advice for speakers, regardless of their subject. Speaking of his parishioners, he said, "I can't give them heaven—if I don't give them a little hell first." This statement illustrates the concept that audience attention is best grasped when you give them what they least expect.

This preacher did *not,* however, imply that you should alienate an audience emotionally to get their attention. Instead, using an unexpected twist goes a long way toward your objective. The firm opening is the verbal equivalent of grabbing someone by the lapel. Sometime it takes that to get an audience's attention.

Give your listeners some very good reasons to be interested in what you're about to tell them. Sometimes, especially for more sophisticated audiences, this can be more important in the opening than summarizing the scope of your subject. *At minimum,* you should have the situation clearly spelled out by the time you've reached your tenth sentence. That surely can be done. In our short example, the speech was well on its way in only *two* sentences. Set the stage—and then move directly into the middle of your speech.

Examples of Good and Bad Openings

By now you know that the important point to remember in speech openings is to get specific early. Avoiding the ambiguous is your primary objective. Here are some examples, both bad and good, to illustrate this principle.

Bad Opening

> *Many of us have no specific goals in attaining financial independence for ourselves and our families. We go about this in an unorganized*

fashion—and with few good results to show for our efforts. This breeds only frustration and discouragement, the first steps to failure. And failure brings no good results for anyone involved.

Good Opening

Are you ready, tonight, to take the first steps to making your dreams come true? Are you tired of punching someone else's time clock—and never being closer to your dreams with any of your paychecks?

Tonight, for the first time, I'll show you a plan to liberate you from the time clock prison forever—and lead to making every dream you ever had come true.

What's the difference between these two openings? The bad opening merely talks about the problem. The audience is more interested in hearing about solutions, not in a recitation of facts they already know.

By contrast, the good opening uses imagery that appeals to the audience. They want to hear about how to get out of their problems and predicaments. Talk about problems later on. But first grab their attention—and challenge them—with a forceful opening.

In Chapter 6, we reviewed the idea that written and verbal communication really weren't much different from each other, except for the form in which they were delivered. This same idea pertains to speeches. Begin your speeches in the same way that you begin an article designed to grab and hold a reader's attention. The concepts are very similar—and yield similar results in both delivery formats.

CONNECTING SECRETS FOR THE MIDDLE PRESENTATION

Some speakers can write and deliver an excellent speech opening, but they run into difficulties when they begin to develop the speech.

The most prevalent problem is a failure to connect segments together into a natural flow. With practice, anyone can develop this ability.

To show you how this idea works, examine the first paragraph of this section. In the two preceding sections, we discussed speech openings that work—and how they work. The first sentence in this section connects this material to the preceding material, offering some sense of continuity to the discussion.

Your objective in beginning to talk about the first aspect of your subject is to connect it to your theme that you emphasized in your opening. Then, build your presentation of one aspect of your subject.

This method helps you to avoid a disconnection in your presentation that jars the audience out of its attentiveness. Once you have grabbed your audience's attention, you don't want them to start thinking of things other than your words. Maintaining a smooth flow, without intellectual detours in your delivery, assures audience attention and gets your message across.

CONSTRUCTING THE MIDDLE OF THE SPEECH

If you have done a good job of opening your speech, you're really more than half way home. You have laid the foundation successfully for the middle of your speech. Now you have to develop the ideas you presented.

The most common fault in delivering the middle of a speech is the failure to logically progress in laying out information. If you're traveling from New York to Los Angeles, you can't start your trip in Chicago. To be successful, a speaker must take his or her listener from the intellectual starting point of the topic and build on it logically.

The construction of this chapter is an example of logical progression. It would have made no sense to put this section at the beginning of the chapter. You don't write and deliver the middle of your speech until you've opened it. The same thing is true about the topics of your speech.

At the beginning of this chapter, as you would do in a speech, I laid the foundation for the rest of the chapter. Since this chapter is written as though I am delivering a speech to you, I used only the sketchiest of notes for the presentation. The total outline for the chapter covers one-half page (double-spaced). The location of each subsection (topic), in relation to the total chapter, was specified. Very little else was included in the outline.

This same approach benefits your writing of a speech. To illustrate, the outline for this chapter (to this point) reads as follows:

Why consultants accept speaking engagements—top consultants' secrets for effective use of the forum—simple rules for effective speech writing—the attention-grabbing opening—example of good and bad openings—connecting secrets for the middle of the presentation—how to construct an effective middle speech.

I wrote this outline well before I started writing the chapter. The main function of this outline is to remind me of the things that I want to tell you. It has no other objective.

Formulating a brief outline helps you to check whether you have a beginning, middle, and end to your subject matter, have logical progression in your presentation, and are staying on target. This is all accomplished before you actually write a single word of your speech.

A good speech should be constructed like a quality garment. The seams should not be visible. With a brief outline you avoid losing the momentum of a bold opening and carry your speech forward logically and smoothly.

EXAMPLES OF APPROACHES FOR THE MIDDLE OF A SPEECH

As mentioned a moment ago, the approach to the middle of a speech is simply a matter of connecting your first topic to the main theme of the speech. Suppose that you were the design consultant for a new bridge in your area. Various groups want you to deliver a speech on how you made the bridge a reality.

You sit down to write the speech. You compose an excellent opening to your speech. Then you launch into your topic like this:

Bad Approach

> *The trickiest part of the project was the insertion of the center span of the bridge. I remember the numerous design challenges involved in making sure that the final product would fit.*

What's wrong with this approach? You're taking your listeners to the end of the process—before you told them how you began. This has one of two results: (1) not giving a clear picture of the process involved, or (2) risking repetition later in the speech. Avoiding this problem is simple.

Better Approach

> *The process of making this bridge a reality began with many hours of work that the general public never saw. The design process for the bridge began with the proper foundation design beneath the water's surface. Various ideas were reviewed—and discarded—until the right specifications were brought together. Here's how we reached our final choice on this important point. We began with . . .*

In this speech opening, you briefly sketched your subject area and talked about how good the final product was. Now you take the listener, by logical progression, into the way it was planned. That's what they came to hear. Begin at the beginning. That's the best place to start any journey.

Each subsequent topic then logically interlocks with the theme you present at the beginning. Jumping back and forth in a subject is *not* recommended. The audience ends up confused and, in some cases, the speaker joins them in that unfortunate intellectual state.

A speaker's confusion may become particularly profound if he or she is operating only from basic notes, not a prepared text. If the speaker jumps forward, he or she may not remember where the jump was from! This unfortunate person won't make a great impression on the audience later as he or she stares at them with a blank expression, not really sure where the presentation is going.

When you deliver a speech, don't use only notes to get your ideas across. I have witnessed several embarrassing fiascos that could have been avoided if this rule had been observed. If you use a brief outline to write the complete text of your speech, your preceding statement automatically suggests to you what comes next. With a thorough knowledge of your subject, you may not even need to refer to your notes after you complete the opening to your speech.

PULLING TOGETHER THE LOOSE ENDS

Although you may be able to start your speech relatively easy, the same may not hold true for reaching a conclusion. Many speakers, particularly neophytes, suddenly find themselves in the same predicament as a beginning tightrope walker. The aerialist is in the middle of the act—and wants to get off without losing it all.

Finishing each topic and drawing the speech to its conclusion is an art. One of the best ways to tie loose ends together is to connect them to your theme. Show your listener how the last topic relates to your theme, developing the scope of your subject. Also, show how the theme contributed to the objective you set before your audience in the opening of your speech.

Earlier in this chapter, we talked about the old speechwriter's advice. This is the point at which you're going to "tell 'em what you told 'em." Just as in a guided tour, you bring your audience back to the point of embarkation. They leave satisfied, feeling that they've seen the full picture and received all the information they needed to fully appreciate the subject.

WRITING THE EFFECTIVE SPEECH ENDING

Assuming that you've followed this process to this point, you're ready (as the tightrope walker was) to get yourself out of your situation as gracefully

164 Speeches: Key to Effective Public Relations

as possible. You have successfully brought your audience through all the elements of your speech, but you really aren't sure how to cap things off.

This is one of the best places to use the illustrative or humorous anecdote to make your message remembered in the listener's mind. An excellent example of this idea was one speech that I heard at an agricultural seminar. The speech was on the use of insecticides and was delivered by a state agricultural agent. He opened his speech, went through his topics, summarized his points, and then concluded with the following:

> *Several years ago, I gave a similar speech to a group much like you. At the end of that speech, I went out into the audience and sat down. A farmer there leaned over and said, "Your speech kinda reminded me of spraying insecticide." I asked him why. He said, "I knew how useful it was. But, boy was I glad when it was over." I hope you'll find these ideas just as useful as that farmer did—and be just as glad. We're done with the spraying again.*

This short example shows how a speech can be brought to a conclusion that clearly tells the audience that it's over—without putting an obvious "The End" tag on it. This speaker drew a chuckle from his audience with the anecdote, connected it with the main theme of this speech, and smoothly made his exit with a summarization that emphasized the importance of his message to the audience.

This is the difference between a successful speech conclusion—and one that leaves the audience in limbo. Observing this rule for conclusions, and applying it regularly, helps you to deliver better speeches.

VOICE ANIMATION SECRETS IN EFFECTIVE DELIVERY

Once your speech is written, the next step is getting it delivered properly. One of the deadliest sins for any speaker is the lack of voice animation. If your speech reaches listeners' ears as a monotone drone, you may instill terminal boredom on their senses. They won't be listening—and might even courteously fall asleep, rather than leave the room.

An important point to remember is that variables in speech volume and pitch can do a lot to emphasize your important points. As you vary your tone of voice, you increase listener involvement in the speech. Your audience becomes emotionally wrapped up in the message being delivered.

This is a serious problem when you deliver your speech from verbatim text. The speech easily falls into a monotone. As your vocal expression declines, so does audience interest.

One favorite trick that some speakers use successfully is to prepare their text with built-in notes on what to emphasize. They do this by varying the way in which the text is typed. The most common method is to capitalize all letters in the words or phrases that the speaker wants to emphasize vocally. Here's an example of the idea.

Text with Emphasis Notes

> *There is NO question that the RESULT of this procedure WILL be favorable. You have CLEARLY DEFINED choices to make in this situation. Your DESTINY is in YOUR hands.*

Read this sample aloud to see how this technique helps to eliminate lack of variety in your tone of voice. You can hear for yourself that there isn't anything flat about the delivery with this technique. You can maintain the confidence enhancing benefit of a totally written speech while eliminating the danger of sounding monotonous.

Preparing the text of your speech in this way has another benefit. In choosing which words to capitalize, you are also mentally practicing its delivery before an audience. That practice gives you an edge in confidence when the moment arrives to deliver your speech before a live audience.

This confidence is readily heard in the speech mannerisms and clarity of delivery. The speaker who lacks confidence has a low voice and an uncertainty in delivery that can't escape notice. In extreme cases, this affects the way in which the audience perceives the credibility of the message.

An excellent way to appreciate vocal variety is to listen to taped speeches of speakers who interest you. With the tapes, you won't be concerned with the body language that they use (our next topic to develop). You can concentrate only on how they vocally emphasize their important points. You'll quickly discover that these variations in voice pitch and volume have the same emotional impact as a physical movement of the speaker.

BODY LANGUAGE AND YOUR MESSAGE

We just discussed the use of vocal inflection as the primary way to give emphasis to your message. This, however, is only half the basic arsenal for the effective speaker. The second half is the use of gestures—or body language.

One of the best ways for a speaker to portray a total lack of confidence is to stand at a podium, holding it like the last hope for a drowning person. The total lack of physical animation before a live audience is a sure way to lose them.

Earlier in this chapter, we briefly discussed some of the techniques used by top speakers. Many of their techniques concern body langauge in speech delivery. Effective body language further wraps the emotional net around your audience.

Successful politicians are adept at using body language in public speaking. Only one man in over 25 years was elected President of the United States without this essential skill. This same principle of body animation can be seen on more regional levels. Can you ever recall a totally unanimated candidate being elected to public office? If it happened, chances are good that the opposition was tainted by political or criminal scandal.

Study successful public speakers. Notice how they use hand gestures and general body movements to accentuate the use of voice inflections for emphasis. Some of the most common gestures are slashing hand movements, pointed index fingers, and wide sweeps of the arms. Richard Nixon, almost single-handedly, made the "V" sign for victory famous.

Developing effective body language technique involves expressing genuine emotion in your speech delivery. If you don't add some emotion, the body language that you project appears artificial. That can be worse than none at all.

One of the best ways to practice this technique is to do it in front of a mirror. Check to see if your movements are natural and fit in with the rest of your delivery style. Do you feel comfortable speaking with the gestures you're adopting?

Some previously unanimated speakers find, to their surprise, that the addition of body movements helps to calm them down in their speech delivery. Most of us feel a rush of adrenalin when we deliver speeches. This comes from natural tension. Body movements help to put this excess energy to good use.

The important thing to remember is that effective body language is *not* the result of nervous agitation. It must be positive and, ideally, correlated with the message you're delivering.

You can make effective use of body language with visual aids as an adjunct to your speeches. This gives you an opportunity to call your audience's attention to the specifics of your visual display by pointing to the display, walking over to it, or making some other gesture in presenting it.

Here's an example of a speech; the suggested body language gestures are italicized and inserted in parentheses.

Body Language Inserts

> There is no reason why you (*point finger toward audience*) can't get good results using these methods. You can see the results by looking at this chart (*point to chart*).

The first line shows results using the old method. This second line (*point to and touch line with your finger*) shows how much better the results are when methods are revised.

Try to visualize this speaker, standing next to the chart, delivering this message (with body language) as indicated. Next, visualize the same words being delivered with a total lack of animation. The speaker just stands there with his hands in his pockets. Which speaker makes a better impression? No one would choose the second speaker.

Why is this choice obvious? The more animated speaker shows a belief in the words being spoken. This speaker also is being doubly certain that we specifically understand which results correlate with each method.

Study your speeches for opportunities to use body language comfortably. Practice using it, even in routine conversations. You may be startled at the increased attention you receive from the people around you.

GEARING UP FOR YOUR TARGET AUDIENCE

Immediately before delivering a speech, many speakers prefer to remain totally out of view. They feel uneasy about their speaking assignment and want to spend time preparing for it privately. Although this idea has some merit, there are distinct disadvantages that can easily work against the speaker when he or she reaches the podium.

If you are an astute observer of human nature, you can benefit from mingling with the audience before your speech. You can assess the mood of your audience. Do they seem relaxed? Or, by contrast, do they seem to have an air of expectancy or tension?

Is the audience's mood conducive to your speech? Will a *straight delivery work well?* Or will more *humor in your speech work better?*

You will also gain audience empathy if you socialize with them before your speech. They will see you as a fellow human being, not just a "star attraction" for the functions that they're attending. This is a tremendous asset in making everyone, you included, feel at ease when you start your speech. You will be talking to "friends," not just a group of nameless faces.

Study facial reactions in the audience. You may spot several people who are positive in their responses to your message. As you speak, focus on their faces. They give you positive reinforcement and improve your level of confidence with each passing word. Few audiences are so totally hostile that you can't find at least one friendly face in the group.

Select these visual targets from various areas of your audience. This allows you to look at almost everyone during the speech and no one in the audience will feel ignored.

As a final note, periodically check the back rows of your audience. In larger facilities, particularly if acoustics aren't the best, your voice won't carry that far back. If you seem to be losing audience attention, speak more loudly on occasion to be certain that they hear you. This keeps their attention on your words and prevents them from being a distracting influence.

CLOSING THOUGHTS

Throughout this chapter, the primary emphasis has been to give you information to write and deliver an effective speech, regardless of the occasion. Although these techniques are important, there is one intangible that simply can't be taught—confidence.

The most important point to remember about audiences is that they consist of people very much like you. They put their pants on one leg at a time—just like everyone else. Don't be intimidated by their presence—unless they're carrying guns and look *very* angry.

Even a potentially hostile audience can be converted to your corner, using wit and humor. Your main objective is to remain confident and calm, even in an adverse situation. Hecklers quickly disperse when they realize that they can't rattle you. That's their primary objective. Don't give them the satisfaction.

Shortly after my second book was published in 1983, I was asked to speak to an informal study group of university students. During the course of my talk, one student openly challenged me, attempting to discredit me. He pointedly asked me what my qualifications were. My response: "The University of Hard Knocks! Next question." The humor defused this heckler—and made fellow students into my allies.

You can attain success with audiences, if you project confidence. They respect your message better—and you gain in prestige. The materials in this chapter help you to achieve these objectives.

CHAPTER

12

SEMINAR POWER: PRESTIGE BUILDER FOR A CONSULTING BUSINESS

One of the essential features of the multiple client marketing program for consultants is the use of the seminar. Spending your time in an auditorium packed with paying clients is more profitable than dealing with individual clients.

Additionally, the seminar promotion process creates a "larger than life" appearance for the seminar headliner. This situation is a great advantage for a consultant, provided that he or she isn't afflicted with excessive modesty. A good dose of self-confidence usually complements the promotional effort.

In this chapter, we take a closer look at seminar organization, promotion, and your later capitalization on the seminar process. Specifically, we examine how seminars build professional image, define seminar markets, and learn to set the parameters for an individual seminar.

Additionally, we review the seminar design process, the solving of common logistical problems, promoting the seminar, and conducting seminar operations. In this process, I show you how to develop a personal following through seminars, how to use personal projection, how to increase effectiveness through flexibility, and how to bring the package to a successful conclusion. This includes the very important seminar follow-up process.

Most consultants find conducting seminars a rewarding experience, provided that they are done correctly. This chapter shows you how to make seminars part of your consulting operations.

SEMINARS AS IMAGE BUILDERS

Few opportunities for self-promotion are more effective than conducting seminars. All well-known consultants with a reputation outside their home area have become known through one of two means: seminars or book publication.

Why are seminars so serviceable as builders of a prestige image? A seminar's package has two distinct promotional sides. Although the seminar's contents are an important consideration to the consumer, an equally important consideration is the person or persons conducting the seminar.

When you conduct a seminar, you are placing yourself in the spotlight. You become part consultant and part showman. The showmanship is what serves to build your public image.

One of the consummate showmen, P. T. Barnum, showed the essentials of piquing human curiosity. Although no one would advocate turning a seminar into a three-ring circus, the promotional principles that this master used show how a relatively unknown promoter became synonymous with an entire sector of the entertainment industry.

Additionally, seminar promotion is generally conducted for a specific target market. You won't be simply advertising in your local newspaper. You will be promoting directly to target customers over a wider area, often on a regional basis covering several states. That alone has a multiplying effect on promotional impact.

A concluding consideration is that seminars have a certain psychological appeal that makes their headliners memorable. In setting yourself up as a seminar headliner, you make a specific statement about your personal qualifications and your knowledge. You are moving yourself away from the pack, converting yourself into a VIP within a professional or business group. This is readily recognized, and accepted, by recipients of your seminar's promotional material.

The key is to balance visible benefits of the seminar with self-aggrandizement. As long as you blend things together well between the two, no one will criticize you for blowing your own horn a bit loudly. Surprisingly, most seminar participants respond favorably to this display of self-confidence, making them more likely to believe in you and the information that you offer them.

DEFINING A SEMINAR'S MARKET

During the routine course of consulting efforts, most of us have had the opportunity to discover numerous potential ideas on which seminars could be based. The key factor in capitalizing on them is in recognizing their value.

An important consideration to the marketability of a seminar idea lies in how common the problem is to your target market. This determines how large your potential seminar market will be.

As an example, if you promote a seminar on how to improve sales for automatic washing machines, you limit yourself to those currently selling, or those wishing to become involved in sales of, these units. Attendance on a regional basis would be limited.

Whenever possible, try to avoid placing artificial limitations on your seminar's market. Unless your professional qualifications and experience are very narrowly defined, look to the idea of cutting across the boundaries of a number of business and/or professional groups. This has an expansive effect on a seminar's market and potential profits.

No two seminars attract an identical audience. Examine each idea carefully. If they are too narrowly defined, you will restrict results. Correcting this weakness often involves modifying the idea to expand its appeal and its marketing base.

As an example, one medical practice management consultant began with a seminar idea that was strictly defined to the practice requirements of orthopedic specialists. Although this was a serviceable idea for a metropolitan market, offering this package to other marketing areas would not have been as profitable.

To compensate for this problem, the seminar was modified to include practice management problems that were common to other practitioners as well. This opened the market to physicians, surgeons, dentists, and chiropractors. It made the seminar package an overwhelming success.

The only caution here is to avoid becoming so general in approach that the seminar fails to satisfy anyone's needs. There is a critical balance to maintain to keep the seminar's marketing appeal high.

USING MARKET SURVEY RESULTS

One of the most common pitfalls in seminar development is to become too emotionally attached to a particular idea, with no marketing potential to back the idea. Sometimes we think that our idea is the greatest thing since sliced bread, only to be greeted by yawns of boredom from our market. That is a very unpleasant, and unprofitable, surprise.

Before too much time, effort, and money is invested in a particular concept, a practical approach is to conduct an informal market survey to see what problems are viewed as important. If you have an extensive list of current clients, you can sometimes do this through informal questions personally delivered.

Unfortunately, this is a relatively slow method for compiling this important data. A more practical method is to assemble a mailing list and to develop a list of common problems. Mail this list to respondents, asking them to rank the contents of the list in order of importance or to individually rate each problem from very important to not important at all.

When you've received your responses and tabulated results, you have a clear focus on which areas will spark seminar interest. You don't have to tell respondents that you're planning to conduct a seminar. Sometimes this has an effect on how they respond to your questions.

In this effort, list general categories, not specific problems. As an example, if you're a general business management consultant, list categories such as office management, employee relations, cost cutting procedures, and customer relations. This will give you direction for idea development.

Keeping your inquiries general rather than specific won't hinder your creativity in idea development. At this stage of the process, you're looking for a direction in which to aim your efforts—not a sharply defined target.

You don't have to survey the entire target market to get usable results. A hundred responses, provided they are from a representative cross-section of your market, gives you an accurate idea of problems common to your target market.

SETTING SEMINAR PARAMETERS

After you have a category listing of market interests, examine these categories for special problems needing solutions. If you can successfully identify a new problem or have an innovative set of solutions to an old problem, you have the basis for a very successful seminar.

The main consideration is the overall length of your seminar. As a practical matter, you can't cover a tremendous amount of material effectively in a very short time. A one-day seminar, covering possibly six hours of instruction, won't allow you to present as much as in a longer format.

You also have to consider the fatigue factor for both yourself and the seminar audience. This can diminish the effectiveness of your delivery and the attentiveness of your audience.

Rather than try to cover a wide area, restrict the parameter and offer more detail in a smaller area. Participants find this information more useful and it provides for better audience response. This will make the seminar process more satisfying for you as well.

If the subject matter is sufficiently complex, you should definitely consider expanding the seminar beyond a one-day format. Although this can pose some logistical problems in the organization process, additional time is preferable to cramming too much together. This makes information undigestible to your listeners.

As an example, one dental practice consultant offers a seminar on operative positioning and instrument transfer. The seminar is narrowed in focus to give seminar participants the opportunity to *practice* the procedures during the seminar—not just listen to someone preaching about them.

The opportunity for a hands-on experience makes a critical difference in whether seminar participants take their results home for effective use. In the final analysis, this is what determines whether participants view your seminars as good values for their dollars—and is the key to repeat business.

OUTLINE APPROACH TO SEMINAR DESIGN

Determining the feasibility of a seminar idea is the real test of whether you should proceed with complete plans. Although most of us view outline formulation with the same excitement as watching grass grow, it's a necessary step to avoid a major expenditure of money and time for an unworkable premise.

The outline, at this point, doesn't have to be detailed. You can simply put in general subject areas to be covered. For multi-day seminars, you might, at this point, indicate what will be covered on each day. But you won't have to go much further than that.

After you've completed this step, let the material settle for a day or two. This technique gives you an opportunity to gain some objectivity that you might not have lost in the excitement of testing your ideas.

When you've determined that this base is solid, you can fill in more detail beneath each individual subject category. This actually becomes a course plan for what will be taught to seminar participants.

The results of your survey serve adequately as information to promote your seminar. Further information helps you to keep your perspective and positive forward motion as you actually conduct the seminar.

Don't become too rigid about the format. Spontaneous participation can cause fewer subjects to be covered—but with much more detail offered in each area. You can build flexibility into the seminar by making a liberal allowance for discussion periods.

Seminar consultants who are too rigid in their scheduling practices overlook an excellent educational opportunity for themselves, not just their students. As these discussions develop, you may find new areas of interest for future seminars. Don't stifle the creative contribution that you receive from this volunteer resource.

As an important concluding note, remember to include a short break period every hour or two during the course of a seminar day. This helps to recharge your intellectual batteries to improve your effectiveness, as well as having the same effect on your students.

SOLVING COMMON LOGISTICAL PROBLEMS

Depending on where your seminar is conducted and the level of responsibility you choose to assume regarding participants' welfare, seminar logistics can be either a joy or a nightmare. The key factors include

1. Extent of seminar package
2. Location
3. Meal availability
4. Lodging availability

Each of these four factors presents its own set of challenges. The extent to which the last three factors are a critical concern depends on the first factor. Let's take a closer look at logistics.

Extent of Seminar Package

The seminar package can vary considerably depending on the individual sponsor. This can range from a series of lectures alone to a complete package that includes meals and lodging.

Each time that you add an additional element, you take on added responsibility. Each element complicates the logistical problems that you face in organization of the seminar.

The logistics factor is balanced out by the increased marketability of the seminar package. We have become an increasingly convenience oriented society. Anything that contributes to this is often viewed favorably.

Even if you don't assume personal responsibility for these factors, you have to be aware of these peripheral issues to maintain a workable seminar. You don't want to wear people out running around for things other than lectures. Fatigue can make seminar participants less receptive—and less satisfied with the package that they receive. This satisfaction factor has nothing to do with the quality of your presentation or your effect personally.

Because, as consultants, we focus on the technical aspects of seminar organization, we may overlook these peripheral factors as too mundane. This can be a serious mistake, giving our efforts an undeserved negative reputation.

Location

One of the most important aspects of successful seminar marketing is the location chosen for the seminar. At this point, you may march out a list of metropolitan areas as the most favorable locations. This is a considerable disservice to your effort.

A metropolitan seminar location has surprisingly little impact on the ultimate success of a seminar. Sometimes it is even detrimental to seminar success.

Objectively speaking, the best location is not dictated by size of city. Instead, the dominant consideration is how central the seminar location is to your proposed market area. As an example, if your market area covered the state of Illinois, Chicago may not be your first choice for a seminar location. It is at the extreme northern end of your market. In this example, smaller cities such as Bloomington or Decatur might be better choices— simply for their more central location.

By contrast, if your market area also included Wisconsin, Minnesota, Iowa, Indiana, and Michigan, Chicago is an excellent choice. It is central to the market area in question.

One of the most popular locations for seminars is at universities. They are natural because of the availability of space for students, possible access to specialized teaching tools, and even dormitory lodging during the summer months (when student loads at the university are low).

A growing number of universities actively solicit seminars during the summer. This brings additional revenue to the university and helps to solve many of the seminar's logistical problems.

Although one-day seminars are not as logistically demanding, the university setting is helpful even in these cases. The university is much more helpful when a seminar is two days or longer. The presence of university facilities is a considerable asset.

Additionally, the communities surrounding universities are equipped to deal with larger influxes of people. Universities often have functions that draw large numbers.

As an example, the university closest to me, Michigan Technological University, hosts a special Winter Carnival that draws several thousand people annually to these festivities. The surrounding community is expanding its lodging facilities, including the entry of chain operations, which will make the area attractive to tourism.

Universities having active programs throughout the year are even better equipped to assist the seminar process. Their surrounding communities can accommodate large numbers of people as well.

Meal Availability

One of the greatest motivators of the human race, aside from the thirst for knowledge, is the hungry belly. You can't escape this factor in any event that lasts more than a half-day.

The best situation is to have meal facilities within easy walking distance or, at most, a very short drive from the seminar location. Because seminars don't have midday meal breaks of more than an hour, your participants can't spend most of that time getting to and from the eating location.

If there is no easy meal availability, you have two choices. You either have to incorporate additional time for meal breaks—or choose another location for the seminar.

In the preceding section, we noted the advantages of the university location. Meal availability is another of their advantages. Most universities have centrally located cafeterias and/or lunch counters that can provide meals for seminar participants.

A good idea, however, is to give some advance warning to these facilities of your seminar's presence. This is essential if your attendance is likely to be large. They have to be prepared for more people.

Most of these facilities can handle several hundred people when necessary. One university has routinely provided facilities (on a rental basis) for regional religious meetings that have drawn several thousand participants. They provide staff to make sure that everyone is deliciously fed.

If you do consider a university location, carefully examine the facility situation—including meals. You may have the opportunity to market a major seminar, with no attendant worries about hungry stomachs.

Lodging Availability

Organization of the multi-day seminar automatically involves overnight lodging. As with meals, lodging should be within easy reach of the seminar location.

Unlike meals, the lodging doesn't necessarily have to be within a few minutes of the seminar lectures, but you don't want the lodging to be many miles away either. This is particularly true if participants have arrived by commercial carrier, rather than driving their own vehicles.

Larger seminar conferences can pose a particular challenge for lodging logistics. Some communities may not have a hundred or more spare motel or hotel units available. There's also the question of accommodation quality. You don't want your participants to be lodged in accommodations equivalent to skid-row dives.

Seminar scheduling should be coordinated with area lodging facilities. There may be other events scheduled for the same area, also making demands on the available lodging. This may seriously impede lodging logistics.

Some locations are popular for this type of operation. This can make scheduling critical to success. Unless you're conducting a seminar for recreational vehicle dealers (who take product samples with them), your prestige would suffer if your seminar participants ended up sleeping on park benches.

You might also check into possible group-rate discounts for seminar participants. If you can guarantee a certain number of occupants through advance reservations, this can give a favorable financial deal to your customers. This is particularly true for larger hotels that have meeting and conference rooms available. They may propose a package deal, including a better rate for conference room rental—if you can deliver additional patronage for their facilities.

Although arranging this involves extra time in the seminar organization process, the favorable impact on your business image can't be underrated. The excellent word-of-mouth advertising generated by extra efforts usually brings in tangible rewards for future efforts.

This is in addition to a possible reduction in costs for your current efforts. You may realize considerably more profit from your seminar effort through this route—without making any sacrifice in the quality of service rendered.

PROMOTING THE SEMINAR EFFECTIVELY

As with most business environments, seminars are in a world of fairly intense competition. To make a marketing impact, you must have some edge over others who are demanding consumer attention.

Although this matter should be addressed in the idea formulation stage of the seminar, no idea, no matter how unique, makes it in the marketplace unless consumers can readily assess its uniqueness. That is where solid promotion enters the picture.

Some fanfare and "hype" is a natural part of any promotional effort. The key in seminar promotion is to deliver this without losing your credibility.

Current advertising psychology for general consumer products has ranged the complete waterfront—from the sublime to the ridiculous. To judge from much of the advertising being ladled to the public, the average intelligence quotient of consumers might well be around 45.

This, for your purposes, is *not* the right approach. A small dose of humor, particularly in electronic media presentations, isn't a bad idea, but you should restrain the urge to be ridiculous or deceptive. Neither does much to boost your prestige image, particularly to those who seek a genuine educational opportunity.

This statement is particularly true for the tendency to inflate claims. As competitive influences become more intense in any given area, there is the strong urge to belabor superlatives. If this becomes business practice, potential customers become confused by these misleading claims.

The best approach to seminar promotion is to make your message results-oriented. Give them facts. Hit hard on those facts that you can positively document. Make a strong issue about documentation. Give them a proven program. This gets customer attention much more quickly than any superlatives you throw at them.

As an example, if your seminar is on business cost cutting techniques, give the prospective customer an average savings percentage for those who have totally implemented your program. You might also go into the range of savings, from the low end to the high.

In some cases, using the range technique in promotion may be more effective than extrapolating an average. There is a very human tendency to commit the upper-end figure to memory, visualizing that their business can achieve similar results.

You won't be telling any lies with this technique. You are merely letting the advertising recipient become your psychological ally in the promotional process.

Regardless of which media you use to promote your seminar, avoid the urge to become long-winded with your advertising presentation. Even in a direct mail presentation, an excessively long pamphlet is mostly ignored. Regrettably, the average attention span for advertising isn't very long.

For direct mail efforts, the standard rule of thumb is that you have to get the reader's attention in the first page of your pamphlet—or you won't get it at all. Don't expect readers to wade through several pages to get enough information to make a purchasing decision. Try to give them that information in the first two pages.

Any materials or information offered after that should be focused on reinforcing a positive purchasing decision. If readers have gone beyond two pages, they are favorably inclined to your ideas. Simply work to bring that inclination into action.

Beyond the active promotion, customer material should also include a fairly detailed schedule of the seminar. This gives the recipient a better picture of the package than can be achieved through several pages of narrative. A well-organized schedule, at least on paper, gives the impression that your seminar will provide a positive learning experience for the customer—the number-one reason for them to invest their money in your services.

Strict reliance on one form of promotion, either electronic or print, for seminars is usually not the best route to follow. You might have good results with direct mail if your mailing lists are good ones. It may even be the only practical approach if your prospective customers are scattered over a wide area.

By contrast, if potential customers are fairly concentrated and in sufficiently high number in the market area, your purposes may be better served through a combination of electronic and direct mail techniques. The electronic media serves to solicit responses from interested individuals or companies. The direct mail effort contains the main information-providing thrust for your presentation.

The main value of seminar promotion aside from direct mail, especially for business and profession-oriented programs, is to provide an information base of potential participants who may not be on any current mailing lists for such services. To a degree, you can develop a personal pool of customers who may not be receiving information from competitive programs. This can be a substantial business advantage.

Additionally, the rate of sales to such respondents is usually much higher than to those receiving a "cold canvass" letter. These companies or individuals have taken the initiative to contact you. They have been partially presold on your ideas. All you have to do then is to reinforce that feeling—and not do something promotionally to lose a golden opportunity for a sale.

As a final note, don't overlook the possibility of advertising your seminar in an applicable business, trade, or professional periodical. If this is done on a properly targeted basis, it can provide participants from a very wide area. Seminars that are sufficiently unique in focus and content can quickly become national events through this advertising source.

SEMINAR OPERATIONS

After you've completed all the necessary planning steps for a seminar, the actual operations of the event may seem like the proverbial "piece of cake." That may, or may not, be true.

Although you are the star attraction for the event, it should never be considered a solo act. There is no way that one single person can coordinate a seminar smoothly without help. You can't be ticket taker, receptionist, and speaker all rolled into one. You won't be able to do any of the jobs well enough if you try it. You'll just be too worn out.

Even though you may be augmented by the staff of the facility that you're renting, you should be ready to provide a receptionist to check in participants with the advance registration lists. If a participant is not registered, and space allows for a last-minute entry, he or she can be registered and the fee paid at this time.

This element of "seminar security" eliminates the possibility that some people might come in without having paid the applicable fee. Such freeloaders would not be fair to those honest participants who have paid to learn from your experience.

The receptionist may also be enlisted to distribute seminar manuals or other literature to participants as they enter the lecture area. For larger seminar events, an additional employee is needed to perform this function. In some seminars, especially with specifically designated seating, these same people perform the role of ushers, directing participants to their appropriate seats for the initial session.

If you are addressing an audience of over 100 people, you should include security measures within the lecture area as well. Although you don't expect trouble, some may arise.

The most pressing potential problem is the illness of a participant. You want them to have access to help as quickly as possible. Additional security for this purpose is appropriate.

In major hotels, this problem is addressed by the facility, removing this concern from your shoulders. This is one big reason why larger seminar events are usually best conducted through a facility that has staffers on duty to address these specialized needs. This eliminates your need to hire temporary employess for your staff to handle these contingencies.

Most universities and colleges, except for the smallest ones, also have a resident police force on duty. You may be able to use this resource for your seminar as part of the package deal, but you should express this in the initial planning stages, not springing it as a last-minute surprise. They may not be prepared to provide this service on short notice.

Although large seminars are usually the most profitable, don't make the mistake of operating in excess of your resources. If there is any question about your ability to provide services, either from a facility or personnel perspective, you are better off to restrict participation at each individual seminar. You can always schedule additional seminars to handle any overflow in clientele.

Becoming seriously overextended in this situation only serves to reflect badly on your services. The resulting inefficiencies can seriously hamper efforts at organizing, and gaining participation in, future seminars.

As a concluding note, there should be a specific plan to provide for the potential medical needs of seminar participants. This is particularly true if your seminar is being conducted during the hottest summer months. Although most lecture areas are in air-conditioned environments, areas outside may not be similarly blessed. This can create some unforeseeable medical emergencies. Failure to meet this problem, especially with larger groups, can bring up the issue of liability for a seminar's organization.

SECRETS TO CREATING A PERSONALIZED AUDIENCE RESPONSE

The personal power that is projected by the most successful seminar speakers is often awesome to behold. Even if you know what is happening, it may be difficult to avoid the "spell" that they weave over an audience.

Some have termed the phenomenon charisma. Other terms have been applied with equal frequency. Regardless of the term used, the result is that the speaker has developed what is almost a "cult following" among seminar participants. People almost literally go anywhere to listen to the speaker—and pay good money for the privilege.

Analyzing this special personal aura is not very easy, primarily because so many intangibles go into the process. There are, however, some tangible factors that can be used by almost any seminar speaker to get some of the same results.

An important factor is "personalization" of contact. Rather than being trapped by a podium, these effective speakers use a mobile microphone that allows them to mingle with their audience. This allows them to reach out and physically touch individual people in the group.

These speakers also make special efforts to dispel feelings of anonymity within a larger group. If someone has a question, the speaker's first priority is to find out the questioner's name. In their responses, the speakers invariably use the questioner's name at least once, if not more often. This interest in an individual's identity has a very complimentary effect that is magnified in direct proportion to the group's size.

This effect is not limited to the questioner. It passes through the entire group. In showing interest in an individual, you are seen as more approachable. This is an important aspect in the general psychology of a successful seminar operation.

The speaker can augment this favorable response by making a mental note of the questioner's name. After a session has concluded, the speaker may come in contact with the questioner during an informal period. If the speaker remembers the questioner, and thanks the person for their active participation, this further flatters this individual. The impact of this gesture can't be underestimated.

Lecturers who have the largest following also have cultivated a strong sense of showmanship. This doesn't mean that they turn a seminar into a three-ring circus in the tradition of P. T. Barnum. Instead, they use their audience's natural inclinations as an allied force to keep them coming back for more.

This statement is not meant only in the physical sense. The successful showman also operates on an intellectual level. Psychological motivations play the strongest role in audience response. Get the audience excited about the message that you are delivering. This excitement, by natural extension, attaches itself to you personally as well.

SECRETS OF PERSONAL PROJECTION

One of the most important keys to effective projection to an audience is a fundamental belief in the message that you are delivering to them. As W. C. Fields once said, "You can't cheat an honest man."

There is considerable truth to this saying. Whenever directness is part of the speaker's demeanor, you'll always have the urge to believe him.

If, by contrast, the speaker equivocates on a subject, you have a naturally skeptical reaction. You just can't trust someone who fails to look you squarely in the eye.

That was one of the strengths of the great circus showman, P. T. Barnum. Although he often pulled practical jokes as promotional gimmicks, he did them with such a direct style that people, even knowing what might happen, still fell for it. Some biographers of Barnum have thought that this master showman actually believed a lot of the nonsense that he dished out. The only other explanation is that he was the world's most astute liar.

Before you get the wrong impression, these references are not being made to encourage you to become a master of deceit. Instead, the example shows that excitement can be generated—even with the truth.

Truth can be made exciting, if you know how to apply the right decorative touches to it. Every advertiser knows how to create presale excitement. Showmanship, in this sense, involves becoming a walking commercial for your own services.

Assuming that your seminar is reasonably well attended, you have also been successful in attracting people preliminarily. Many of these same attention-grabbing concepts are beneficial in delivering the product as well.

The late Liberace, one of the greater pianists of the twentieth century, was also one of the greatest showmen. His personal following was based on the flashy apparel that he wore to make an entrance on stage. After he received the audience's accolades, he invariably removed a considerable amount of the glitter before actually sitting down to deliver his performance.

The removal of the extra glitter, in itself, was a display of the genius of his showmanship. He knew that, after the entry applause was over, it had served its purpose. He didn't want it to interfere with audience perception of the actual performance. He didn't want his personal appearance to compete with his music.

This illustrates a key element of personal projection that you can apply to seminar programming. Give your entry into the seminar a sufficient buildup for your audience. Raise their expectations—and then deliver on them.

One of the least logistically complicated techniques, especially applicable to an auditorium, is the use of the darkened room with a stage spotlight for your entrance. When background lighting is cut down and a spotlight is turned on, a psychology of expectancy is created in an audience. People naturally want to find out who, or what, fills that specially lighted area.

After the introduction is over, the normal lighting can be restored. The technique has accomplished its desired objective. You have the audience's attention.

Active audience participation during the course of an event helps to keep that interest alive and fresh. If you have a demonstration to conduct, ask for an audience volunteer to help with it. It's part of the show—and a learning experience for the volunteer as well.

Two magician showmen, David Copperfield and Harry Blackwell, almost invariably ask for an audience volunteer during their acts. When this involves someone without prior knowledge of the trick (when none is required), it offers a spontaneity to the event that cannot be duplicated.

There is an unspoken flattery associated with audience participation. Sharing the spotlight with someone "famous" is an experience that affects even the most sophisticated audience. Even the most jaded individual gets some vicarious satisfaction from the experience.

When these techniques are coupled with effective body language (see Chapter 11 for details), you have the capacity to hold an audience firmly in your grasp. If you don't use some showmanship in your presentation, a seminar can become boring for all involved. Even the most exciting information, if presented in a dull way, can be an intellectual anesthetic for an audience.

FLEXIBILITY SECRETS FOR SUCCESS

Although a rigid approach to seminar subjects can be efficient, it may not be the most effective way to get the job accomplished for your audience. As you get into the seminar, there may be some areas in which considerable interest and numerous questions are generated. This can quickly throw the best laid plans into the trash can.

This can be a golden opportunity for you—or a total disaster. Everything hinges on your attitude to changes in the basic plan.

As you proceed with your presentation, draw your cues from audience response. If an area of your subject is not drawing response, give it only the most cursory of reviews. This allows you to shift gears to compensate for audience imposed changes.

In some cases, the priorities of your audience may come as a complete surprise to you. This is particularly true for the first time that you give a particular seminar. You might end up going back to the planning stage before offering the seminar again, incorporating changes that are gleaned from audience priorities.

Don't attempt any radical changes, however. Every audience is not identical. If you carry your generalizations to the extreme, you will find yourself constantly in a redesign mode. That won't prove beneficial for the long-term profitability of your seminar efforts.

If you see the situation potentially getting out of control, channel discussions into scheduled periods provided for that purpose. Although you don't want to be too rigid about it, there may be others in the group who are seeking different information. Allowing one or two individuals to command a disproportionate share of time is not fair to the remainder of your group. You are in control of the situation, if you choose to exercise it.

If in doubt, check audience reaction to the situation. If you sense interest rather than impatience, let the situation unfold. The result may be an extremely important educational experience for all concerned, including the consultant conducting the seminar.

WRAPPING UP THE PACKAGE

One of the unique aspects of the seminar experience is that it can develop a life of its own, outside of the direct control of its creator. A spontaneous learning experience is one of the greatest joys that a person can experience.

This can, however, offer an extra challenge when the time to conclude the seminar arrives. It can be compared to trying to dismount from a horse while it's at a full gallop. A smooth landing on the ground is not always guaranteed.

The most common method is the summary approach to seminar conclusion. After all the scheduled subject matter has been covered, the conclusion covers a brief review of the whole seminar. This is followed by a final question-and-answer session to clear up any remaining problems or points of misunderstanding.

As this reaches its conclusion, the seminar speaker's final role is as a motivator to follow-up action. You want your audience to go out and apply the information that they've gained through your efforts. This is what they paid their fees for.

This involves a psychological shifting of gears from the role of instructor to that of cheerleader. You want to fire up their enthusiasm.

In your final comments to the group, aim for the benefits "sales pitch" that initially drew your participants to the seminar. You've given them the needed information to perform the great expectations with which they arrived. The rest is up to them. They must go out and implement the miracle for their businesses.

You won't necessarily have to project the same zeal as a television evangelist, but the idea is the same. You're now preaching to the "converted," those who share your enthusiasm for the ideas presented. Your concluding words imply the same message as the evangelist, though in a temporal sense: "Go—and 'sin' no more."

SEMINAR FOLLOW-UP IDEAS

When you have brought your seminar to a successful conclusion, there is often an accompanying sense of relief. After assuring yourself that you weren't insane for having launched the enterprise, you may have the urge to let the situation mellow.

While this is valid from a technical viewpoint, failure to follow up on your seminar participants abandons a golden opportunity to gain important marketing information. You should, at minimum, incorporate a small questionnaire for participants to fill out at the conclusion of the seminar—or when they have returned to their home bases.

A short time, possibly a week, might actually be beneficial to gain a more accurate appraisal from this survey result. Participants have been given an opportunity to reflect on their seminar experience and can provide potentially useful comments.

Although this survey can prove quite useful, a note of caution should be sounded. Not all comments should be given credence. Some people often tell you what they think you'll want to hear, not their true impressions. Take comments, particularly those of glowing praise, with a bit of healthy skepticism.

One positive indicator is if respondents show an interest in possible future seminar offerings. This indicator also provides a marketing base that gives you an advantage when you begin other marketing efforts.

Another follow-up technique is the use of a newsletter, as described in Chapter 10. This provides a vehicle for continuing contact, the "personal touch," and an opportunity to promote additional ideas. This keeps your customers aware of future seminars that you might offer—and creates a sense of anticipation that can be used when you initiate new seminar marketing efforts.

CLOSING THOUGHTS

Throughout this lengthy chapter, the primary focus has been to condense the sometimes complex process of conducting a seminar. The process can be rewarding to the participants and to the consultant, both intellectually and financially.

At several hundred dollars per participant, the gross income from a well-attended seminar can be impressive by anyone's standards. Few of us can turn our backs on gross revenues of $10,000 or more *per day*.

The key to maintaining a good seminar system is to balance product quality with cost control considerations. You can accomplish both objectives—if you plan for it.

Although the recommendations on showmanship can be considered as "frills," the other recommendations are basic to the operation of a successful seminar. Coverage here is admittedly limited in scope. The total subject could be, and has been, treated in a book of its own.

Our focus has been primarily on those areas that are most likely to cause trouble in organizing and conducting the seminar. With the information contained here, you should be ready to implement a successful seminar that will add substantially to both your prestige image and your business bank account.

CHAPTER

13

WRITING SEMINAR AND INSTRUCTION MANUALS

An integral part of making seminar programs successful is to provide something tangible for the participants to take back with them. This necessitates the preparation of some form of written materials, the most common of which is the seminar manual.

The most successful of such efforts serve two connecting purposes. First, and most important, a manual provides a complementary addition to the verbal and visual presentations conducted at the seminar. There is a definite reinforcing effect that a manual provides for the participant.

The second purpose is to provide a measure of instructional continuity after the seminar is over. Suppose, as an example, that a participant forgets the specifics of a topic discussed at the seminar. If the manual is well prepared, he or she can check its contents for the answer.

A third distinct, but auxiliary, benefit is that the manual may be a product to be marketed to clients who cannot attend the seminar in person. They may wish to purchase the manual instead, extending the impact—and the total profitability—of your seminar presentation. You can, in effect, reach hundreds of additional people who might not otherwise benefit from your expertise.

In this chapter, we review the manual preparation process from beginning to end, including using the seminar outline as your starting point, developing the manual outline, style and substance in content, the "come back for more" theory, the writing process for manuals, standard preshipment manuscript checks, packaging for shipment, the printing production process, page proofs and galleys, receipt of the completed product, distribution procedures in seminars, and independent supplementary sales. This chapter shows you how to effectively capitalize on this important avenue to get your message to its desired destination.

OVERVIEW OF THE PROCESS

Unlike the process for preparing the newsletter, as reviewed in Chapter 10 of this book, setting up and writing a seminar or instructional manual is not something that can be accomplished in a single evening or two at the dining room table at home. There is considerably more planning and effort involved in this endeavor.

You probably won't spend as much time on a manual as I have spent writing this book, but you can expect to spend a considerable number of hours immersed in the planning and writing process—if you expect a final quality product.

Seminar manuals should accurately reflect the contents of the seminars with which they are associated. Although they serve a complementary purpose, manuals should also be somewhat tangential to the oral presentations. Seminar participants, after having their interest peaked by the seminar leader, have a natural desire to learn more about the subject being presented. The seminar manual can help to, at least partially, satisfy that need.

This is the perspective from which you begin the process of preparing a manual outline. This outline, like the seminar outline itself, is an important part of the manual writing process because you can check your thinking for continuity and sense of direction *before* you have invested a large number of hours in the project.

When you have an outline, your next step is to sit down and write the actual manuscript. Depending on the length of the manual, this may take anywhere from a week of spare evenings to a month or more. It also depends on how productive a writer you are.

After the writing is completed, check your work carefully, package it for the printer, and then follow the printing process through the galley stage to the completed product. Unlike books that are handled through commercial publishers, you are primarily responsible for every stage of the process. Others may be doing the actual work for you in terms of printing, binding, and so on, but the responsibility for supervision rests primarily with you.

To further assist you in understanding the manual writing process, let's break it down into its individual parts for closer and more detailed examination.

COMPARING SEMINAR AND MANUAL OUTLINES

If you have a reasonably comprehensive outline for the seminar that you plan to conduct, the largest part of the manual outlining process is already done. Seminars generally focus their attention on three, four, or possibly five subdivisions of a basic topic. Sometimes, for longer seminars, this can be expanded to eight subdivisions. They are generally in bite-size chunks to assure that materials covered won't be outside the listeners' attention spans.

Examine your seminar subject closely as you prepare the manual outline. As an example, if you are conducting an office management seminar, you may be including the subject of microcomputer information management, focusing on one particular aspect of making the job easier and even more efficient. Time limitations within the seminar format may not allow you to reveal small details of the techniques being discussed. Your seminar manual is the place to slip in such information.

Let's say, as an example, that your seminar is divided into six informational parts. Each of these parts can be divided into two subcategories. You can do this in the seminar manual, by offering 12 shorter chapters, and getting into more detail than you can give during the seminar.

The chapters in your manual don't have to be book-length chapters. There isn't an arbitrary chapter length for *any* book, seminar or otherwise. Say what you want to say, wrap it up, and move on to the next chapter in the manual. I do, however, caution you against being *too* brief in your manual presentation. Especially when they buy a manual as an independent product, most buyers want to feel that they're getting some value for their money.

To give you a reasonable estimate of printed page length for a manual based on the size of the manuscript, the ratio for a standard-size book is from 1.75 to 2 double-spaced manuscript pages per printed book page. Therefore, a manual of 100 book pages has 175 to 200 manuscript pages. Generally, it isn't advisable to have a manual shorter than 60 or 70 printed book pages.

As you make your outline, keep this fact in mind. It helps to assure that you include enough topics to get an adequate-length manual.

Here's a little trick that I find very useful when planning larger projects, such as this book. I sit down with a legal pad and, at the top of the sheet, jot an opening chapter title. At the bottom of the sheet, I write down a concluding chapter title. In doing this, I have defined my beginning and conclusion. After that, I fill in nothing but chapter titles for materials in-between these points.

At this point in the process, I'm only thinking in generalities. I don't try for specifics in this initial session. I don't even try to develop an engaging or interesting chapter title now. The first note that was the genesis for this chapter was one word on the legal pad sheet. It read, "Manuals".

I don't go any further with the process until I'm satisfied with this preliminary list. After I am satisfied with this list, I go back and fill in each chapter's contents. Here, I turn to my word processor to speed up the process, but the general idea is that I don't invest an enormous amount of time on an idea that simply refuses to come together in a coherent fashion.

When you've decided on the subject subdivisions to be included in your manual, examine each from the same perspective that you would use if you planned to write a journal article about it. In effect, that's what you're doing as you prepare the manual.

Don't try to be ultraspecific as you fill in the contents for each chapter in your outline. My working outline for this section was only four words in length: "developing the manual outline." I have a few other notes available for myself as I write this, in case I need to refer to them. But I don't put myself in a complete intellectual straitjacket as I write. If you're too detailed in the outline process, you may never get around to actually writing the manual.

If you feel the need for this psychological support, keep your notes separate from your working outline. The working outline, if it is excessively cluttered with peripheral notes, may be difficult to judge for its clarity and sense of direction for each individual chapter. Whenever you sense weaknesses in the direction of the chapter, this is the time to make changes—not after you've invested hours in the writing process.

If your schedule allows for it, particularly with first efforts at manual authorship, allow the completed outline to sit for a day or two. This gives you a fresher perspective from which to judge its contents. The creative process wraps an author up in it emotionally. This can cause an excessively rosy impression of the effort.

STYLE AND SUBSTANCE IN MANUAL CONTENTS

All too often, seminar manuals tend to be little more than loose-leaf "notebooks" of the seminar itself. They have little or no independent identity and, as a result, offer little additional contribution to the seminar process. By any standards, they are not acceptable products to market.

When manuals do make a decisive difference, they are somewhat tangential to the main seminar, offering additional information that the reader does not otherwise receive. That's a very practical application for the manual.

The most successful seminars tend to narrow the focus of attention to a smaller scope, offering more detail within that fixed area. If the manual does no more than offer repetition of this narrow scope, it serves only a limited function. To offer the greatest value to the seminar recipient, the manual should at least attempt to interrelate the narrowed focus with the more general subject.

Let's take an example to show the concept in action. Assume, for the sake of discussion, that you are an office management consultant who has devised a new filing system that is far more efficient than any other in use. The initiation, implementation, and use of this system is the basis for your seminar.

During the main part of your seminar, you will undoubtedly focus almost all your attention on the procedural logistics of starting and maintaining this new system in the seminar participants' offices. There is no argument that this is the correct way to approach the situation.

The key point to remember is that seminar manuals assist participants to follow through on what they have learned. This requires some measure of motivation. Without a tangible reason to do so, many people who attend seminars often fail to take recommended actions—even if they fully comprehend the need within their organizations.

This is where the tangential element of the seminar manual comes into play. Although your manual would supply memory refreshing notes on seminar contents for the reader, your focus should shift considerably from procedure to rationale. Manual readers usually have much greater motivation if they can focus on the reasons behind the recommendations. During the seminar, you've already pounded the "how" into their heads. Use the manual forum to pound in the "why," thereby multiplying the motivation factor for action.

Closely allied to the motivation issue, the style of manual presentations can have a considerable impact on the seminar process. One of the most common errors made in writing seminar manuals is to drastically differ the style from that used in the actual seminar.

In other chapters of this book where writing was discussed (see Chapters 6 and 10), we reviewed the importance of having the written word reflect the way the writer speaks. This is particularly important for the psychological reinforcement process involved with seminar manuals.

As readers review seminar manual contents, they should be able to mentally hear *you* in the words that they read. This spurs memories of what they heard you say in your seminar presentation, helping to augment the manual text. You might even consider special memory jogging references within your manual text to capitalize on this factor. You might use something like the following:

Do you remember that special filing trick that we reviewed on the first day of the seminar? This is the place where you can really benefit from its use in your office.

Take your reader back, through both the manual's style and content, to relive their seminar experience. This helps them to recapture the feelings of motivation that they experienced within the group—and carry it through to successful implementation.

THE "COME BACK FOR MORE" THEORY

One of the thorniest ethical issues involved in developing both seminars and their associated educational materials is the question of "how much is enough" information. You want to give participants a sufficient banquet of information to temporarily satisfy their hunger, but you don't want to give them so much that it totally eliminates their future need for your services, either personally or through other seminars that you might offer in the future.

Although it's true that there are "seminar junkies" (people who attend almost anything even vaguely resembling a seminar), most seminar participants are people of serious intention. They want to take back solid information that they can use immediately. If they don't get some information, they won't feel that they've invested their seminar fee wisely. Feeling cheated, they definitely will *not* be "coming back for more."

The major reason why most seminars are so narrowly focused is that they can offer sufficient detail to satisfy customers without selling out the entire store in one shot. As long as seminar participants know, in advance, exactly what they will receive for their fee, there is no ethical question involved in the practice. No one can legitimately expect you to condense the contents of years of experience into a couple days worth of lectures.

Effective seminar manuals and seminars permit readers to master a technique that was foreign to them prior to participation in your group. This mastery, and the sense of satisfaction that it generates, is the key to getting participants to come back for more. What is more ethical than creating a satisfied customer?

THE ACTUAL WRITING PROCESS

Most of us could summon the self-discipline necessary to write an isolated magazine article or two, sandwiched within our schedule of other activities, but the prospect of tackling a writing project that is closer to book length is an entirely different matter.

Having written more than one manual, I can speak from personal experience regarding the discipline that is involved. It isn't easy. But it isn't as difficult as some people have you believe, either. The key is to break the emotional and intellectual barrier that seems to form itself around the book-length media.

After you have developed your outline, the largest challenge of the project is behind you. The job is organized. Now all you have to do is write. That's where the discipline comes in.

A moment ago, the reference to magazine articles was made to help you develop the psychological frame of reference that is required to complete a book-length project. By segmenting your project, viewing each chapter of a seminar manual as you would the authorship of a magazine article, the project won't seem as formidable. If someone asked you to write 8 or 10 magazine articles, you would probably figure that you could squeeze that into your schedule. But a book, you say? Never!

Let's not kid each other. We just kicked the number-one excuse for inaction right out the window.

Now that we've agreed that you have the time, let's talk about the actual writing process. In writing these 10 "magazine articles," you have to set aside specific time to devote to writing. Assuming that your manual has 10 chapters, you have to write between 160 and 250 manuscript pages (double-spaced). This length will more than satisfy any seminar participant, giving them a manual that is, at minimum, over 90 printed pages.

An important key to avoiding writer's block is to allow sufficient time for the writing process. If you have a tight schedule, you'll find yourself feeling rushed. The result is reduced productivity in the time that you spend writing.

From an intellectual viewpoint, writing a book-length manuscript is somewhat like running a 10-kilometer race—if not the Boston Marathon. This is no 100 yard dash that you can complete with a single burst of energy. You have to pace yourself to maintain your feeling of accomplishment and keep your motivation high.

For myself, I consider a single writing session that produces eight manuscript pages a reasonably good output. I often go beyond that at a single sitting. I don't set up emotional barriers making productivity standards so high that they block me from starting at all.

Getting that first page in each writing session under your belt is often the most difficult part of the mission. After you have written the first page, a considerable number of additional pages follow. My favorite psychological trick is to mentally give myself a day's vacation—when I only *absolutely must* write two pages. Usually I keep writing well beyond those two pages—even if I'm tired. But I've given myself that "steam vent" to satisfy the too-occasional case of spring fever that afflicts us all.

Incidentally, at the eight page per day pace, a 160-page manuscript gets completed in 20 sessions. See? We aren't talking about signing your life away. In less than a month of spare-time effort, you have the project totally nailed down.

As with any skill of value, experience is usually the best teacher. The first effort is usually the most difficult to complete. If you're slightly better than a hunt-and-peck typist, you can probably type out a first draft, with the eight-page quota, in two or three hours per sitting. Assuming that you're relatively organized in your effort, that first draft, with only minor editing, will probably be your final draft as well. This is the level that you can achieve—with experience.

As you write, try to mentally visualize the reader. You are "talking" to that person. You probably would have little or no difficulty in personally talking to that person. To construct your manual, simply write down what you have to say to the reader.

If you can remove the intellectual barriers that block written communication (see Chapter 6), you may end up surprising yourself with your productivity. On one occasion, in writing one of my books, I sat down to write and found myself so totally immersed in the chapter's subject that I couldn't stop until I had the chapter completed. Almost seven hours and 30 manuscript pages later, the chapter was completed. (The chapter passed through into a commercially published book with only a few copy editor's marks in the process.)

Admittedly, this type of productivity is the exception, not the standard rule. It does, though, give you some indication of the potential within the human mind for concentrated effort—if its power is unchained from psychological barriers.

As a concluding note to this section, try to avoid writing sessions in which you absolutely must stop in 15 to 30 minutes. Often, once you start developing a specific avenue of thought, you can really get rolling. Being forced to stop prematurely, sometimes in the middle of an explanation, may cause difficulty in picking up the process where you left off. This frustration may impede your writing efforts, making the process far more difficult than necessary.

Select a time for writing that allows you to singularly focus your attention on your subject. By minimizing distractions, you can unfold the creativity that makes your first manual—and any future efforts—a virtual breeze to complete.

PERFORMING THOSE LAST-MINUTE CHECKS

After you've finished writing the manual, you are entitled to a few moments of self-congratulations—indulge yourself. But the job isn't finished quite yet.

Before you send the manuscript off to the printer, check it over to find possible errors in your copy. Your first priority will be factual mistakes. Be certain that these don't slip into the completed product. You don't want your credibility to go down the drain.

When you've corrected factual errors, read your manuscript with an eye toward picking up spelling and punctuation errors. The primary problem with the self-publishing route is that you are responsible for absolutely *everything* surrounding the manuscript. You won't have the benefit of a copy editor to correct spelling errors, punctuation gaffes, and sloppy syntax. As writer, editor, and publisher all rolled into one, your desk deserves the same plaque that decorated Harry Truman's in the Oval Office. It read: "THE BUCK STOPS HERE."

You generally won't have to retype the manuscript to make minor corrections. Corrections, neatly penciled in, are easily handled with no noticeable reduction in efficiency.

Also check to see that any illustrations that you are including in the manual are properly referenced in your manuscript. This is a common mistake, particularly for first-time manual authors. Readers who find unreferenced illustrations are sometimes confused about their relevance to the printed text.

When you have completed these checks, your material should be ready for shipment to the printer. That step, with the few hints that follow, can make a considerable contribution to the total efficiency of your enterprise.

LET'S PACK IT UP

Packing up a manuscript for shipment is generally a fairly routine matter, but there are a couple of points, connected with a printer's production processes, that should be considered when you do your packing.

Because your printer will likely handle the layout process for your manual, they want to have any accompanying illustrations separate from the main manuscript, but clearly labeled. Some authors, thinking that it helps the printer, put their illustrations within the manuscript, approximately in the location at which they will appear in the manual.

This practice only contributes to confusion. Illustrations are generally handled by a different department than the main text of the manuscript. If they are not separate, all your material goes to one department. When your illustrations are discovered within the manuscript, they will then be separated and sent to their appropriate destinations.

Label your illustrations by the chapter in which they appear. If you want to further categorize them, you can pack each chapter's illustrations into their own manila envelope within the main package. Each envelope is then labeled accordingly, such as "Seminar Manual—Chapter 1 Illustrations."

As a special note regarding photographs, label all photographic prints on the reverse side for easy printer reference. Do not, however, write directly on the back of the print paper. This leaves an impression on the print itself, adversely affecting the results of reproduction. Instead, use press-on labels. Write on the labels before transferring them to the backs of the photos that you're packing. You'll effectively safeguard your investment in manual illustrations.

Regardless of what method you use for shipping a larger manuscript, sturdy external packaging is recommended. Most package handlers are not noted for their delicate touch, except for packages that are boldly labeled as fragile. Almost everything else gets tossed and turned upside down. A manila envelope, strained to its maximum capacity, might not weather the storm very well. If the package comes apart, valuable materials may be lost in transit.

THE MANUAL PRODUCTION PROCESS

After you've successfully delivered the manual materials to the printer, you generally have a wait of several weeks. During this time, production steps are being accomplished that have a direct impact on the finished product that you'll be presenting to seminar participants.

Unless you are submitting "camera ready copy" (meaning that your manuscript pages are of good enough quality to photograph and your book will look just like the manuscript), the printer typesets your manual. While typesetting is being done, you are asked to choose the manual's binding.

Seminar and instruction manuals are generally bound in paperback format or in hardcover ring-binder format. Paperback binding is considerably less expensive. The main disadvantage to the paperback option is that it is also cheaper in appearance. If you're charging several hundred to a thousand dollars for the privilege of attending your seminar, this less prestigious appearance may not be as well received by your participants.

The ring-binder format is also of utilitarian value if you decide to provide updates or a newsletter as an additional future service. Your recipients can put this material in with the rest of the printed matter as a unified package. That's an efficiency consideration that your recipients value.

If the manual's long-term durability is an objective, you may want to consider an option that some printers offer—ring reinforcement on the pages. Depending on the printer, this can add five percent to the total cost, but this option virtually eliminates one of the most frequent complaints about ring binders—pages tearing themselves out with regular use.

You are also asked to approve the cover design before the total units are manufactured. This is usually given in the form of a paper copy of the final design.

Finally, you are given (in most instances) a page sample to approve the type style. This helps to prevent one of the most common causes of printer-customer dissatisfaction with the finished product. (We'll give more attention to this in the next section.)

After your prepublication decisions are completed, the number of copies that you ordered are printed in flat page units. Commercial presses are generally capable of printing on larger sheets of paper, putting several manual pages on the side of one sheet. These sheets are then cut and organized in sequence to form the completed product.

One option that few first-time publishers are aware of is to have more pages printed than you expect to use. Having only a portion of your press run bound as completed manuals helps to reduce your preliminary costs. It also gives you faster response time if customer demand exceeds conservative initial projections. These extra pages are stored in the initial press run form (uncut) until you are ready to proceed with more bindings.

After the press run, the cut pages are bound, packed, and shipped to you. The job is done—and you're on your way to a successful seminar.

GALLEY PROOF REVIEW

Just prior to publication, many printers provide "galley proof" pages that contain the entire contents of your manual. They are in sheets considerably longer than standard book pages. This shows the result of the typesetter's efforts.

You are asked to review these proofs for *typographical errors only!* I emphasize because too many authors succumb to the temptation of rewriting their books at this stage of operations. You have no business doing this now. You should have been completely satisfied with the book *before* you put it in the printer's hands.

Check the proofs thoroughly. This is a safeguard against potentially embarrassing errors. Although typesetters are very conscientious in their work, they're human—like the rest of us. An occasional error is possible. I've even had one or two typos get past me into a published book (which proves that I'm as human as the typesetter).

After you're done with this process, return the proofs to the printer. They will note any corrections that you made on the proofs, and correct the typesetting.

As noted a moment ago, the review process is for printer's errors only. Most printers have a stipulated limit on the amount of changes that they will make with no increase in the printing fee. Some may be very stringent in this area. Commercial publishers generally limit this to 10 percent. After that, the author bears the cost of additional composition and typesetting.

The key element here is that a relatively minor change can have a considerable impact on the amount of new typesetting required and the total printing cost. As an example, if you decide to take out an entire paragraph early in a chapter, this may eliminate one page from the total—and require renumbering of the pages from that point on.

Few of us can afford tinkering with a book's contents after it has gone to the typesetter. Do your best, hand it in, and then keep your blue pencil firmly sheathed. Failure to do this can prove very expensive for your publishing enterprise.

A page sample is a randomly selected page that shows the type styles that are used for headlining, chapter titles, and the main body of copy. This page sample is not a complete set of proofs for your entire manuscript. It serves only for approval of style, not accuracy of content. Most printers do not require their return. Just remember to complain *before,* not after, your manual is published—if you feel it's warranted.

RECEIVING THE FINAL PRODUCT

After all the effort is completed, you're likely to be anxious to receive the bound copies of your personal masterpiece. Welcome to the club! This is especially true of a first effort. Most veterans of several such efforts are a bit less excited.

If you've done all the preliminary work, you're likely to be very satisfied with the final results. After a minute or two of self-congratulations, you'll be faced with the stark reality of the sheer number of books that must be handled in some coherent fashion.

When you receive your shipment, check it immediately to be certain that you received what you ordered. Also, count the number of copies that you received. Some printers may occasionally have an overrun (meaning that you receive a few more copies than you ordered). That isn't a deadly sin. It is important that you don't have a shortfall, particularly if the printer bills you for the full amount.

After you've satisfied yourself on this point, you may have to store some of your copies—if you have more than your seminar requires. As with the newsletter operation discussed in Chapter 10, store these manuals close to the area where your distribution operations will be. You won't want to indulge in a lot of wasted motions to get the job done.

We mention this here simply because it is a logical adjunct to the receipt of the product. After a seminar is completed, there is usually some demand generated by word-of-mouth advertising. You should be prepared for this by a little advance planning.

As a final note, check the packing boxes for the presence of a printer's invoice. Some printers make it a practice to include their invoices with the product being shipped. Checking for this can prevent receiving one of those aggravating (and prestige dampening) notices that your payment is past due.

SEMINAR DISTRIBUTION PRACTICES

There is no standard rule for the distribution of manuals at seminars. Some seminars offer the manuals right away. Others choose to wait until the conclusion, providing them as an inducement not to drop out prematurely.

The determining factor is the contents of the manual. If recipients would find it valuable as a follow-along text during the seminar, they should receive them right away. If not, reserving them for the conclusion is not a major problem.

A practical method around this problem is to make a portion of the seminar fee nonrefundable. This covers the cost of the manual, allowing you to distribute the books immediately as participants come to the first seminar session.

This method also allows you to use the manual as an auxiliary text to assist in the mechanics of presenting the seminar. That can be a valuable help to you. By combining manual contents with visual aids and your oral presentation to the seminar audience, you can give a well-rounded program that makes all participants feel that they've received full value for their money.

To assist the word-of-mouth advertising process, also consider offering special reply cards to participants, urging them to pass these on to colleagues who were unable to attend the seminar in person. This broadens your audience, your seminar's total impact, and the contents of your bank account. Many consultants who offer seminars find that this can easily expand their manual circulation by 5 to 10 percent. Some have experienced a doubling of sales through this technique.

As a final note, don't forget to have some extra copies of your manual available at the seminar. You may have some last-minute registrants come in who will need a copy. You can also suggest that some particpants may want to purchase extra copies for their company's use or to satisfy a request of a colleague who was not able to attend. With a little imagination in your approach, you can get considerable marketing mileage from the manual—and enhance your prestige in the process.

INDEPENDENT SUPPLEMENTARY SALES

After the conclusion of a successful seminar, the impact on a consultant's business is usually considerable. Rave reviews from participants can generate considerable publication and service sales for months ahead.

Sole dependence on this factor is not, however, recommended. A seminar that is well attended can be a springboard for manual sales that often multiplies total circulation many times over. The key is to use the concluded seminar itself as the catalyst in the marketing effort for the manual.

Hollywood movie moguls have long recognized the excellent marketing tandem of a good motion picture and the book on which it is based. The same principle is applied.

Your advertising could be directed somewhat as follows:

You've heard about the great seminar! Now, available while supplies last, is the important book on which that seminar was based!

An important consideration in this effort is timing. You don't want to begin your advertising the day after your seminar is over, but you shouldn't wait for a month or two either. Let some of that favorable notice precede you. Then start your advertising!

If you're planning to advertise in a monthly journal, ask them about their delivery schedule to subscribers. Sometimes a journal is sent out in the month preceding that listed on the cover. You don't want to have that type of advertising appear *before* you've actually conducted the seminar. It would wreak havoc on your credibility.

This adjunct marketing consideration may be a factor for you to consider in scheduling the seminar itself. Having a seminar scheduled early in a month gives you a practical advantage from this perspective—and gives you the kind of one-two marketing punch that makes your seminar a very successful enterprise.

CLOSING THOUGHTS

Aside from the obvious monetary gains that a manual provides, one of the major intangible benefits that you derive is enhanced credibility. There is something unique about the printed word, even in our electronically oriented age, that delivers a special power. Authorship, rightly or wrongly, has a mystique about it. It can almost be called a celebrity factor.

If you happen to have authorship to your credit *before* you conduct a seminar, the marketing advantage can be enormous. Even if the book was not a huge commercial success, the simple fact of authorship is what carries the clout.

As an example, one consultant conducted seminars for several years before having a published book to his credit. His seminars, before this publication, were moderately successful efforts, but, as he put it, they "weren't something to write home about."

This is in great contrast to the results that he obtained *after* his book was published. The average attendance for his seminars *tripled* in the several years after the book came on the market. Using his authorship as a marketing tool, he imparted the prestigious aura that drew an audience.

The process described in this chapter can bear similar fruit for your seminar efforts. The postseminar marketing efforts can set the stage for even more successful seminars in the future.

As a concluding note, many of the elements we discussed in the production process of a manual will also be true if you are published by a standard commercial publisher. The primary difference is that the decision-making authority is in the hands of the publishing house.

Self-publication, as outlined in this chapter, can be an adventure in itself. For materials directed at a specific seminar, it is the only logical choice. The information offered here makes this effort a productive one—with results that you'll be proud of for years to come.

CHAPTER
14

PROMOTING INDIVIDUAL CONSULTING: KEY TO LONG-TERM SUCCESS

Throughout the course of this book, the emphasis has been on mass marketing and in consulting for more than one client at a time. You have the impression that consultation with an individual client is unprofitable.

Although it's true that your per hour gross income from individual consulting is never as high as that obtained from group consulting, you can't afford to ignore it. One primary reason is that, if you are considered unapproachable individually, you will lose your appeal to a mass market.

When you remove the marketing gestures, purchase decisions are made on an individual basis. The collective effect of numerous individual decisions determines the effectiveness of any mass marketing program.

In this chapter, we focus our attention on the value of the one-to-one consulting adjunct, the interrelationship between individual and mass consulting efforts, how these two distinct entities help to promote each other, individual consulting as a stepping-stone, and an analysis of what constitutes a satisfied customer. The key to balance in a consulting business is to maintain a sense of perspective in both areas, an increasingly difficult challenge if most of your efforts are for the mass market. This chapter helps you to maintain the balance that contributes to your ultimate success.

ONE-ON-ONE: THE IMPORTANT ADJUNCT

Traditional marketing wisdom, especially when applied to consulting, dictates conducting marketing efforts on an individual basis with potential clients—rather than using the mass market strategy advocated in this book. There are specific times, however, when there is no substitute for individualized attention to client needs.

This is particularly true when client circumstances are considerably different than the norm for a particular business or professional group. Standardized mass instruction does not meet the client's specific needs. Standardized instruction brings these clients a considerable distance toward their goal of a business solution, but there are specific gaps that remain unattended.

These gaps are the province of the individualized consulting effort. If these gaps are not being addressed, clients feel that some vital ingredient is missing from your consulting program.

One consultant who regularly conducts seminars has established a reply card program within the seminar for participants who wish to retain her services on an individualized basis. Her seminars yield the vast majority of her individualized consulting clients. Generally, her well-attended professional seminars yield between 5 and 10 percent of individualized consulting clients. "Sometimes," she once mused, "you get paid to advertise."

As it applies to seminars, her statement has more than a small grain of truth to it. But, as many very successful consultants have discovered, there is a circle effect between individual and seminar consulting. Many individual consulting clients often attend seminars given by their consultants and seminars often create specific needs for individualized consulting services. It's a continuing chain that is almost self-perpetuating for the consultant's profit.

Strict reliance on the group idea, although initially profitable, sometimes creates customer disenchantment. In granting individual services, you can capitalize on the "celebrity factor" that is directly connected with conducting seminars. You will inevitably become the subject of very favorable verbal advertising within the client's group.

One of the most common pitfalls into which seminar consultants fall is that of being almost totally unapproachable on an individual basis. Because of the impact of mass marketing, this becomes a reflexive act of self-preservation. They become concerned that they'll have no private life left at all.

Although this is a legitimate concern, establishing a mechanism for controlled access is well worth the effort. The individualized client feels especially honored for having been singled out for the attention. They, in turn, will sing your praises to colleagues. This is, of course, contingent on your ability to provide a solution to the particular problem involved.

THE INDIVIDUAL CONSULTING/SEMINAR INTERRELATIONSHIP

As indicated a few moments ago, conducting seminars tends to impart a measure of "star status" on the consultant. This enhanced visibility, augmented by well-orchestrated marketing, tends to make its beneficiary seem somehow larger than life. This can sometimes prove to be the proverbial two-edged sword—you have to live up to these higher expectations.

The result, as noted earlier, is that clients feel especially honored to rub elbows with someone who has a greater than average professional status. In dealing on an individual basis, however, you may have the problem of breaking away from this celebrity factor to get at the true nature of the client's problem. They are so much in awe of the image that *you* have helped to create that it impedes the more natural flow of consultant-client communication.

In the tandem of seminars and individualized consulting, the role of the latter is to focus on specific areas of difficulty in implementation within the client's business or professional activities. If the client has been paying attention in your seminar, you won't have to review basic principles. You can zero in on the specific problem—and solve it.

The one major drawback of individualized consulting assignments that are gotten from seminars is that you aren't likely to get many easy cases. These clients have more difficult challenges that aren't as responsive to remedy. You covered the easy problems in your seminar. Now you have only the tough jobs left.

PROMOTIONAL CONNECTOR PRINCIPLES

As a practical matter, few consultants can effectively jump directly into seminar consulting without having established a reputation on the individual level. The primary danger for most seminar consultants is that, in having tasted seminar success, they lose sight of the fundamental roots that formed the foundation for that success.

Many of the most successful seminars have been developed through direct observations made in the process of individual consultations. This is the type of real-world experience that is very promotable.

When consultants become strictly oriented to seminars, becoming immersed in an almost sterile pseudoacademic environment, they can lose touch with the changing realities in their chosen consulting field. Although they may do extensive reading on the newest developments, this isn't usually as effective as being present where these developments are being applied.

Although some consultants have fallen into this pitfall, these statements are not intended as an implied indictment of the seminar system. They are raised as a caution to a consultant who considers a single-minded adherence to seminars the guaranteed road to personal fame and wealth.

In the short term, you may achieve fame and wealth, but, if an audience perceives that you are not in touch with the real world, they will stop attending seminars. To borrow a political analyst's aphorism for voter apathy, your audience will "vote with their feet" in increasing numbers.

Any consultant who assumes that a single seminar will guarantee fame and fortune is living in a dream world. The best place to get salable seminar ideas for future efforts is through individualized consulting. It is also the proving ground for ideas—and gives them increased credibility when presented to a larger audience.

This increased credibility is a key element in making a seminar eminently salable to a mass audience. Ideas that are at the philosophical and/or procedural forefront within a given field have the greatest drawing power for an audience. People have a natural interest in anything new—or in something old that is presented from a new perspective.

Seminars, in turn, help you to place your finger on the mass market "pulse." What are the individual concerns that propel mass interest?

Successful seminar speakers are often envied. Aspirants to this fame and fortune often wonder about the "secret formula" for this success. As simplistic as this may sound, the successful ones have done the research to answer the question raised in the preceding paragraph.

Within the seminar setting, you can promote the success of your individual consulting efforts by carefully noting the questions that are raised, not just the answers that you provide. These questions may also contain the seeds for another seminar idea—if you can perceive a particular trend from their content.

As a concluding note, don't allow the seminar to become a totally one-way learning experience. Discussion periods, customarily built into the seminar format, are an opportunity for the sharing of ideas. Be open to the ideas of others. Some seminar participants may have tried a number of ideas that have met with some measure of success. These discussions can often serve as the research vehicle by which you can determine future avenues for both individual and seminar consulting efforts.

INDIVIDUAL CONSULTING AS A STEPPING-STONE

Another important role for individual consulting is for the consultant who seeks to make fundamental career changes using the seminar format. Some may find that a particular business or professional group's needs have been essentially met. Others may find themselves growing weary of talking about the same subjects repeatedly to different audiences. There is a basic desire to shift gears professionally in an effort to maintain personal enthusiasm, an essential ingredient to the successful seminar.

In this situation, the consultant has to "go back to the drawing board." Just as he or she developed a professional reputation that launched previous seminars, the same applies for a basic change in audience. You must become known to a group before you can be an effective audience drawing force.

The main difference in this situation is that you won't be going back to square one totally. By having a previous seminar background, your primary objective is to develop identification with a group. They need to know that you understand their particular concerns—and are sufficiently knowledgeable to offer solutions that are worth the price of admission.

In the process of mass marketing either a product or individual, there is a tendency to stereotype the "package" being presented. Although this has considerable value for purposes of consumer identification of the product or service being presented, this stereotyping can sometimes become a trap of our own construction.

Breaking out of this trap may not be very easy. Being identified with a particular area may be as much a curse as a blessing. Although it serves you well within an established framework, your knowledge and abilities may be questioned in other areas.

This is particularly true in some of the more technical professional positions. Some may assume that anyone who is not a direct contemporary "can't walk and chew gum at the same time" in their field. You have to prove your knowledge to gain wider acceptance.

Individual consulting, not the larger audience, is the place to prove your knowledge. In the direct one-on-one discussions, your abilities to analyze and solve problems will receive a thorough test.

As an example, a consultant specializing in medical practice management procedures may want to broaden horizons to include all professional practice management. Many similarities exist in this area, regardless of the professional group involved.

However, the consultant will have to prove to an attorney, for instance, that he or she is versed in the specific differences found within a legal practice. Successes in these individualized efforts become the springboard for launching seminars that, in this case, are directed to a legal audience. The satisfied customer is the basis for further progress.

IS YOUR CUSTOMER SATISFIED?

One of the most ambiguous aspects of any business, consulting definitely included, is to determine what constitutes a satisfied customer. Although there is the consensus that a lack of complaints is a favorable indicator, this isn't always accurate. You just may not have been confronted by the customer about them.

Although the consultant-client relationship does represent a different set of circumstances from the standard commercial enterprise, there are similarities. You, as some of my other readers probably did, may have questioned the use of the term "customer" in relation to your clients.

The key here is your psychological frame of reference. We often tend to elevate the consultant-client relationship above the level of mundane commercialism, losing sight of the fact that many of the same rules still apply. We can't repeal the rules because of psychology.

Our true objective is to have a customer who is not just satisfied, but enthusiastic, with the quality of services rendered. This completes the full circle that we started at the beginning of this book. The satisfied customer enhances your image, making it more marketable. This draws more customers that, when satisfied, add to your prestige.

With this in mind, let's take a look at what constitutes a satisfied customer. Check each item that applies to your client.

Satisifed Customer Checklist

( ) Customer volunteers positive feedback to initial recommendations.
( ) Customer takes steps to implement recommendations.
( ) You and customer agree on realistic expectations.
( ) Customer indicates that expectations have been met or exceeded.
( ) Customer specifically compliments results.
( ) Customer volunteers possible referrals, without your suggestion.
( ) Customer supplies actual referrals.
( ) Customer shows no hesitation in payment.
( ) Customer shows interest in further services.

Of this nine-item checklist, a score of less then five for a customer indicates some potential problems. In the range of five to seven, you are doing reasonably well. They probably won't be giving you a lot of free advertising, but they won't be negative either. A score of eight to nine is an indicator of the "prestige builder" client that truly contributes to your success.

CLOSING THOUGHTS

Throughout the course of this book, our focus has been on the capacity to take an essentially individualized endeavor, as consulting is, and convert it into a commodity that can be promoted through the mass market media. We've also discussed the practice modifications that are needed to serve an expanded market.

As each succeeding chapter has unfolded, the range of the market gradually expanded. In some instances, this can create a national and international marketplace.

In this chapter, however, our focus has come back to the basis of mass marketing success—the individual customer. The mass market, contrary to the tone of some advertising, is not a mindless horde that follows anything blindly. At least it isn't true for potential consulting clients.

Regardless of the product or service involved, it is the large number of *individual* purchasing decisions that determines the success of mass marketing efforts. In focusing our attention on the larger group, we can fall into the trap of forgetting this essential truth.

Although the techniques discussed throughout this book are designed to reach out to a group, you are fundamentally playing to an audience of one. If you can maintain this important balance in your perspective, the materials in this and all the other chapters of this book will contribute to the full measure of your future success.

INDEX

Advertising:
  budget range for, 33, 34
  cautious approach in, 50
  cramped copy in, 73
  feedback concept in, 74
  "good taste" in, 73
  newspaper, 44, 45
  pitfalls in newspaper, 65
  radio, 46, 47
  reply coupon design in, 74
  slogans in, 64
  television, 47
  trade journals, in, 45
  trade journal articles as, 45
  writing newspaper, 64

Barnum, P. T., 170, 182, 183
Blackwell, Harry, 184
Body language, 5, 6, 165–167
Budget, advertising, 33–34
Business relationships, 15

Checklist:
  Colleague Influence, 13
  Marketability, 7
  Satisfied Customer, 211
  Self-Perception, 12
Client:
  respect and trust of, 18
  eye contact with, 20
Clothing, 4–5
  men's, 4
  women's, 4
Colleague Influence Checklist, 13
Consultant as "miracle worker", 20
Consulting services:
  "celebrity factor" in, 207
  changes in emphasis, 209–210
  controlled access, 207
  customer checklist, 211
  customer, satisfied, 210–211
  drawbacks of, 208
  establishing need for, 28, 29
  "get paid to advertise," 207
  getting past celebrity, 207
  mass market, 211–212
  one-on-one approach, 206
  reply card for, 206
  seminar connection, 208
  seminar discussions as research, 209
Coupon, reply, 74

Developmental priorities, 8, 9
Direct mail:
  conversational tone in, 16
  PC trick for, 18
  "Personal and Confidential" in, 17
  two tips for, 17
Directories, phone, 42
"dovetail" concept, 56, 66–67

Electronic media:
  authorship adjunct to, 53
  five stages of, 52
  reducing gamble of, 52
  shared cost promotion for, 53
Expansion, mass market role in, 24–25

Friendships, true quality of, 14

Hairstyle, 3–4
Humor:
  as "salt," 23

Humor (cont.)
  in business cards, 22
  use of, 22

IBM, 50
Image:
  your current, 2
  packaging, 23
  "Product," as marketable, 10
  prestige, 75

Jewelry, 4
Journals, see Trade journals

Literary marketplace, 80

Manuals, seminar:
  additional sales for, 203
  advertising, 203
  authorship mystique, 203-204
  celebrity factor, 203
  "come back for more" theory, 194-195
  extra copies of, 202
  galley proofs for, 200-201
  illustration labelling, 198
  invoice, printer's, 202
  last-minute checks, 197-198
  major output example, 197
  manuscript lengths for, 192
  manuscript packing, 198-199
  overview of, 190-191
  outlines for, 191-193
  page sample for, 201
  production process for, 199-201
  psychology of writing, 195
  purposes of, 190
  receiving, 201
  reply cards in promotion, 202
  storing and distribution, 201
  style, 193-194
  style example, 194
  time of distribution, 202
  writing process, 195-197
Manuscripts:
  trade journal requirements, 77-78
  self-service pitfall in, 79
  magazine rights for, 78
Market, concerns of, 21
Marketability Checklist, 7
Media:
  basics of, 42
  electronic, 43
  message repetition in, 42
  "perishable," 43
  selection of, 51-53
Monotone voice, 6

Newsletters:
  article length for, 141
  article series for, 141
  banner design for, 142-144
  banner samples, 143
  as broadcast adjunct, 49
  "camera-ready copy" for, 149
  distribution of, 151
  ethics of, 49
  illustrations for, 146
  length of, 141
  objectives of, 130-131
  organization of, 140
  overview of, 130
  page proofs for, 150
  page size for, 147
  printer selection for, 149-150
  samples of, 132-139
  success story for, 152
  type styles for, 145
  writing headlines for, 145

Newspapers:
  advertising fees in, 60
  cost-effective approaches, 61-63
  daily vs. weekly, 57-59
  display advertising in, 62
  fee variations in, 62

Index 215

layout design in, 60–61
page location in ads, 62
press releases for, 63
two-column idea, 62
understanding processes of, 56–57
writing ads for, 64

Outline:
changes in market, 37
dangers in, 36
"elapsed time" method in, 38
implementing market, 36
sample market, 38–39
stage marketing, 34–36

PBS programming, *see* Public Broadcasting System
Press releases, 63
Prestige, responsibility of, 20
Priorities, developmental, 8, 9
Public Broadcasting System, 48

Radio:
ad timing in, 83, 92–93
advertising tone in, 88
alternatives, 87
comparing stations in, 84
costs of advertising in, 86–87
median age indicators, 85
music in, 85, 91
role in combination media, 93–94
sample commercial script for, 89
sound effects, 91–92
sound mixing in, 90
station image in, 84–85
terminology, 82–83
writing ads for, 89
Reply coupons, 74
Response, individual basis of, 15
RTP principle, 18

Scandal, 36, 37
Scripts, television:
camera angles in, 103
expanded format in, 103–104
glossary of terms, 102
program "teaser" in, 106
public service, 105–106
rules for, 100–101
sample, 101
writing short, 104–105
Self Perception Checklist, 12
Seminars:
as image builders, 170
charisma as factor, 181–182
conclusion of, 185–186
defining market for, 171–172
direct mail promotion for, 179
extent of package, 175
flexibility secrets for, 184–185
follow-up to, 186
humor in, 178
income from, 187
journal promotion for, 180
location of, 175–176
lodging for, 177–178
logistical problems of, 174–178
manuals, *see* Manuals, seminal
market surveys for, 172–173
meal availability for, 176–177
medical needs of, 181
multimedia approach, 179
operations of, 180–181
outline approach, 173–174
personal projection in, 182–184
personalized response to, 181–182
promotion of, 178–180
psychological shift, 185
results range statements in, 179
setting parameters for, 173
staffing for, 180–181
summary approach for, 185
Speeches:
audience mood for, 167
beating pressure of, 155–156
benefits of, 166
body language in, 165–167

Speeches (cont.)
  fees for, 154
  hecklers, 168
  middle presentation for, 160-163
  nine point plan for, 157
  opening examples for, 159-160
  outline use in, 161
  overview of, 154
  practice techniques for, 166
  publicity value of, 155
  rules of, 156-158
  seeds of influence in, 154
  voice animation in, 164-165
  writing openings for, 158-159
  writing ends for, 163-164
Stage Marketing Outline, 34-36
Surveys:
  assessing results of, 31
  and direct mail, 30
  "flattery factor" in, 32
  market, 29
  passive respondents in, 30
  and promotions, 31
  rate of response in, 31
  recipients of, 32
  response "clusters" in, 32
  restricting size of, 30
  telephone canvass, 30

Television:
  animated graphics on, 99-100
  background factors, 97
  broadcasting costs, 110-111
  cable, 48, 114-120
  as educational forum, 107-108
  general environment for, 98
  "grapevine" advertisement, 99
  as image builder, 108-109
  interviews on, 109
  lighting for, 97-98
  production principles of, 96
  public service programming, 106-107
  satellite, 48, 121-124
  script terminology, 102
  shooting script, 100-101
  station management in, 126-127
  station ownership in, 124-126
  studio audience in, 107
  visual impact in, 98-100
Trade journals:
  advertising in, 72-73
  authored articles in, 75-76
  "bio notes" in, 75
  data in advertising, 72
  definition of, 79
  editors, 71
  editorial focus of, 72
  humor in, 80
  market information for, 70-71
  overview of, 70
  study requirements for, 71
  "typical reader" statistics, 71-72
Turner Broadcasting System, 48
Type styles, 145

Voice Projection, 6

writer's block, 76-77
Writer's Digest Books, 80
Writer's Market, 80